Hollywood Renaissance

HOLLYWOOD RENAISSANCE

Diane Jacobs

South Brunswick and New York: A. S. Barnes & Co.
London: The Tantivy Press

A.S. Barnes & Co. Inc,
Cranbury, New Jersey 08512

The Tantivy Press
Magdalen House
136-148 Tooley Street
London SE1 2TT, England

Library of Congress Cataloging in Publication Data

Jacobs, Diane.
   Hollywood Renaissance.

   Bibliography: p.

   CONTENTS: John Cassavetes.—Robert Altman.—Francis
Ford Coppola.—Martin Scorsese.—Paul Mazursky.
   1. Moving-picture producers and directors—United
States—Biography. 2. Moving-pictures—United States.
I. Title.
PN1998.A2J28   791.43'0233'0922 [B]   76-18796
ISBN 0-498-01785-0   U.K.: SBN 0-904208-17-6

For my mother and father

Acknowledgements

I would like to thank the following for their help in providing prints, illustrations, and other material for this book: Josh Bagley, Marion Billings, Joseph Brenner Associates, Columbia University, Films Incorporated, Lincoln Center Film Library, Mary Margaret Miller, The Museum of Modern Art Film Study Center, Paramount Films, Stuart Rosenthal, Nancy Schwartz, Charles Silver, 20th Century-Fox, United Artists, and especially my editor, Peter Cowie, whose assistance was invaluable.

NB: additional pictures for this volume were kindly loaned by Jacobo Brender/Elio Mujica, Derek Elley, Allen Eyles, Barnie Pattison, and Stuart Rosenthal.

Contents

Hollywood Renaissance

Warren Beatty and Julie Christie in one of the new Hollywood's most difficult yet rewarding movies, McCABE AND MRS. MILLER

Introduction

The history of America in the early Seventies reads something like a lobotomy of the late Sixties. The socio-political imbroglio that led New Deal historian Richard Hofstadter to label the previous decade "The Age Of Rubbish" was beginning to disperse, but then so was the liberating energy behind it. Two years into the Nixon administration, 1970 looked bleak indeed. The "Revolution" was as dead as Ken Kesey's McMurphy, and while the Big Nurse of power politics was busy filling in the chasm between Woodstock and Wall Street, the next decade seemed destined to inherit only a residue of disillusioned flower children, as effete as the cardboard caricatures in Robert Patrick's timely, distasteful play, *Kennedy's Children.*

While historians were busy painting the gloomy picture of a decade of reaction and backlash, Orson Welles came out with a decidedly felicitous prediction for the Seventies in Hollywood: Rome might be burning, but Nero's orchestras were fiddling *beautifully.* After nearly thirty years' worth of battling an ungrateful and intractable Indian Giver, Welles himself was resigned, not without a trace of bitterness, to the exile of Prospero; but for the young — "everyone and his idiot brother" owning a camera — there was a field day ahead. "When the arts and skills combine for anything from films to football," writes Welles in *Look's* "But Where Are We Going?", "combine with passion and purpose in the brief explosion of a nation's cultural energy — this sudden harvest of grace is not invariably subject to the rule of seasons. Quite often a country seems to come into a golden age as a poet gets his inspiration. There is no reliable calendar for such beginnings."[34]

It is not entirely far-fetched to speculate that the political energies of the Sixties were cathartically channelled into the arts — and particularly the popular arts — of the Seventies. As with the movie boom in the Thirties, a period of cinematic "rebirth" seems to have been gestating within the frenetic activity of the previous decade. What the advent of sound and the stock market crash were

11

to the Thirties, Woodstock and Watergate have constituted to the Seventies. Most of the so-called new directors rolled into Hollywood at the apex of the youth cult and on the crest of *Easy Rider,* Dennis Hopper's low-budget, youth-oriented gamble that grossed $50 million at box-offices and has accorded its dubious "auteur" a pivotal role in film history. *Easy Rider* is a convenient landmark: like Godard's *Breathless* (significantly predated by Claude Chabrol's *Le beau Serge*), it was merely the most conspicuous of any number of symptoms of change. One could convincingly argue, for instance, that it was Cassavetes's grainy, improvisational *Shadows,* released in 1960, that served as stylistic progenitor of this new school of film-makers and that with *Catch-22* Mike Nichols, the first director since Welles to obtain right of final cut, was harbinger of the relative artistic freedom to be enjoyed by the Coppolas, Altmans, and Mazurskys.

Some will argue that there is no such animus as a "New Hollywood," that inspiration so mercurial and privy to the whims of what Welles calls "ugly, greeds, little hustlers"[34] (translation: the producers and distributors) can scarcely be discussed as a movement: that with the first substantial financial thaw, studios will return to doing what they alone know best. Indeed, they will say that with Steven Spielberg's *Jaws* and conceivably even Martin Scorsese's *Alice Doesn't Live Here Anymore,* the artists have already buckled under to the bankers, that the "personal" film-making community which congealed so precipitately has begun to dissolve or alchemise just as fast. After all, *Easy Rider,* once a household word, is now all but forgotten. As Blake Edwards remarked, "It used to be that there were ten directors you were sure of. Now a director has one great success and three failures and you look back and say, 'What did I ever see in him'?"

The fact that Welles's "harvest of grace" has not turned out so unadulterated as the sunset finale of an "old" Hollywood film, is in keeping with the mongrel nature of both the art and the industry. That villain distributors have not been reduced to grovelling at the feet of heroic directors/artists does not mean that the latter have not won a degree of influence; and if the issues are more befuddled than they appeared in 1970, still a renaissance of sorts has begun to take shape. The New Hollywood is not all that different from the Old. Were the Fifties' films of Nicolas Ray any less "personal" than Bogdaovich's *oeuvre* thus far? No. (Although, to give them credit, Hollywood's contemporary directors, unlike their French New Wave counterparts, are more inclined to emulate than to disclaim their immediate predecessors.) Are the new directors inured to the money sirens? Certainly not. If Scorsese made his *début* feature on a shoestring — $35,000, he nonetheless proceeded to spend $85,000 of Warner's finances on a single day's shooting for *Alice Doesn't Live Here Anymore* — and loved every minute of it.

After all, it was Broadway's "good news" and not Hollywood's that "the best things in life are free"; and I'll agree with Scorsese that *Mean Streets* as well as *Who's That Knocking?* might have profited from a few extra thousand dollars. Coppola, the Hearst of this coterie, bought the right to make *The Conversation* with *The Godfather,* and his autonomy, not unlike the Corleones', is safe-guarded by an organisational fortress (including, among other plums, a directorship of Cinema 5) the Don himself might have coveted.

As a financial entity, the studio (with the notable exception of M-G-M) has not collapsed over the past fifteen years, nor has it as yet been challenged by a more viable institution. Although small artist-controlled companies like Coppola's now-deceased Zoetrope and the Director's Group have assumed a very real and salutary role, and while stalwart independents like John Cassavetes and Joan Silver *(Hester Street)* have enjoyed moderate success peddling their projects, risks are still too great for the average director to make it on his own. Cassavetes, for instance, had to mortgage his house in order to make *Woman Under the Influence.*

In certain respects today's director actually suffers from the gradual attrition in the expansive structure of heyday studio oligarchy. "I think what's changed," Mazursky told me, "is that the great monolithic figures — the Harry Cohns, Jack Warners; those great mastodons that were strong and powerful, angry and primitive, are not there anymore. They left a stamp on so many movies that my childhood was probably a vision of those men. Somewhere along the line Jack Warner must have been an *auteur.* That quality is gone from Hollywood today." Martin Scorsese is particularly conscious of the discrepancy between venerable studio directors like Howard Hawks and John Ford, who were able to churn out four pictures a year because they had the studios behind them, and the ostensibly autonomous new director who has difficulty producing one. (Robert Altman, who has been releasing films biannually, is an exception; and Brian De Palma was at one point equally prolific with his low-budget films.) "In the old days, you made three pictures a year: if two of them flopped and one was a hit, you were O.K.," says Scorsese. "Michael Curtiz was under contract to Warner Brothers, for instance — never made a picture for another studio; and he was ensured a job, a contract, a picture, a salary."[17] This uneasiness about where financing for the next film will come from is a disconcerting corollary to autonomy.

In his "Look" article Welles gleefully compares Hollywood in 1970 to a "nervous old lady." "She needs youthful hands to guide her," writes Welles. "The trust is rather touching, slightly ridiculous, and very hopeful for the future of American films."[34] The saga of the early Seventies has scarcely borne out the "nervous old lady" analogy: to begin with, "young" directors like Hal Ashby and Robert Altman were older than most of the "hustlers" themselves; and, indeed, their hustle was doubtless as well polished, it being no secret that the movie directing business is as competitive a field as one can find — be it the old or the new Hollywood one is out to conquer. "You're only as good as your last film" is an adage as relevant today as ever. The prodigious commercial success of *M*A*S*H*, for instance, was ancient history by the time United Artists got around to rejecting *Nashville,* and even *Bob and Carol and Ted and Alice* couldn't find Paul Mazursky work for two years following the commercial-critical failure of his second film, *Alex in Wonderland.*

What distinguishes the films of this first half of the Seventies is neither artistic superiority nor administrative autonomy — but a happy combination of the two, a fusion of ability, accessibility, and yes, inspiration, at a fortuitous juncture in time. Someone got it into his head that an amorphous under-30 audience did exist out there, that it was tired of the costume drama and the safe situation comedy, and that with business so bad anything new was worth a try. The phenomenon that resulted was not a matter of one or two outstanding individuals — of a prodigal Welles or Huston — but of a conglomeration of talent descending upon Hollywood and insisting on having a say in the future of movies. As Mazursky pointed out, for the first time American directors were making "personal" films that were packaged as such.

Altman, for instance, may make one film for United Artists, the next for Paramount; but each is an "Altman" film with an Altman crew and cast and look. This evolution can in part be attributed to the permutations in the role of the producer, as Jerzy Toeplitz astutely analyses it in *Hollywood and After.* Until the Fifties, the producer was almost always on the payroll of a particular studio: responsible for not just one, but several studio films simultaneously. For this service, he would receive a percentage of the profits as well as a salary from the given studio. Today, few producers are bound by contract to a particular studio (although in practice they often develop such working relationships), and none is ever responsible for more than a given work at a time. Thus, the producer-director liaison has further eroded the studio, while contributing to the glory of the director. "The emphasis has shifted 180 degrees," writes Toeplitz, "the producer and director have become allies, held together by a common aim. No longer can a studio count on the producer's support in opposing the director's views."[30] Toeplitz also points out a substantial rise in the number of independent productions in recent years. In 1970, for instance, independents represented 43%, while Hollywood companies constituted 57% of film output. The number of independently produced films expanded from 19 in 1968 to 107 in 1972.

On the other hand, studio pictures like *The Towering Inferno* and *The Exorcist* and *Jaws* are alive and well and often serve as umbrellas for the art film. *Jaws* is a particularly interesting case, as it will doubtless be remembered as a Zanuck-Brown Production, although it was directed by Steven Spielberg, whose *Sugarland Express* (directed at age twenty-five) had been hailed as commensurate to *Citizen Kane* just the year before. It is as if after painting *Guernica,* Picasso got it into his head to make an Excedrin commercial; but in Hollywood such juggling is accepted with aplomb.

Paul Mazursky's *Alex in Wonderland* (an autobiographical reverie) is itself a reliable document of the spirit of Hollywood in the early Seventies, as enjoyed by a very privileged few. Donald Sutherland plays the Mazursky character — a sensitive young soul whose first film (suspiciously like *Bob and Carol and Ted and Alice*) has dazzled him into inaction: everything and nothing is possible. Mazursky himself plays the attentively hip producer who can't offer this instant super star enough: won't he accept a Chagall painting, a trip to Europe with no strings attached? "You want to do the same picture you just did," he inquires pusillanimously, "or is your head open to anything?" In *Alex in Wonderland,* Mazursky employs Fellini as a loving foil for the hoopla of the Hollywood system; but the very fact that he was allowed to use Fellini and Jeanne Moreau in the context of his own Sunset Boulevard carnival is a tribute to the Wonderland of a Hollywood that indulged him. The off-camera epilogue to the film is equally revealing of Hollywood's vicissitudes. *Alex's* poor reception and its director's subsequent status as overnight hot potato were indications of the more ignominious aspects of success in a dreamworld.

But it is not my intention to give more than a cursory glance at the financial situation in Hollywood. The films themselves are what I will be concerned with here and financial exigencies only as they affect a critical examination of a movie. Film is, by definition, a commercial vehicle, affected (though not necessarily afflicted) by the popular market. Mazursky and Altman are no more exempt from the tastes and whims of a mass audience than were Sturges and Huston: they have merely found new ways of approaching traditional problems.

As Welles pointed out, it is almost impossible to chart beginnings, which are more often than not many half-starts converging. For convenience's sake, I have chosen the year 1970 as a point of departure, selecting as subjects only those directors whose major works were made after that date. The choice was painful, as it meant eliminating major figures such as Arthur Penn, Roman Polanski, Sidney Lumet, as well as distinguished if less accomplished directors such as Mike Nichols. Having to limit my subject, I also give short shift to comedians like Woody Allen, Mel Brooks, and animator Ralph Bakshi, all of whom deserve recognition, had I but world enough and time. . .

Having set my terms, I will now immediately protest stipulator's licence and include John Cassavetes, who made his first film ten years before 1970, but whose unified body of work and unflinchingly personal, if ever-controversial style has served as example and in certain cases model for the generation to come. I have also dedicated chapters to Robert Altman, Francis Ford Coppola, Paul Mazursky, and Martin Scorsese: a "Pantheon" chosen purely on the basis of my own bias and in light of the films released when this book goes to press. There are other directors — George Lucas and Terrence Malick in particular, whose works I greatly admire, but who just have not made enough films to merit extensive analysis.

I quickly protest that in general I have adhered to the director as auteur approach as the least fair system except for all the others. Collaboration has always been a working principle in Hollywood, and many screenwriters, editors, and cameramen as well as actors will naturally come up in my discussion. While Anita Loos was doubtless as much a collaborator as Joan Tewkesbury and William Cameron Menzies's cinematography as distinctive as Vilmos Zsigmond's; only recently have the various limbs of film-making assumed importance in their own right. An increasingly media-sophisticated audience has come to recognise film as both multifaceted and organic; and the proof is that outside as well as inside the trade certain expectations are set up by the announcement of a Robert Towne screenplay or camera work by Laszlo Kovacs.

The number of directors working within or on the fringe of Hollywood today is legion, and I cannot hope to do justice to them all. As Blake Edwards so aptly remarked, yesterday's prodigals are tomorrow's has-beens; and by the same token fledgling directors are coming into their own every day. No one who saw *Boxcar Bertha*, for instance, would have guessed that Scorsese would go on to make a work as pungent and complex as *Mean Streets*. On the other hand, Peter Bogdanovich's *Last Picture Show*, hailed rather hyperbolically by *Newsweek* at the time as "the most important work by a young American director since *Citizen Kane*" has been succeeded by the beautiful, shallow *Daisy Miller* and the lacklustre *At Long Last Love*. Tomorrow he may make the most exciting film of the decade. Any list is by definition anachronistic almost as soon as it hits the page; and so I have merely compiled an assemblage of post-1970 directors at work now or in recent past, whose films have shown promise. In each case, I list here only the best known of the director's films as a means of identification.

Besides the five I have already mentioned, I would include Woody Allen *(Love and Death)*; Hal Ashby *(The Last Detail)*; Ralph Bakshi *(Heavy Traffic)*; Noel Black *(Pretty Poison)*. Peter Bogdanovich *(The Last Picture Show)*; Mel Brooks *(Young Frankenstein)*; Brian De Palma *(Phantom of the Paradise)*; John Hancock *(Bang the Drum Slowly)*; Dennis Hopper *(Easy Rider)*; George Lucas *(American Graffiti)*; Terrence Malick *(Badlands)*; John Milius *(The Wind and the Lion)*; Bob Rafelson *(Five Easy Pieces)*; Michael Ritchie *(Smile)*; Jerry Schatzberg *(Scarecrow)*; Steven Spielberg *(Jaws)*; Howard Zieff *(Hearts of the West)*.

The screenwriters to emerge in recent years include Willard Huyck and Gloria Katz *(American Graffiti)* — a married writing team along the line of Frances Goodrich and Albert Hackett, Ruth Gordon and Garson Kanin; Paul Schrader *(Taxi Driver)*; and Joan Tewkesbury *(Nashville)*. Of contemporary screenwriters I find Robert Towne most impressive, portraying an intuitive sense of character and the ability to insinuate affecting relationships into exceptionally cogent scripts, which include contributions to *Bonnie and Clyde* and *The Godfather* as well as the script for *Chinatown*, *The Last Detail*, and shared credit on *Shampoo*.

Visually, the influence of the two Eastern European cameramen — Laszlo Kovacs and Vilmos Zsigmond — is conspicuous in the films of Bogdanovich, Altman, Rafelson, and others. The nicest qualities of *A Cold Day in the Park*, for instance, revolve around the Canadian atmosphere, evoked through juxtapositions of interior warmth and a pluvious, raw outdoors. Kovacs describes the shooting as "an exercise in lighting", as he shot ninety percent of the film from the inside of the frustrated young heroine's apartment; and it is the texture he

Hollywood movies of the Seventies: CARNAL KNOWLEDGE (above), and THE LAST PICTURE SHOW (below)

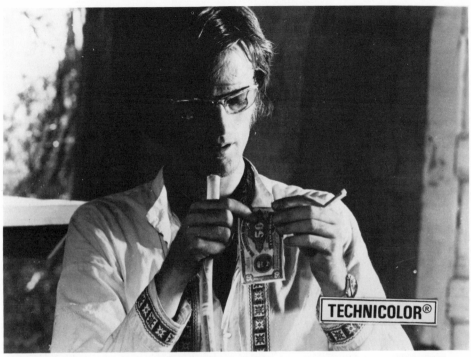

Above: Peter Fonda in EASY RIDER. Below: Jack Nicholson in THE LAST DETAIL

thus managed to evoke that is most interesting in what is otherwise a very uneven early Altman film. In a later Altman work, Vilmos Zsigmond's use of "flashing" (a technique conceived with Altman as a means of re-creating the feeling of an old colour photo) is responsible for much of the elusive, lyrical quality of *McCabe and Mrs. Miller.* Haskell Wexler is to be credited with the purposely sullied effect of the colour photography in *American Graffiti.*

Of the actors to emerge as emblematic of the New Hollywood, Jack Nicholson is certainly the most visible. Besides starring in *Easy Rider, Five Easy Pieces, The Last Detail, One Flew Over the Cuckoo's Nest,* etc. ad gloriam; he has also co-directed (*Head,* with Bob Rafelson), directed *(Drive He Said),* and done a stint of screenwriting *(The Trip, Ride the Whirlwind).* Robert De Niro, who first appeared with a superb Harvey Keitel in Scorsese's *Mean Streets,* has gone on to play the dying ball player in John Hancock's *Bang the Drums Slowly,* the Marlon Brando role of Don Vito in *Godfather II,* and the schizophrenic hero of Scorsese's *Taxi Driver.* Both Nicholson and De Niro have worked in Europe under Antonioni and Bertolucci, respectively. Similarly, Ingmar Bergman created *The Touch* with Elliot Gould, an Altman/Mazursky discovery in mind. Other Altman discoveries or re-discoveries include Keith Carradine, Shelley Duvall, Karen Black, Julie Christie, John Schuck, Sally Kellerman, Louise Fletcher, Donald Sutherland, and more which I will discuss in my Altman chapter. Paul Mazursky gave Ellen Burstyn her first ample role in *Alex in Wonderland* (she went on to win an Oscar in Scorsese's *Alice Doesn't Live Here Anymore*); and Bogdanovich "found" Cybill Shepherd (admirable in *The Last Picture Show* and Elaine May's *Heartbreak Kid;* a miscast Galatea in *Daisy Miller* and *At Long Last Love*) and the extremely talented Madeleine Kahn — equally active in Mel Brooks's repertoire. John Cassavetes, the actor's director, has elicited stunning performances from Peter Falk, Lelia Goldoni, Ben Carruthers, Lynn Carlin, Seymour Cassel, John Marley, Ben Gazzara, Jenny Runacre, himself, and, most notably, his wife Gena Rowlands.

In *From Reverence to Rape,* Molly Haskell speaks convincingly about the dearth of interesting women's roles in recent years and of an equally discouraging wane in the number of talented actresses. "From a woman's point of view," she writes, "the ten years from, say 1962 to 1973 have been the most disheartening in screen history. In the roles and prominence accorded women, the decade began unpromisingly, grew steadily worse, and at present shows no signs of improving."[15] Given a viable, if limited number of women writers and/or directors, such as Susan Sontag (Director: *Promised Lands*);

Penelope Giliatt (Screenplay: *Sunday, Bloody Sunday*); Joan Didion (co-writer of screenplay: *Play It as It Lays*); Joan Silver (Director: *Hester Street*) — where, she asks, are the actresses to portray these women's dramas? From the sketchy list I've compiled, it become evident that if we still lack women thespians to compete with Bette Davis, Jean Arthur, and Katharine Hepburn, the past few years have at least brought us a few tentative steps toward both the incisive woman's role and the women to play it. In addition to Ellen Burstyn, Madeleine Kahn, and Sally Kellerman, we have Shirley Knight giving her best performance since *The Group* in Coppola's *The Rain People,* and Lelia Goldoni (first appearing as a very young woman in Cassavetes's *Shadows*) and Diane Ladd staging comebacks in Scorsese's *Alice Doesn't Live Here Anymore.*

What distinguishes the film-makers of this New Hollywood? Like the French and Italian New Waves, they are excruciatingly conscious of their medium and its history, by and large equipped with technical machinery and facilities not available to their predecessors. While they did not arise uniformly from the womb of the Cinémathèque or "Cahiers du Cinéma," many of them (Lucas, Coppola, Scorsese, Milius) attended film schools, while others, Bogdanovich the most prominent example, began their careers as film critics or *aficionados.* Another group, led by Altman and Mazursky, served apprenticeships in television, while Howard Zieff came to movies from a prestigious career in advertising. Unlike the French Nouvelle Vague, they have no collective axe to grind, politically or aesthetically. Many of them were given their first opportunity to direct in Roger Corman's Grade-B pictures (Coppola's *Dementia-13,* Scorsese's *Boxcar Bertha,* Bogdanovich's *Targets*) and remain intrigued by the exploitation film to this day. Coppola, who made a few "nudies" when starting out, still toys with the idea of making a pornographic feature; and Scorsese is not ashamed that the only way he was able to get *Who's That Knocking?* released was by inserting a nude scene — and at considerable trouble and expense. (He was in Amsterdam at the time and had to fly Harvey Keitel over to shoot a prurient dream sequence.)

As I mentioned earlier, rather than slighting Fifties and Sixties directors like Penn, Lumet, Nichols, Edwards, or the earlier Huston, they tend to admire all previous cinematic eras, albeit to varying degrees. Penn's *Bonnie and Clyde* has been re-made in one form or another so many times that "criminal couples" like "road pictures" now constitute a separate *genre.* In 1974 alone we had Altman's *Thieves Like Us,* Malick's *Badlands,* Spielberg's *Sugarland Express.*

The most representative Seventies films have by and large been *genre* pictures. It is not in *The Conversation,* an oblique study of a loner as helpless as the subject of a de Chirico painting in his archaic environment, that we get the true sense of ruthless power hunger and indefatigability that was Watergate, but in *The Godfather* (s). At their best, these contemporary westerns, capers, musicals, and gangster films have reflected a tension between nostalgia and immediacy, homage and idiosyncrasy, much as Truffaut's *Shoot The Piano Player* set up a dialectic between Hitchcockian suspense and Truffaut's own more reflective sensibility. In *Badlands,* for instance, Malick acknowledges the Nicholas Ray vision of malleable libidinal energy within a working morality, but uncovers only the vast banality of his James Dean look-alike of a mass killer. The film is successful because it both pays tribute to and verges from its source. *Paper Moon,* on the other hand, reaches back for an "authentic" depression ethos, and despite some hilarious scenes with Madeleine Kahn, finds only *kitsch* and *genre* details and a cloying nostalgia. What renders *Shoot The Piano Player* and *The Bride Wore Black* interesting is that Truffaut is *not* Hitchcock; the problem with recent Bogdanovich movies (*Targets* was an admirable *début* and *The Last Picture Show* very affecting) is that he is neither Hawks nor Welles nor Sturges nor McCarey, but then neither has he evolved a personal style with which to offset his often provocative observations about directors he makes no bones about imitating.

Altman is another interesting case. His *Long Good-Bye* may have audiences clammering for *The Big Sleep;* his *McCabe and Mrs. Miller* might elicit outrage and unflattering comparisons to the West of Ford or Hawks. Nonetheless, they never fail to approach the original from an interesting angle and a respectful distance.

A tendency toward cultural autobiography tends to characterise the fictions of the mass media, and the *genre* films of the Seventies are particularly insidious in this respect. It is not coincidental that of all American films, European cultists should have been most fascinated with the *genre* picture (particularly the western and the gangster film)—for the *genre* is the most perfect sublimation of the American experience. The western has traditionally represented America as Americans would like to see themselves. In *Who's That Knocking?,* the hero J.R. stares incredulously at a heretical girl who has just stipulated that she does not like westerns. "Everybody should like westerns—solve everybody's problems if they liked westerns," retorts the Scorsese surrogate. (Interestingly, Scorsese arranges that the girl really *does* like westerns, thus showing up as hypocritical the protests of those who claim not to thrill to the cult of rugged macho individuality.)

If the traditional western has confirmed DeToqueville's observations on the American spirit, the gangster film has served subtly to undermine these tenets of optimism. Robert Warshow gave a marvelious definition of the cinematic gangster as he had evolved by 1954. "The gangster is lonely and melancholy," he writes of characters like Big Louie and Little Caesar, "and can give the impression of a profound worldly wisdom. He appeals most to adolescents with their impatience and their feeling of being outsiders, but more generally he appeals to that side of all of us which refuses to believe in the 'normal' possibilities of happiness and achievement; the gangster is the 'no' to the great American 'yes' which is stamped so big over our official culture and yet has so little to do with the way we really feel about our lives."[32]

The old gangster is alive and well (which means seconds away from death) in films like *Bonnie and Clyde* and in the spate of drug movies like Ivan Passer's *Born to Win.* But directors such as Malick and Altman have taken the gangster film one crucial step further. While the old gangster is a loner, the new one travels with a woman (granted, the woman rarely understands his motives any more than the girl comprehends the ethos of her western hero); and while the traditional gangster is wedded to the shadows of the city, his modern counterpart is mobile, nomadic, always on the run. But, most important, while the classic gangster stuck out in relief against the social forces of law and order that would ultimately confound him, the gangster of the recent *genres* is camouflaged by his moral environment. The marshal's first reaction to catching Kit in *Badlands,* for instance, is, "He ain't no bigger than I am!" In similar fashion, Boyie of *Thieves Like Us* is developed as anything but an iconoclast: he's a drifter who fell in with bad company, and certainly no more lethal than Mattie's husband whose release is assured by his death.

These revisionist views of the traditional American *genres* are counterbalanced by a more wistful stance; and one could divide the "new" *genre* films, like revised studies of political heroes, into two schools: those that look back with nostalgia and those that look back with prescience. Both tend to see little to recommend today. *Paper Moon,* for instance, attempts to foil modern cynicism and the nightly newscast much as the Thirties films foiled the Depression. In retrospect, the New Deal years look rather quaint and flat and naïve. After all, petty gangsters capitalised on Bibles rather than heroin. Altman, on the other hand, imbues the past with the seeds of the present; and even such pleasantries as coke bottles and Southern drawls are deceptively innocuous. Thus, *McCabe* tells us that the

West was won with power—not ingenuity, expedience—not sacrifice; while *Thieves Like Us,* though winsome, sees betrayal and survival as the dominant American *motifs*—even way back then.

Two exceptional *genre* pictures of recent years are illustrative of these opposite camps in the nostalgia struggle. As both George Lucas's *American Graffiti* and Terrence Malick's *Badlands* will be referred to time and again in the body of the book, I would like to discuss them briefly here. Both films take place at approximately the same time: late Fifties, early Sixties, and reflect their directors' shared provincial roots—Lucas, small-town California; Malick the American Southwest. *American Graffiti* is essentially of the things-were-better, personally and nationally, school of thought; while *Badlands,* documentary in tone, intimates that there is little discrepancy between then and now. Lucas's film is autobiographical, and Malick's bears an uncanny ressemblance to the real-life story of nineteen-year-old Charles Starkweather and his thirteen-year-old girlfriend who harassed the Midwest in the late Fifties. Malick, however, denies any biographical intentions.

Both films are scrupulously disciplined (compare *Mean Streets, Shadows*), but *Badlands* is the more laconic of the two, its documentary approach balanced by a limpid precision of style. Similarly, the obscurity of his subjects (two nobodies only recognised for their dastardly deeds) is ironically offset by the effulgence of the brittle images. The most objective of the "couples that kill" pictures, *Badlands* has little desire to indulge its twenty-five-year-old garbage collector killer, Kit (Martin Sheen), who looks strikingly like James Dean and models himself accordingly; or his girlfriend Holly, the film's fifteen-year-old narrator, who talks like a movie magazine. *Badlands* has been described as a little gem; and that is precisely the way it looks—crisp, irridescent and inpenetrable.

The narrative begins as Kit sets off on a shooting spree, having murdered Holly's father (a sign painter who disapproved of the liaison and paid for it) and set the house blazing. Like Louis Malle's Lacombe Lucien, Kit is as amoral as neanderthal man; and unlike Arthur Penn, Malick doesn't encourage sympathy for the young outlaw. We are not forced to condemn him, however, as Malick has cleverly placed his subjects under a microscope, removing them from the province of conventional morality. Like Kit, fascinated with immortality through artifact, and Holly, preoccupied with subliter-ary description, Malick focuses on detail rather than design. The beginning, for instance, is bathed in pastels, suffused with the warmth one might associate with attic smells or the look of tea dances in the Old South. In one scene Holly wears a green dress and sits on a lavender couch—the two muted colours creating a mellow, aged effect. Throughout the film Malick conscientiously undermines the killings by concentrating, like his characters, on the environmental data: the flowered wallpaper, the music sheets burning, the setting sun, the colour of the fire (set to Passion music—a superimposed correlative for Holly's movie magazine melodrama).

Kit preserves his artifacts as lore: some of their possessions he sends up in a weather balloon, others he burns; his own body he donates to science—a nice American reversal of the Egyptian pyramid as immortality guarantee. Holly, who never mixed well at school, is busy trying to relate her saga in the manner of a movie magazine—her closest association with celebrity before she met Kit. "Suddenly I was thrown into a state of shock," she says without a trace of emotion; "Kit was the most trigger-happy person I'd ever met." Holly cherishes no Hollywood illusions about spending old age with her outlaw lover: even as they set off she wonders whom she will eventually marry; and without a choke in her voice she tells of finally linking up with her trial lawyer while Kit is sentenced to death.

Badlands is itself an elegant document of boredom and anonymity. It is a painless film and, as such, has been labelled as cruel and immoral: it is not. Rather, the film is unpejorative—the underside of the American dream seen without glamour or pathos or bile. Like *The Great Gatsby, Badlands* is about a sector of the American culture inured to pain and beyond the comprehension of artist and audience alike. Fitzgerald showed us the bored rich, Malick the bored poor. In both cases, it is the style of presentation and not the ostensible subject that is elevating.

American Graffiti is an equally memorable, but much more affecting film. Its advertising campaign asks, "Where were you in '62?"; but it really doesn't matter what one's answer is. Those who have little nostalgia for the late fifties and whose high school years were deprived of roller skating waitresses and double chubby chucks, of racing cars and "cruising", have nonetheless been intensely affected by this unsentimental tribute to the universal phenomenon of lost innocence. Lucas tells his tale (like Scorsese's *Who's That Knocking?* and *Mean Streets*) to the score of contemporary rock music and sets the action during one final night in Modesto, California, with its proms, its cars, its closure—and its very beguiling promise of love. The alternative is to leave for a college education in the East.

Lucas has said of his comment on America: "There's no message or long speech, but you know that when the story ends America underwent a drastic change. The early Sixties were the end

of an era. It hit us all very hard."[11] This aspect of the film I don't
accept. If, indeed, America ever was innocent, it surely was not in
the year following the Bay of Pigs. Nor does it appear, from Michael
Ritchie's 1975 *Smile* that the Sixties have done much to mitigate
either the insularity or the conviviality of complacent smalltown life
in California.

What *is* moving in *American Graffiti* are the portraits of an
aging car racer, a bungling girl-crazy "Toad" (Lucas says this
character is he), a high school President in love, the town intellectual
torn between the known and the unknown. The rites of passage each
undergoes in his own personal, undramatic fashion are universal: it is
Eve yearning for her apple, innocent and precocious and scared all at
once.

Andrew Sarris was offended by the blonde in the white
Thunderbird whose image continues to haunt Curt, the intellectual,
after he has decided to leave Modesto for college in the East.
"Fellini," writes Sarris, "transformed Anita Ekberg into a Roman
goddess not merely through his personal genius, but through a
cultural tradition that he shares with his countrymen, a tradition in
which a sexually repressed Italian male waits to be liberated by a
Gothic invasion from the icily inhibited North."

I would argue that a similar romantic/sexual sensibility is at
work not just in Lucas, but in Scorsese, Coppola, Mazursky, and
Rafelson, to name just a few of the new directors still enthralled with
American variations on the Roman goddess *motif.* We find the icy
blonde goddess issuing promises of salvation and sex in *Who's That
Knocking?, The Godfather, Carnal Knowledge, McCabe and Mrs.
Miller, Blume In Love, Taxi Driver,* and *Five Easy Pieces.* Curt of
American Graffiti is very much the inhibited adolescent in awe both
of sex and of the American dream of gold; and the recondite blonde
in the Thunderbird who whispers "I love you" and disappears in the
night, encapsulates both. She is also very similar to the girl that
Bernstein speaks of in *Citizen Kane:* he saw her only once on a ferry,
and yet not a day has passed since that he has not thought of her.
That girl is as important to the American cinema as she is to the
Italian. She is Robert Frost's "Path Not Taken": sacrifice, and at the
same time the intimation of a salvation that might have been.

Apart from a predilection for *genre,* nostalgia, and, often
blonde goddesses, it is difficult to codify the "personal" directors of
the New Hollywood, either stylistically or thematically. If they are
unusually compatible socially, their films are as heterogeneous as
those of Godard and Resnais, Fellini and Visconti. Realism and plot
aversion have often been invoked as coalescent factors in the films of

such otherwise dissimilar talents as Coppola, Scorsese, Mazursky, Cassavetes, and Altman. Neither hold up in an examination of Coppola, for instance, but it is viable to examine the various angles of realism employed in the films of Scorsese, Cassavetes, and Altman.

Cassavetes and Scorsese are concerned with the texture of reality as it feels in the motion of every-day life and with an atavistic exploration of the function of the camera. Thus, even *Minnie and Moskowitz* and *Alice Doesn't Live Here Anymore*—their most mythic films, respectively—feel compelled to remind us that the camera is ambulatory, that it is an uneasy magnet, often clinging to viscera rather than fact. For instance, when Alice appears most secure, the camera continues to rove apprehensively. Cassavetes in particular is wedded to interiors and small groups: concerned that he should only infrequently permit a moment that might be construed as purely aesthetic or universal. Scorsese is more concerned with atmosphere— with the feel of the streets of Little Italy and in *Taxi* with an almost tactile, sultry New York summer in which freak passions breed and explode.

In a discussion of *M*A*S*H* Altman told an interviewer that he wanted audiences to note the arbitrary nature of their experience, the fact that had they looked through another window, they would have seen a different pageant, but distilling life down to the same emotional experience. I have labelled Altman's peculiar species of realism—his use of garbled voices, unstructured dialogues, simultaneous experiences—actualism, inarticulacy and simultaneity being no more "real," in a visceral sense, than coherence. In fact, the disjointed conversations and inaudible soundtrack effects draw attention to the autonomous prerogatives of the filming process and away from the film's mythic power in much the same fashion as the camera's uneasiness in the Scorsese and Cassavetes works.

A complaint one often hears is, "Those new directors can handle actors, but they just can't tell a straight story." Vanished continuity and a narcissistic preoccupation with style did not originate with film. Self-dissecting and disjointed art has characterised the Twentieth century from Braque to Joyce to Robbe-Grillet to Webern. Inactivity as subject matter is as prevalent in the plays of Beckett as in the films of Resnais; it is at times fascinating, at times banal. Simone de Beauvoir nicely sums up the worst of narrativeless art in a discussion of the *nouveau roman*. "But in the 'objective' school," she writes in "Force of Circumstance", "the justification and the discoveries coincide: the Revolution has failed, the future is slipping from our grasp, the country is sinking into political apathy, man's progress has come to a halt; if he is written about, it will be as an object; or we may even follow the example of the economists and technocrats who put objects in his place; in any event, he will be stripped of his historical dimension." [5]

The multiplicity of film, as of music, affords it an edge over words and paint: hard as it may try to appear unilateral, resonances of dimension will surface. There are moments in the Altman or Cassavetes *oeuvre* guilty of this sin of abject objectivity, but their films never dismiss life, or even story, so peremptorily. Cassavetes's interest in the diurnal is more like that of Le Nain or even Brueghel than that of the cubists or expressionist painters. Through his actors' intuitions the everyday comes alive, just as De Palma's sense of rhythm furnishes continuity in his disjointed plots. Altman and Mazursky are particularly interesting in this context, falling into both the story-nonstory, mythic–anti-mythic arenas. *Thieves Like Us* and *Bob and Carol and Ted and Alice* are traditional narratives, for instance, while *Brewster McCloud* and *Blume In Love* are disjointed.

If one becomes too intrigued with the prevalence of so-called realism and plotlessness in new director films, he has only to look at masterpieces of storytelling like *The Godfather* or scrupulously evoked myth like *Alex in Wonderland* for counterpoint. Reality is a tricky term to begin with. Which is more real—the palpable flush of a Rembrandt bather or the unchastened angularity of *Les Desmoiselles D'Avignon; The Sorrow and the Pity* or *Grand Illusions?* Which is more natural, the prose of Zola or the poetry of e.e. cummings? In discussing the postwar Italian directors André Bazin once said, "They all reject implicitly or explicitly, with humour, satire, or poetry the reality they are using . . .";[4] and this definition could be applied to the best works of Cassavetes, Scorsese, and Altman.

The classic, "mythic" directors invest their films with a reality of emotion, at times more compelling than authenticity. The *motifs* of *The Godfather*(s) (power, family, loyalty, ruthlessness) are every bit as tenable as those of the low-budget *Mean Streets.* Coming of age is as identifiable—maybe more so—in Mazursky's *Next Stop, Greenwich Village* as in Cassavetes's grainy, improvisational *Shadows.*

I suggested earlier that the social and political energies of the late Sixties were channelled into the arts of the Seventies. On the surface this seems unlikely as contemporary films have a way of avoiding social and political issues: a good many deal with the distant past or with the Fifties, a time more congruent with the present than the previous decade. Joseph Heller once postulated that it was all but impossible to write an important war novel until twenty years after the fact, and decades are not much different in this respect than wars. The imminence of film gives it greater latitude than the novel form; and thus *The Bicycle Thief, Paisan,* and *Open City* have held up as art as well as document, much as a fine still photograph combines intuition with the momentum of actuality.

But these films are exceptions and not rules. It is improbable that Marcel Ophuls's *The Sorrow and the Pity* or Louis Malle's *Lacombe Lucien* could have been made ten years earlier; and by the same token *Paper Moon* or *Thieves Like Us* would have been inconceivable as Depression works.

Involving as it does so many sacred cows and betrayed illusions, the Sixties will be a tough era for the American artist to tackle head-on for many years. Like *The Graduate,* Bob Rafelson's *Five Easy Pieces* is an interesting case in point. A slickly photographed, often hilarious film about the scion of a wealthy musical family who leaves the wealth and the glory because it isn't "real," *Five Easy Pieces* panders to the *clichés* of the time without affording an artist's perspective on them. The drifters are "hip"—the cop-outs (Catherine, played by Susan Anspach in particular) settle down with the squares. Commitment is impossible. Andrew Sarris called the film "A testament to the thrilling danger of just living and bumping into other people on the way to the cemetery." At the time I felt precisely that—but seeing it five years later without the imminence and the shared cultural assumptions, the film's flaws stand out in sharp focus. As a work of art, the best things about *Five Easy Pieces* are the truly superb Jack Nicholson performance and the evocation of place and time, rather than the portrayal of the inner conflicts of self-absorbed hero Robert Eroica Dupea, a portrayal which panders to nihilism without justifying it. Nor do the anti-Hollywood, anti-commercial jokes hold up well.

What is moving and true in the film is Karen Black's evocation of the abrasive, demanding envoy of a reality that elitist Dupea will never be able to embrace and the sad-eyed devotion of Bobby's concert pianist sister (beautifully played by Lois Smith). What also distinguishes *Five Easy Pieces* is the lyricism that both Rafelson and Dupea appear to be fighting: the lovely pictoral texture of the stultifying Puget Sound home; the marvellous 360 degree panning shot that tracks from Dupea's hands (as he plays the piano) to Catherine's to the pictures on the wall, and which renders Dupea's confession that he feels nothing while he plays, irrelevant. The other image that remains haunting is the conversation between Dupea and his mute father in a wheelchair: a communion much more profound than Dupea's self-pitying relationship with the universe at large. The latter appears pedestrian in retrospect, rendering his probable escape to Alaska no more innovative in concept than the traditional

Opposite: Martin Sheen in BADLANDS Two of the most successful "new" films of the period: FIVE EASY PIECES, with Jack Nicholson (above), and AMERICAN GRAFFITI, with Candy Clark, Charlie Martin Smith, and Ronny Howard (below)

Hollywood ride into the sunset of an equally undefined irresponsibility.

More than any other medium, film responds to the psychic needs of the time: *Five Easy Pieces* was a viable response, but it has not held up as art. The films that do work both as art and as socio-political comments are as a rule based on sublimation. Directors like Cassavetes are not members of this school. Cassavetes is concerned with an element of the population unaffected by the changing decades. They are not even concerned in any fundamental fashion with what it means to be an American. *A Woman Under the Influence,* for instance, is not a timely complaint: it is the chronicle of an ancient, universal dilemma, focusing on a woman who has no conception of the implications of Women's Lib.

Nonetheless, as a rule the directors of the Seventies are usually concerned with the American experience. Love stories, for instance, are few and far between. Instead, from *Easy Rider* through *Nashville* we see again and again a veiled preoccupation with the strictures of American life, the death of the American dream, the plastic essence of what has been termed Americana. It is interesting to note that the 1968 *Easy Rider* saw youths assassinated at the apex of the youth movement, while *Nashville* assassinates its vacuous if harmless Establishment heroine at a time when Establishment figures are acknowledged as viable authority by most Americans—old and young alike.

Big government and business are explored at oblique angles in the films of the Seventies. Ironically, both *Nashville* and Brian De Palma's *Phantom of the Paradise* chose the music industry as bastion of Big Business: rock having served as the poetry of Sixties idealism, its appearance in these films reflects a particularly cynical disavowment of singer-prophets like Bob Dylan. Similarly, we watch the army squelch life out of the little man in pictures like *Cinderella Liberty* and *The Last Detail.*

As I will point out in my chapter on Altman, the progression of that director's films from *M*A*S*H* to *Nashville* can be viewed as a sociological litmus test of the spirit of the times. *M*A*S*H* for instance, its replete with smug anti-war, anti-Establishment jargon—very much a reflection of the optimistic irreverence of the Sixties. God-believing Establishment figures like Major Frank Burns would soon be carted off to the asylum. *Nashville,* on the other hand, looks over its shoulder at *M*A*S*H* with contempt. Keith Carradine as rock singer Tom lambasts a very sweet, gentle soldier. Here the military figure is the nice guy: the rock star is a phoney liberal.

America's gluttony for power has been most extensively charted

in the films of Francis Ford Coppola. *The Godfather* (s) could well
be analysed as allegorical: the American Dream turned inside out. All
the traditional virtues: loyalty, equal opportunity, diligence, spunk,
are invoked. Much more than *The Conversation,* a film intrigued by
the involuted mentality of a cipher, *The Godfather*(s) are films about
the ramifications of Watergate and the assumptions that precipitated
it. They are the ideal wedding of gangster and western *genres:* the
hero/villains of Puzo's story have the virtues of the western hero
(loner mentality meshed with respect for family values, personal
property, and honor) and of the outcast gangster. They are
simultaneously crooks and good guys like the Merry Pranksters or
Bonnie and Clyde (and unlike Keechie and Boyie of *Thieves Like Us*
and Kit and Holly of *Badlands*). By establishing them as such
Coppola has subtly ruled out the viability of unblemished heroism in
America today, of success untempered by compromise. A confused
religious zeal is similarly at work in Scorsese's *Mean Streets* and once
again in the convoluted altruism of Travis in *Taxi Driver.*

It is nonetheless false to assume that all the films of the early
Seventies paint the future of America as unremittingly bleak. What
Lucas looks back at with nostalgia in *American Graffiti,* Michael
Ritchie points out as timeless in *Smile,* where we see a small town in
Southern California as involuted and yet as wholesome and charming
(portrayed through the beauty pageant contestants) as Modesto in
the late Fifties, early Sixties. Mazursky and Scorsese, on the other
hand, paint a picture of America and Americans as changing, as torn
between a viable past and a potentially appealing future. In *Bob and
Carol and Ted and Alice* Mazursky shows us sophisticates whose
intellects want to swing, but whose instincts are back in the Middle
Ages.

In *Blume in Love,* Mazursky is dealing with a hip, liberated man
who fools around with his secretary, but will die if he can't win his
wife back. Like Leo McCarey, Mazursky is ever-lovingly conscious of
the discrepancies within his characters that transcend the sociological
conditions around them. Alex's dilemmas are variations on those that
must have beset Shakespeare, and *Next Stop, Greenwich Village* is an
hilarious Twentieth century version of the Oedipal myth. With
Mazursky the fact that sentiment wins out is less a comment on the
times than a conviction about humanity. And thus his view of
America, as seen through the Esalen-obsessed California, the movie
industry, a semi-free lover, a New York Lear, a Fifties' would-be star
are tempered by a personal hunch, like Robert Browning's in "Love
among the Ruins," that "love is best."

Of the timely films, the most optimistic work comes, surprisingly, from the man who gave us the failed saint of *Mean Streets* and the crazed cipher of *Taxi Driver. Alice Doesn't Live Here Anymore* is not without its darker undertones, but it is also a glimpse of the other side of *Nashville*. Scorsese's study of Middle Americans today concentrates on their humour, their tenacity, their ability to help each other survive and, just maybe, ameliorate. Unlike *American Graffiti* or *Paper Moon, Alice* points out that looking back is at least in part a function of dream and retroactive wish fulfilment, nicely portrayed in the florid hues of the opening shots of Monterey. Instead of looking nostalgically to the past, Scorsese sublimates and creates tension by imbuing his experiences and emotions in the Robert Getchell/Ellen Burstyn *Alice,* a whole country away from the New York of his own past. Scorsese sees life as neither better nor worse in any absolute sense today than yesterday, but he insists that the present offers opportunities an older generation, be it Italian or Anglo Saxon, would never have dreamed of. Alice, for instance, has ample trouble leaving her nest in New Mexico, but her mother's generation would never have left at all.

Like Mazursky in *Blume,* Scorsese shows us the triumph of love when Alice gets her rancher; but he shows us something a bit more polemical as well. "There's got to be another way," says Kris Kristofferson's rancher to Alice; and it is probably the most optimistic line to be uttered in a film of the early Seventies. Altman ends *Nashville* with quasi-plastic Americans clinging to each other and their tenuous roots as protection against the even less appealing threat of insanity and chaos. *Alice* is a small step forward, out of the mess we've made for ourselves and that has been bequeathed to us, into a future that we may make brighter. It is the traditional American optimism of Vidor's little man, still willing to believe, despite obstacles and downright proof to the contrary, that Gatsby's waves need not bear us ceaselessly into the past—that there is a future ahead.

Such is the specious optimism of the mid-Seventies. About Hollywood, these directors, if not quite so enthused as Welles at the turn of the decade, are decidedly more hopeful. As a rule, they have been given artistic control and thus responsibility. What they have done with these will be the subject of the book. Have these so-called new directors created works of genius? I think it is too early to judge. Have they made films of enduring quality? I believe so, and that is what I will attempt to analyse, making critical judgements only when they seem in order.

John Cassavetes

Of all the directors I will be discussing, Cassavetes is considered to be the least palatable. I have called him the "father" of the New Hollywood in that his fascination with realism and the actor-based narrative set the stage for the "personal" styles of the school of directors that invaded Hollywood over a decade later. Cassavetes is *not* the Godard of American cinema — an iconoclast, yes, an innovator, no. His peculiar genius is intuitive and more often than not abrasive; and those who assiduously avoid each new Cassavetes film miss a footnote and not a landmark in film history. I have included him because he *does* appeal to my taste, and rather than taking on the impossible task of converting his detractors, I will adhere to analysis of the works themselves.

To Claude Chabrol's classic abnegation of the Nouvelle Vague: "There are no waves - new or old - there is only the ocean," John Cassavetes might be inclined to quip, "There is no ocean - only water." Neo-experimentalist, self-professed "amateur," commercial pariah, the fledgling whose *Shadows* was hailed as harbinger of an American New Wave, has matured into something of a mutant. While the Hollywood "art" periphery was capitalising on the viability of counter-culture cinema with *Easy Rider, Hi, Mom!, Head, Woodstock,* etc., Cassavetes was wielding a hand-held camera in the inertia of suburbia; and later when cult, nostalgia, and Americana became fashionably emblematic of what Welles termed the youthful "harvest of grace," he was still wallowing in the everyday, chronicler of the middle-brow, middle class, Middle American: perennial losers and survivors.

The least congruous of the so-called new directors, Cassavetes is the easiest to situate and the most elusive to formal analysis. Cassavetes once told an interviewer, "I am more interested in the people who work with me than in the flim itself or in cinema," [19] and for better and for worse his films bear him out. In Kierkegaardian tradition, Cassavetes's *oeuvre* asserts that ineffable passions rather than abstract thought capture the meaning of life; and

35

John Cassavetes as he appeared in his own film, HUSBANDS

like Vidor and Capra, his five major films thus far deal with the egos of the unremarkable. While directors such as Altman and Scorsese (superficially, Cassavetes disciples) are transmuting improvisation and the rough edges of selective reality into rhythm and myth, Cassavetes continues to distill susceptibilities down to their most idiosyncratic fibre. *Mean Streets* is, for instance, as much the tale of a failed saint as of a small-time gangster, and *Nashville* is as obtrusively concerned with the ethos of Watergate as with the country music racket. *Woman Under the Influence,* on the other hand, is the story of facial tics and small betrayals: an isolated narrative preoccupied with instinctual realism.

John Cassavetes was born on December 9, 1929 in New York, the son of Greek immigrants. His father was a Harvard-educated businessman with a knack for making and losing millions; and Cassavetes was raised in *Husbands* territory, the Long Island towns of Sands Point and Port Washington. One of his most vivid recollections from childhood is of how he chipped his teeth in a fight and, unable to afford caps, refused to smile for years — an anecdote which makes one speculate on the strained smiles and laughter in his films. At Colgate University the plays of Robert E. Sherwood spurred Cassavetes to enroll at the New York Academy of Dramatic Arts, from which he graduated in 1953. Unable to find work on Broadway, Cassavetes drifted into James Dean-type roles on television and slowly made his way into such films as *The Night Holds Terror* and *Edge of the City.* Cassavetes still refers to himself as a "professional" actor and an "amateur" director, as most of his films have been financed by his acting career. In 1956 he began conducting a "method" workshop for unemployed actors, and in an interview on "Night People" - a late-night music and talk show - he mentioned the possibility of turning an especially successful improvisation into a film. Small contributions began pouring in from listeners, and thus began *Shadows* and Cassavetes's *métier* as director.

In defence of Cassavetes's prodigal inconsistencies, I have always been tempted to invoke Emerson's "A foolish consistency is the hobgoblin of little minds." As frequently as he hits the mark (usually the solar plexus), he misses it, and even his greatest admirers admit his films to be erratic. "I know people who are sensational one minute and bastards the next," Cassavetes once said. "Terribly funny one minute and morose the next."

Cassavetes's art is as replete with dichotomy as with uneven quality: he yearns for the sanguinity of Capra and makes *Faces;* bemoans the social *status quo* and hedges the polemics of change; elevates the everyday to art, but refuses to turn around and intimate a cosmic truth from the evidence of the specific. Like his characters, Cassavetes is proud of his insouciance, his irascibility, the deliberate paradoxes of his life and his *mise-en-scène.* As he expressed it, if you take eight months to shoot a film and four years to edit it (*Faces*), the result is scarcely accidental.

Yet, despite the tenaciously capricious nature of both director and *oeuvre,* a stylistic-thematic consistency does suffuse all his major works from *Shadows* to *Woman Under the Influence,* and it is thus possible to talk about Cassavetes's films not just as a series of fortuitous "privileged moments," but as a unified body of work. In a discussion of the postwar Italian directors André Bazin once reflected, "They all reject implicitly or explicitly, with humour, satire, or poetry the reality they are using", and this definition might well be applied to Cassavetes, whose most outstanding works *(Husbands* and *Woman Under the Influence)* are notable less for their intractable integrity than for their humour and compassion. Just as his denigration of style ultimately emerges as a style in itself, so his penchant for the antic and the small-time idiosyncratic is as much a credo as Frank Capra's affection for the small-time sublime.

The most distinguishing quality of Cassavetes's peculiar brand of realism is its Pirandellian flavour. In *Shadows* the characters use their personal names, and almost all the later films feature members of the Cassavetes family, with Gena Rowlands serving as a kind of American Stéphane Audran to Cassavetes's Chabrol. In *Woman Under the Influence,* Cassavetes uses not only his wife and children, but his mother and in-laws as well. While Altman may insinuate Julie Christie and Elliott Gould into the mainstream of *Nashville* as a kind of "in-joke," Cassavetes's interlacing of personality and actor is of a more subliminal nature.

In a "New Yorker" review of *A Child is Waiting* — Cassavetes's exceptionally moving, if flawed third feature — Brendan Gill puts his finger on the symbiotic relationship between art and life that renders Cassavetes's films both compelling and exceptionally unnerving. "But since *A Child is Waiting* is a study of defective children," he protests, "and since Mr. Kramer [producer] and his colleagues have chosen to use a large number of real defective children, including Mongolian idiots, to tell their story, they have produced a picture that is itself radically defective, being neither true documentary nor true work of art... One doesn't cast an authentically crazy old king as Lear,"[13] he adds.

If Cassavetes has not yet managed to cast a crazy old king as Lear, he has done his best to fuse fantasy and reality beyond differentiation. We can appreciate a John Wayne film, for instance, without taking into consideration the actor's right-wing politics; but we can scarcely watch *A Child is Waiting* or *Shadows* or even *Husbands* without confusing the viscera if not the intellect of character and player. This is not to intimate that Gena Rowlands *is* Mabel; obviously she is not. But *Woman* coaxes us to believe that if Rowlands were a lower middle class housewife, she would probably behave in a comparable fashion. Cassavetes piques the star system's Achilles heel when he shows us real retarded children playing retarded children *(A Child is Waiting),* a real unknown playing an unknown (Hugh Hurd in *Shadows*), three aging adolescents facing mediocrity and mortality that are and yet are not those men (Cassavetes, Falk, and Gazzara in *Husbands*). It is in the shady area between life and fiction that Cassavetes's films are both most effective and most disquieting — less than myth and more than fact.

The nature of Cassavetes's visual style: the shaky camera, the rough-edged texture of his most finished prints, is somewhat unique, even by neo-realist standards. (Critics suggest, less generously, that his is a bastardisation of neo-realism.) Of the classic directors, Cassavetes's stylistic philosophy comes closest to that of von Stroheim: both sharing a fascination with the particular and a thinly disguised indifference to in-depth generalisation of the abstract. Cassavetes is of the neo-realist and deep focus school of thought in that his images retain what André Bazin has called "the ambiguity of reality"; and yet the predominant aesthetic and thematic repercussion of his interpretation of form (or anti-form, as the case may be) is an unwavering myopia. Renoir's cinema, for example, sets up a tension between pantheism and solipsism by examining man in his environment: Cassavetes does precisely the opposite, employing a visual stringency that ignores extrinsic factors, be they natural or supernatural, and thus imprisons his characters within the "Huis Clos" of existing, inter-personal relationships.

Eschewing metaphor on the one hand and the painterly image (with its intimation of hidden alternatives) on the other, Cassavetes's myopic lens denies man the option of either escape or of metaphysical redemption. Cassavetes's few "open" shots of the environment — Benny and his friends exploring the sculpture garden in *Shadows;* Minnie, Zelmo, and Moskowitz tousling in the parking lot of *Minnie and Moskowitz;* Mabel watching for her children's school bus in *Woman:* tend only to underscore the alienation of the respective characters from the exigencies of the outside world. Like Vidor's magnificent final shot in *The Crowd,* Cassavetes's tentative detours into a hostile universe prove only that the characters who loom so large in the eyes of one another are but "as flies to wanton school boys" to the gods and society at large. They are American iconoclasts in the loneliest sense of the term.

Yet, anonymity is never a major preoccupation with Cassavetes. Like Capra in *It's a Wonderful Life* or Cukor in *The Marrying Kind,* he prefers to show us the microcosmic joys and tribulations of his familial community, leaving us to discover their diminutive stature in the world at large. Neither are Cassavetes's characters nourished by the cosmos that scorns them. On the contrary: for all they gleaned from London *per se,* the aging adolescents of *Husbands* might just as well have flown to Westchester. (The Italian neo-realists, on the other hand, were very much wedded to a particular place and time.)

The intransigence of Cassavetes's universe — its inherent resistance to change — is abetted by the myopic lens, but is confirmed in a plethora of circuitous narrative improvisations. With the exception of the youths in *Shadows,* all of Cassavetes's characters are sloping downhill on the parabola of life, and with sisyphean resignation they continue to push the same stone toward an unrelenting mirage of horizon. The situations may change, but the dilemmas remain the same. (*A Child is Waiting,* for instance, opens with the traumatic arrival of one child at the institution and concludes inauspiciously with an equally traumatic arrival of another.) Cassavetes describes the sequential nature of *Shadows* saying, "they [the scenes] were predicated on people having problems that were overcome with other problems;" and this pattern recurs pretty consistently throughout all Cassavetes's works.

Like John Updike's Rabbit, Cassavetes's characters nearly always maintain a strain of rebellion from a dimly remembered adolescence when more seemed possible, but like Zavattini (one of the writers Cassavetes most admires), Cassavetes creates personalities to be played upon. The involuted thinking of the atrophied little man is articulated most explicitly by Cassavetes himself (as Gus) in the subway sequence of *Husbands.* Describing the parasitic though process of the athlete *not* dying young, he says, "When you reach twenty-seven you know you'll never be a professional athlete — then you reach thirty and you watch others to see when they're gonna give up."

Although *Husbands* is Cassavetes's most perfect enunciation of the adult-child unable to grow and explore, unwilling to accept and mature, all his films are absorbed with the self-thwarted. What many have decried as redundancy in Cassavetes's *oeuvre* is merely an affirmation of stasis. (Many of the same or similar jokes are, for instance, repeated again and again, and sequence often follows upon similar sequence.) The inability to articulate or pray and thus

Cassavetes with Peter Falk and Ben Gazzara in HUSBANDS

intellectualise or transcend one's way out of the labyrinth of diurnal reality is also a recurring *motif.* The scenes of studied laughter and frenetic truculence in *Shadows;* the spasmodic mouth and limb games between husband and wife in *Woman;* the singing in *Minnie:* all these are manifestations of psychic impotence, outlets for those unable to project through the barriers of physical reality. Cassavetes's characters don't die or walk out (Harry in *Husbands* is a possible exception, although we have no idea how long he will remain in London); they pace and vomit. In fact, it is considered a deficiency of spirit *not* to seek recourse in the physical. Gus's ultimate put-down of Harry in *Husbands* is a disdainful: "You can't even vomit!"

Cassavetes' camera is essentially as Puritanical as it is myopic. The director himself constantly protests his resistance to aesthetic beauty and form *per se;* and the number of "pretty" shots in his films can probably be numbered on one hand. There is a muted shot, for instance, in *Husbands* where Peter Falk's face blends with that of a moon-faced Chinese girl just before love-making — an image all the more remarkable because its fragility is foiled by the asperity of the preceding sequence. A similar interlude appears in *Shadows* (Lelia and Tony face each other in bed), and there is a parallel silhouetting

of Nick and Mabel on the staircase in *Woman Under the Influence.*
All these shots possess the muffled contours of an Ingres portrait,
and all, either by design or intuitive continuity, record moments of
physical blendings and mental or emotional attrition. (Nick and
Mabel no longer possess a connubial sureness of one another; the
Chinese girl and Peter Falk's Archie cannot exhange a word of
conversation; Lelia says she never thought "it [sex] could be so
awful".)

Despite these notable exceptions, it is the characters and the
actors, rather than the structure and the images that dominate
Cassavetes's screen. An actor himself, Cassavetes has stated repeatedly that it is the actor's and, by implication, the character's
perspective that is vital — not the director's. In his criticism of
Stanley Kramer's editing of *A Child is Waiting* (he found the end
product too sentimental due to unnecessary cross-cutting), he made
an extremely thoughtful comment to Joseph Gelmis: "To tell the
truth as you see it, incidentally, is not necessarily the truth. To tell
the truth as somebody else sees it is, to me, much more important
and enlightening."[12] *Shadows* was entirely improvisational, with
each actor constructing his or her role and thus ingesting a peculiarly
individual vision of the truth. Contrary to popular opinion, the later
films are all fully scripted, but they are written to be attenuated
through the sensibilities of the actors involved. Thus, as with the
retarded children in *A Child is Waiting,* Cassavetes's later works very
cannily incorporate the discipline of a scripted production into the
realism of an apparently improvisational performance.

There are, of course, moments when Cassavetes's assiduous
resistance to visual metaphor relents, and raw emotions are complicated by a conscious structural technique. In *Mean Streets* and
Alice Doesn't Live Here Anymore Scorsese uses a jolting camera to
underscore the instability of his characters' lives; and this is a
technique which Cassavetes uses constantly, probably both consciously and intuitively. In *Minnie and Moskowitz,* for instance, we
watch a bibulous Minnie wending her way down a steep staircase
toward a waiting taxi. As she prepares to leave the house, we are
given a shot revealing the precipitous angle of her imminent descent
— an image as psychologically jarring as Hitchcock's use of Mt.
Rushmore in *North by Northwest* and Chabrol's manipulation of
jagged cliff in *Que la bête meure.* The shot lasts only a second, but its
deliberate brutality very effectively and wordlessly foils Minnie's
apparent stability, under-scoring an inherently fragile and vulnerable
position *vis-a-vis* the whims of the universe. It is characteristic that
while Hitchcock and Chabrol pointed their cameras at cliffs,

Cassavetes finds mortality lurking in the mundane slope of a flight of stairs.

Is Cassavetes truly as pessimistic as his characters and images imply? I would say both yes and no. A comparison between the conclusions of *Woman Under the Influence* and Scorsese's *Alice Doesn't Live Here Anymore* is helpful in understanding the nature of Cassavetes's pessimism. The Hollywoodish conclusion of *Alice,* with the suggestion that Alice has found a meaningful relationship with her rancher,intimates that despite the handicaps, of the past and of the lingering Middle American ethos, there is hope that redemptive love and earthy intelligence will lead our hero and heroine toward something a little better than what they have known.

It is this style of hope that is conspicuously absent in Cassavetes's work in general and in *Woman* in particular. Yet, when discussing *Woman* in an interview with David Sterrit, Cassavetes said, "I really think *A Woman Under the Influence* is a new film... a film that says we're not so evil as we are caring." [29] The optimism in Cassavetes' films — and there is a specious brand of optimism in all his works save *Faces* — emerges not from growth, but continuity; not from altruism, but selfishness; not understanding, but sentiment. In a discussion of *Husbands* Cassavetes said, *"Husbands* is about feelings and sentiment, and sentiment is selfish. We try to prove that selfishness is important, a way to stay sensitive." Mabel and Nick know nothing about Women's Lib — for them, it might as well be an exotic sect flourishing on Mars. They are troubled and destined to remain so — beyond the reach of sociology, religion, wisdom. But they are also in love, and Cassavets encourages us to feel the work-a-day miracle of this compensation.

The camaraderie in *Husbands* is handled in similar fashion. "Besides sex, and my wife's very good at it," confides Harry, "I love you guys best". Uneasy affection of like for like (the opposite of homosexual tenderness), the inability to come to terms with the emotional demands of romantic sentiment: these are undercurrents skilfully sheathed by frenetic activity and ribald humour. Cassavetes's characters have built fortresses against the truth: brought to the precipice they will invariably move back. There is no way out, Cassavetes says repeatedly, but there are fringe benefits along the way.

The most effective moments in Cassavetes's films are un-chartered and unexpected: the painful breakfast sequence between Gus and his English girl in *Husbands;* Lelia's morning-after sequence in *Shadows;* the closing moment in *Woman Under the Influence* where Mabel and Nick undress for bed: imperfectly wed, but committed. It is Cassavetes's belief in the spontaneity of emotions and his unswerving integrity in evoking them that elevate his films beyond moments and improvisations.

SHADOWS

If Hollywood had deigned to take note of *Shadows* at all, it would have been as a kind of bar-room *Sacre du printemps:* a syncopated narrative, *tour de force* for a trio of nameless thespians, and clearly a box-office albatross. Considering Cassavetes's own acting background and the proliferation of *Nouvelle Vague* and neo-realist films at the time, *Shadows* was a superior, but scarcely revolutionary first directorial endeavour. Like the Bill Denny character of Altman's *California Split* (a role that would have suited him perfectly), Cassavetes has always operated on the level of gut risk rather that startling innovation in both financial and artistic arenas; and the history of *Shadows* is remarkable for its timely intelligence rather than bludgeoning genius. (Oddly enough, as consistently as daring has distinguished Cassavetes himself, it has eluded the characters of his imagination.)

Conceived in a workshop for unemployed actors, *Shadows* was fittingly catalysed by the small contributions of an amorphous band of late night radio enthusiasts. (Cassavetes first off-handedly mentioned the idea of filming his improvisation in an interview with Jean Shepherd on "Night People," and $20,000 came dribbling in.) Like his father — a businessman never known for moderation — Cassavetes then gambled his own money and what funds he could scrounge from show business friends on a $40,000 16mm unscripted endeavour that was neither feature nor *cinéma vérité,* neither experimental chic nor Hollywood material.

Virtually ignored in the United States, *Shadows* managed to win the Critics Award at the 1960 Venice Film Festival, returning home to be acknowledged, if not exactly acclaimed by the *New York Times* as "fitfully dynamic, endowed with a raw but vibrant strength." Meanwhile, the film was accruing a considerable art house reputation, and critics and audiences alike were beginning to hail it as a kind of American *Breathless.*

Indeed, *Shadows* does possess many *Nouvelle Vague* ingredients — although to my mind, it is more early Chabrol and Rozier than Godard. Featuring unknowns Hugh Hurd, Lelia Goldoni, and Ben Carruthers — all maintaining their own names — *Shadows* is Cassavetes's most elastic film and his solitary investigation of youth to date. Shot intermittently over a two year period in and around the Times Square area of Manhattan, it chronicles the rites of passage of three members of a parentless black family in which the sister and younger brother pass as whites. Despite the uncharacteristic emphasis on off-beat youth, *Shadows* contains most of the elements that will appear in Cassavetes's later works: the Pirandellian framework; the shaky, hand-held camera; the myopic lens; the pre-eminence of character over structure and actor over audience.

Like Chabrol's *Les cousins, Shadows* revolves around the activities of one apartment (his camera underscores its insularity by closing in on a buzzer while eschewing all but a few open shots of the New York setting) and is concerned with the symbiotic relationship of violence and *ennui,* bravado and vulnerability. Through a series of loosely constructed anecdotes, *Shadows* takes an aging jazz musician, a truculent post-adolescent, a plucky dilettante to the brink of understanding and leaves them in a moment of revision.

Unlike its *Nouvelle Vague* antecedents, however, *Shadows* is more preoccupied with mediocrity than with libidinal virulence — with that apocalyptic moment in which one realises not so much that one can kill or be killed, as that one can be passed over. This fear of impending mediocrity is to be found in almost all the later films. Even the commercial *Child is Waiting* portrays Judy Garland as a woman afraid that age will catch up with her before she has accomplished anything worthwhile.

Despite the rough texture of the cinematography, Cassavetes's camera is more docile in *Shadows* than in his later works. There is a swift but elegiac sequence in Central Park and a leisurely stroll through the Sculpture Garden at the Museum of Modern Art: two of the handful of outdoor sequences in Cassavetes's *oeuvre.* Throughout the film the jazz music of Charles Mingus and Shifti Hadi rubs against the rough-edged cinematography and the incubated improvisations: its now doleful, now fervent tones underscoring the flailing and futile energy of the unexceptional multitude.

For purposes of analysis, it is easiest to see *Shadows* as a function of its three main characters: Hugh, Benny, and Lelia. Hugh, the jazz musician, is on his way downhill before the picture begins. In the opening sequences we see him as a frazzled father figure (lending his brother money, babying his sister) and an artistic ego shamed into introducing the "girlies" in a second-rate nightclub. The one obviously black member of the family, Hugh carries with him the perpetual stigma accorded a Negro in the white Fifties; and like the Jimmy Stewart protagonist of *It's a Wonderful Life,* he has grown testy watching the eclipse of the wanton American Dream.

One of the most moving scenes in the film is the sequence where Hugh plays the trumpet in a shabby nightclub in Philadelphia. Cassavetes handles the scene much as Chabrol handled Ginette's theatrical interlude in *Les bonnes femmes:* juxtaposing the expectations of the artist with the indifference of the audience. In *Les bonnes femmes,* we see Ginette's friends giggling, and in *Shadows* we watch the desultory chatter and phlegmatic yawns of the clientele in a bawdy club.

The difference is that while Chabrol's cinematography elevates Ginette's performance to a metaphysical level (we see Ginette herself looking up to the lights, rather than out to the audience), Cassavetes refuses to lend myth to Hugh's music. Throughout his uninspired performance, culminating in the premature arrival of the "girlies," an uneasy camera roves from the audience to his averted face, emphasising his unmollified discomfiture.

Twenty-year-old Lelia is the most attractive figure in *Shadows:* a flirtatious, indulged virgin, caught between the riskless play of childhood and the burgeoning desires of a young woman. To Hugh, she is the "baby," a child to be petted, kissed, and worried over. To David, her sexually unappealing novelist friend, she is a wide-eyed pupil who can proclaim with assurance reserved for untried wisdom: "If you're yourself, you won't get hurt."

Lelia Goldoni in SHADOWS

If tragedy is commensurate with hope, then the only real tragedy in *Shadows* is Lelia's, as she passes so quickly from play to love that one senses she may never again expose herself to tenderness. Before meeting Tony, her first lover, Lelia embodies all the frustrations and impatience of pampered youth. At twenty, she feels that life is already passing her by. "I feel like I'll never be smart," she murmurs petulantly," and I'll never get the things I want in life." She kisses Tony histrionically in the midst of a literary party, but once alone in his apartment she demurs, sensing the tenuous nature of her freedom.

The aftermath of Lelia and Tony's love scene is one of the most poignant sequences in any Cassavetes film. As their two heads rest side-by-side (an image picked up again in *Husbands* and *Woman Under the Influence*), physically aligned and metaphysical worlds apart, Lelia blurts: "I didn't know it could be so awful."

With the exception of small children, Lelia and Benny are the only two uninitiated characters in Cassavetes's works, and their "coming to life" is thus all the more beautiful and terrible for its isolation. Pauline Kael has compared Lelia's disappointment at physical love to the Lynn Carlin character's reaction to adultery in *Faces*, but the comparison is unjust.

Lynn Carlin's vomiting is really much closer to that of the men in *Husbands*: an impotent recoiling from the limitations dictated both by her society and her emotional framework. Lelia is experiencing the first tremors of life – an intimation of potential ecstasy and commensurate despair, while the wife in *Faces* is merely reaffirming her own mortality.

Benny is the most typical Cassavetes character in *Shadows*: the superficially happy-go-lucky "nice guy," whose buoyancy and passivity conceal a wealth of violence and tenderness. With luck, Benny will grow from swilling beer with his shiftless friends into the routine existence of an unquestioning middle class. Without luck, he will merge, as he does in the final scene, with the torpor of the city – a city more insidious and no less oppressive than Vidor's.

Like *Les cousins, Shadows* is about spoiled youth awoken to its vulnerability. The party scenes are replete with pretension and self-consciousness. While the students of *Les cousins* played Wagner and discussed Nazis, the "hip" younsters of *Shadows* play jazz and use words like "wow" and "making the scene." They talk a lot about freedom and self-reliance, but they take cabs home and (some) are repelled by the notion of inter-racial sex.

As in *Husbands* and *Woman Under the Influence*, it is the family—imperfect institution that it is —that salvages its tired segments, no match for the tidal mysteries of an unkind world. In the end, Hugh and his manager Rupert have sworn allegiance against the indifference of the hypothetical audience; Lelia is holding tight the warm body of a less challenging love potential; and Benny has gone off alone to come to terms with some nasty wounds picked up in a fight with a stronger gang. Badly shaken by the fight, Benny speaks for Hugh and Lelia as well when he tells his friends, "You want me to be corny and say this has taught me a lesson. O.K. — it's taught me a lesson."

FACES

Following the relative commercial success of *Shadows,* Paramount contracted Cassavetes to make a series of artistic, low-budget films, a partnership that came swiftly to a halt with the failure of *Too Late Blues* — a commercial version of the first film, which I have been unable to see, but which pleased neither critics nor the public at the time. Stanley Kramer produced Cassavetes's third film, an underestimated picture starring Judy Garland and Burt Lancaster in a semi-documentary on afflicted children, told with classical Hollywood pans and zooms and a steady camera. Despite its overt didacticism, *A Child is Waiting* is a surprisingly moving and provocative statement, suggesting much more than the traumas of the retarded child. In one rather understated sequence a father deplores the fact that the most his son can aspire to is a life as a dish-washer or a basket-weaver. The response — "I often wonder how far the rest of us get" — echoes throughout all of the more sophisticated, more idiosyncratic works.

Kramer and Cassavetes had a dispute over the editing of *A Child is Waiting,* and Kramer eventually supervised the final print himself. Cassavetes denounced the result as overly sentimental and at that point terminated his commercial film-making career. With the exception of *Minnie and Moskowitz,* all his other films have been independent projects — the finances accrued from friends, unsalaried actors, and predominantly his own resources. (In the case of *Woman Under the Influence,* Cassavetes had to mortgage his house, and the venture did not begin to pay off until years later.) Even with *Minnie and Moskowitz* Cassavetes gave Universal a run for their money: when he disapproved of their publicity campaign, he began conducting his own press screenings.

Faces was shot in eight months and released four years later. Featuring John Marley (winner of Best Actor in Venice), Lynn Carlin, Seymour Cassel, and Gena Rowlands, it was greeted with

Lynn Carlin (foreground) in FACES

raves and verbal brickbats, but little in between. It is his most
comprehensive, least elastic film — an uncompromising dissection of
a fourteen-year-old middle class marriage in in the grainy, *cinéma-
vérité* style of *Shadows*. A dolorous film, *Faces* is set chronologically
in the late Sixties, a factor more significant to its tone than its
atmosphere. For all the social upheaval in America at that time
affected them, the characters of *Faces* might just as well have been
living in the previous century. Nonetheless, the uneasiness of the
time did affect Cassavetes, who discussed the late Sixties as a period
when private sentiments protruded timorously, if at all, upon the
bludgeoning abandon of society at large. "The problem with the
people in America is that they are so politically oriented," he said at
the time, "so economically oriented, that they keep what they really
feel, their private thoughts, quite to themselves."[4]

Like *A Child is Waiting, Faces* was based on a projected rather
than an experienced reality and used improvised feelings, but
scripted dialogue. Cassavetes told Patricia Bosworth of the "New
York Times:" "I was bugged about marriage. Not my marriage
...About the millions of middle-class marriages in the U.S. that just
glide along."

Faces opens as a movie within a movie — a rather gimmicky
device, unworthy of Cassavetes or the serious *timbre* of the film.
There is an interesting twist to the Pirandellian aspect of *Faces*,

however, as Gena Rowlands plays the call girl Jeannie rather than the central figure of wife or wife-to-be she will enact in Cassavetes's later films. It is as if Cassavetes has chosen not to insinuate his own felicitous marital experience into the sour conjugal arrangement at the core of *Faces* and has instead attributed the frazzled, winsome qualities of the later Minnie to a more wanton, more glamorous Gena as a very unwhorish whore.

Cassavetes wields a brash camera in *Faces:* presenting an irreconcilable impasse at which the characters are unable to function either within or without the nuclear family structure. It opens with Dick's (John Marley) after-work rendezvous with a call girl and ends as his wife Maria (Lynn Carlin), having confessed that she no longer loves him, makes a desperate attempt to avoid her spouse as they cross along a narrow staircase. In between, Dick returns to spend an amorous evening with Jeannie: the call girl, and the solitary character capable of experiencing love without shame or posturing. Maria invites a young cross between gigolo and T-Group leader to share her bed and then attempts to kill herself in the ensuing self-consciousness and remorse. We conclude that neither fidelity nor infidelity agrees with either partner.

The extravagant physical gestures and child play which appeared first in *Shadows* are redoubled in *Faces.* Maria masks her confusion with a high-pitched laugh. Jeannie communicates with

John Marley caught in one of the many close-ups deployed by Cassavetes in
FACES

Dick in nursery rhymes (they are most fond of Peter Piper), and the characters that congregate at Jeannie's and the discotheque banter and sing, but rarely with any conviction. Jeannie is an exception.

The scene most remarkable for its portrayal of skittishness between the sexes is the dinner table sequence where Dick and Maria discuss Darlene and Freddy — a comparable *bourgeois* couple with grown children and marriage on the rocks. In order to relieve the tension of obligatory comparison, Dick and Maria laugh uproariously with all the crudity, but none of the exuberance of the men in *Husbands.* It is a prolonged scene — unconfortable to watch; and Cassavetes intensifies the isolation of each character by cutting from one to the other, rarely portraying both husband and wife in the same frame. As they laugh at ostensibly shared jokes, the camera jolts uneasily — capturing a terrifying mutual uncertainty that underlies half a lifetime of intimacy.

The waning of love is a profoundly disturbing topic, and rarely does art portray two ordinary people whose love degenerates not to lust or hate or friendship, but apathy and confused distaste. Cassavetes is not so facile as to place the blame on either party. Dicky is a less unappealing character, granted; but Maria, with her pretences, her *facades,* her very real confusion, is somehow more pitiable. Her situation is not unlike that of the elderly woman in Bergman's *Scenes from a Marriage,* who requests a divorce, admitting; "I have the capacity to love, but it is all bottled up."

Faces is Cassavetes's only film in which the viability of the nuclear family is seriously challenged. (One of the most distasteful moments in the film comes when Maria kisses her husband's face placatingly, with neither passion nor affection, and giggles. Moments later we see him out of bed asserting: "I want a divorce.") It is also the only Cassavetes film in which no children are involved — with the exception of *Shadows* which is concerned with characters themselves only a step out of childhood. Cassavetes tends to measure the felicity of family arrangements by the proclivities of the children: thus, the child becomes the measure as well as the protector of connubial affection. The happiest marriage in *Husbands* is ostensibly Gus's, and it is thus fitting that we should see *his* children rather than Archie's at the end. In the visual epilogue of *Minnie and Moskowitz,* we also meet a brood of healthy children, surrounded by doting parents and grandparents: hence, a happy ending.

Although the nuclear family suffers erosion in *Faces,* the alternatives are equally importunate. Maria and her friends find Chett (Seymour Cassel) at the discotheque, and one croons that he "succeeds where science fails". Yet, he is far from a viable alternative to familial affection. "Cry, cry — that's life," he drawls with the easy wisdom of Esalen or Encounter Group therapy; but like all Cassavetes's adulterers, he is quick to hit the roof when the husband threatens to appear.

Jeannie, while sympathetic, is an equally unsatisfactory foil for Dick's predicament. Jeannie is the mythic female: whore, mother, healer; but Dick is unable to accept reciprocal love outside the learned strictures of marriage. When they awaken the next moring, he feels compelled to demean her. He tells her she makes lousy eggs and then adds, "You're wearing false eyelashes — you're stupid."

A discrepancy between the sexes is emphasised in *Faces*. Cassavetes has said that he finds women simpler than men; and here they are both simpler and more tortuous. As in *Husbands,* the men relate more convincingly to their male companions and competition than to the opposite sex. The women, on the other hand, are portrayed as predatory or salacious in groups, unable to function without a man's attention. (Jeannie again is the exception. Like Lelia of *Shadows,* she is open to experience. When Dicky tells her to be herself, she replies candidly: "But I am myself — who else would I be?") When Chett insults Maria's friend Louise, the other women chortle among themselves. "You know something — this is going to put her back on the couch for another twenty-five years," one of them gloats.

The conclusion of *Faces* is Cassavetes's most pessimistic statement. When a cuckolded Dick returns from his night of adultery, he is greeted with the unvarnished truth. "I hate my life," says Maria. "I just don't love you." The camera follows them as they switch places, seeking and avoiding one another along the dank, narrow staircase: two little people, not so unlike the couple in Cukor's *The Marrying Kind.* They are a bit wealthier, a bit more sophisticated — and they have no reservoir of affection to draw on. It's early morning, and one can't help wondering if they will still be performing the same ritual at the end of the day.

HUSBANDS

Cassavetes deems *Woman Under the Influence* his finest film, and I think he's justified; but *Husbands* is his fullest, most anarchic work, depicting the widest spectrum of emotional experience and capturing moments which range from tediously actor-indulgent to sublime. The saga of three aging suburbanites out to expiate the death of a fourth buddy with a vengeance, *Husbands* is also ribald, witty, and at times cruel. Played by Cassavetes, Peter Falk, and Ben Gazzara (who struck up a real-life friendship during the shooting), respectively, Gus, Archie, and Harry commence a four-day binge in Port Arthur and tie it up in London. Although only one of their wives is portrayed (and she in a far from felicitous context), *Husbands* is again concerned with the nuclear family — here in absentia — as well as mortality, with the dilemma of structure and mobility, independence and responsibility.

During their brief hiatus from work and family cares, Archie, Gus, and Harry do their best to return to activities associated with puberty. They play basketball, swim, bait vulnerable adults, get stinking drunk. In London they pick up three attractive girls in a gambling parlour, sleep with them, and begin to experience the disquieting emotions of love and guilt. Gus and Archie precipitously return home where they belong, leaving Harry (whose wife has made it clear she no longer wants him) to London and an indefinite tenure of liberty.

Andrew Sarris said of *Husbands* that it "never really rises above its best moments scattered here, there and everywhere, and the best moments themselves fail to accumulate into the majestic pile of feelings that the formal sublimity of a Mizoguchi or a Ford or an Ophuls or a Renoir can give us."[2 5]

True, Cassavetes frustrates the formalist's anticipation: fragmenting images, refusing to shoot to the momentum of a crescendo or even to build an aesthetic sand castle. Yet, what is remarkable about his works and *Husbands* in particular is their amplitude. Cassavetes said recently: "I would like the audience not really to relate to what's going on on-screen, but to relate to their own lives while they're watching it." In this respect, *Husbands* undoubtedly succeeds — and what is more conclusive proof than that Betty Friedan hailed it as a masterpiece of Women's Lib?

In *Rabbit Run,* John Updike recounts his protagonist's mixed feelings at the death of his son in a reverie on flesh and happenstance. "Rabbit resents her [his wife] being able to walk; resents her not dying of remorse and shame. What kind of grief is it that permits them to walk? The sense of their thick bodies just going on, wrapping their hearts in numbness and small need, angers him. They walk with their child through streets they walked as children... Why does anyone live here? Why was he set down here, why is this town, a dull suburb of a third-rate city, for him the center and index of a universe that contains immense prairies, mountains, deserts, forests, coastlines, cities, seas?"[3 1]

It is feelings such as these, never articulated, which haunt the heroes of *Husbands*. Like *Rabbit Run, Husbands* revolves around a masculine ethos of competition, virility, physical prominence and verbal reticence. When Gus speaks French in the London casino, for instance, we are as taken aback as if Humphrey Bogart had broken into Latin in *The African Queen*. These athletes outliving their laurels look somewhat incongruous even in their own offices. Gus doubles over in laughter before his sedated dental patient, suggesting that he regards his role as grown-up dentist in the line of a cosmic prank.

The least athletic of the three, Harry is always a little isolated from his cronies, suspicious of their physical intimacy. When he confesses that he doesn't understand people who play to win Gus and Archie regard him with the same alarm Hawkeye accords Painless in *M*A*S*H* when he learns that the dentist views poker as "just a game." Later Gus berates him, only partially in jest: "You can't even vomit" — e.g. you can't express sentiment and anguish in the terms of our physical code. Yet, it is Harry ("homo Harry," they quip) who articulates one of the pivotal dilemmas of the film: "except for sex," he admits, "and my wife's very good at it, I like you guys better."

The uneasiness inherent in male-female relationships — in sex as opposed to basketball, reciprocity rather than camaraderie — is depicted in *Husbands* with a subtlety and a credibility practically unparalleled in cinema. Cassavetes's men are forever denying his female characters their intelligence and idiosyncrasies. In *Woman,* for example, Nick is only capable of approaching Mabel as wife and mother — he cannot see her as an individual. Dick of *Faces* and the one-night adulterers of *Husbands* feel compelled to treat their extramarital sexual companions as whores. Paradoxically, it is also Cassavetes's men who are incapable of extricating sex from love, whore from angel. Archie, for instance, says of a girl he could not exchange one word with (but slept with): "I'm in deep trouble emotionally. I don't want to go home. That Chinese girl — I'm crazy about her."

To make a rather far-fetched comparison, most of Cassavetes's women are parallel to Keaton's women: idiosyncratic, lively, relatively complex; but Cassavetes's men regard them in a distortion of the Chaplin "pedestal" perspective, as if by their very "femaleness" they are made to be cherished and thus feared. The most happily married, best adjusted of the three husbands, Gus is thrown off-balance by a roguishly attractive English girl he seduces into antic, bullying, mutually fulfilling sex the first day in London. Yet, thoroughly unliberated male that he is, Gus, (like Dick of *Faces*) is

Peter Falk, Ben Gazzara and John Cassavetes "on the town" in HUSBANDS

forced to badger her in order to mask his own vulnerability. "I hate aggressive women," he announces at breakfast the next morning, and proceeds to deride her. Later he pleads with Archie, "We got five children between us, two houses, two garages..."

The cruelty of the male is underscored throughout *Husbands.* In one scene in the London gambling parlour Archie heckles a particularly pathetic old woman — lips twittering, eyes appealing. He flatters her and then drops her with a guffaw. At the bar all three men torment a lady whose singing is no more strident than their own; and in one excruciatingly truculent scene Harry nearly kills his wife because she won't love him.

As in *Rabbit Run,* the dissatisfied neo-adolescents find various ways of fighting the myopia of their existence and the encroachment of age. At one point Archie, the least bright of the three, tells Gus: "He [Harry] went into the house this morning because he was supposed to. That's wrong... I can't put my finger on what's wrong with that, but that's wrong." Like children defying their mothers, Archie and Gus refuse to change clothes, vomit with gusto, take off at a moment's notice for London.

Ultimately, however, they return to Sands Point for the not so simple reason that they must. They have five children between them, two houses, and, we presume, love as well as commitment. They've had a glimpse of London, but it's no more real to them than Brooklyn is to the Italian scumbags of Scorsese's *Mean Streets.*

Gifts in hand, Archie and Gus are not returning to the *"Huis Clos"* of *Faces.* Gus's children are the most refreshing images in *Husbands;* and their appearance at the end is peculiarly auspicious. In the children a mystical bond of love is introduced as antidote to the compelling, restricting responsibilities of adulthood. It is almost as if, looking into his daughter's suddenly teary eyes, Gus has travelled the cycle from death (the funeral in the opening scene) to birth; and in so doing has begun to grow up.

MINNIE AND MOSKOWITZ

Cassavetes's "entertainment" film, *Minnie and Moskowitz* is neither realistic nor the least bit credible plot-wise. The tale of an impossible mating of prom queen and car parker, it matches a wasp sophisticate (Gena Rowlands) with a bungling, long-haired, good -for-nothing New Yorker (Seymour Cassel) and leaves them baby-making in an ever-sunny, fecund L.A. When the film opens a pretty, blonde Minnie is unhappily involved with a married man (played by Cassavetes) and disillusioned with the un-Hollywoodish bent of her real life. "You know I think movies are a conspiracy," she tells her friend Florence. "They set you up to believe everything." (Obviously, she has not seen *Faces.*) Weaned on Bogart, she is not quick to accept chance acquaintance Seymour Moskowitz as answer to a woman's prayers. "Seymour, that's not the face," muses Minnie, as she scrutinises Moskowitz's unremittingly prosaic mug. But he's determined they'll marry, and marry they do; and the whole Cassavetes-Cassel family gets into the act with Gena's brother as minister; her mother playing Minnie's mother; Cassel's mother playing the bridesmaid Florence; and Cassavetes's Mama outshining them all as a strident, incredulous Jewish mother. ("You mean to tell me she's not pregnant?" gasps Mrs. Moskowitz, realising that Minnie is marrying her son by choice.)

"Films that really impressed my life as I look back on it seem to all have been made by Frank Capra," said Cassavetes after making *Shadows. "Mr. Smith Goes to Washington, Mr. Deeds Goes to Town, It's a Wonderful Life* — that sort of thing. Those films showed the beauty of people having some kind of hope and dignity no matter in what strata of society they moved."[33] While Cassavetes shares Capra's sentiment, dignity and hope are qualities conspicuously

Gena Rowlands and Seymour Cassel, the ill-matched pair of lovers in MINNIE AND MOSKOWITZ

missing from the bulk of his films; and his affection for Capra the storyteller is rather like the yearning of the intellectuals of the *Nouvelle Vague* for the intuitions of Hitchcock. *Minnie* is a pleasant exception: far from a masterpiece, it is a buoyant, back-handed tribute to Hollywood in general and romance in particular — with the repeated humming and singing of "I Love You Truly" a fitting paean to Capra's *It's a Wonderful Life.*

Like Scorsese's *Alice Doesn't Live Here Anymore, Minnie* reflects the advantages as well as the disadvantages of a commercial product — of the sublimation of personal obsessions within the context of upbeat comedy. Earlier I mentioned the shot where Minnie leaves Florence's apartment: a vertiginous overhead stressing the precipitous nature of Minnie's helter-skelter existence. There is also an unsettling degree of physical violence in *Minnie.* Like slapstick comedians, Cassavetes's characters never seem to incur bruised bones or slashed faces, but the continual tousling — particularly in sexual arenas (Minnie is initially so rough with her married lover we presume him an intruder) — under-scores both a fear of tenderness and a prescience of psychic danger.

The complexities of love are also insinuated into the fantasy framework. Minnie's outrageous lunch date Zelmo; her married lover; the lonely bridesmaid Florence: all of these are the underside of Hollywood romance — the side Cassavetes is habitually inclined to explore. In one scene we are privy to a mini-*Faces,* with the adulturous husband returning to discover that his wife has attempted suicide. The darker aspects of romance are again alluded to when the lover, accompanied by his son (coincidentally, Cassavetes's real life son) confronts Minnie at the museum to sever their relationship. "I keep remembering the laughs we had," he tells the bruised, indignant Minnie; and we witness the first almost viable alternative to marital fidelity. Typically, the Cassavetes male is uncomfortable with the concept of divorce, and the children tip the scale in favour of the family — sending the confused lover back to the lacerations of a *Faces*-like impasse.

But these are merely undertones in what is essentially whimsy. Minnie and Moskowitz are beautifully mismatched, sharing little save blonde locks and a determination not to be lonely. She owns an extravagantly furnished apartment — he's broke; she drinks Vermouth-Cassis, which he's never heard of. Cassavetes never develops their characters beyond caricature, and it would be presumptuous to speculate on profundities in their ludicrous liaison. For instance, we never have any idea who Minnie really is. Does she work as curator or receptionist at the museum? Does she love Moskowitz, or merely snatch at the chance for a lopsided Hollywood sunset? We are not meant to know, and the ins and outs of marriage are left to his next and most profound work, miles out of Hollywood and deep in the reality of Middle America.

A WOMAN UNDER THE INFLUENCE

After two years spent in search of a distributor, *Woman Under the Influence* opened at the 1974 New York Film Festival. Cassavetes had originally conceived of *Woman* as a theatrical *tour de force* for Gena and a treatment of the much-neglected "woman problem" from a female perspective. When Gena balked at portraying the emotionally draining role of Mabel nightly on stage, Cassavetes mortgaged half his home, called up friends and family, and began another unsalaried production.

Once again an exploration of middle class (this time lower middle class) marriage at metaphysical crossroads, *Woman* is Cassavetes's first confrontation with the awesome nature of connubial love. While the final image of *Faces* leaves husband and wife confined to raw mutual distaste, *Woman Under the Influence* concludes as Mabel and Nick prepare for bed. In *Woman,* Cassavetes's always superb acting is elevated to the sublime with Gena Rowlands's flailing, inarticulate Mabel masterfully embodying the ambivalence and the depth of the ailing female — liberated or not — and Peter Falk brilliantly interpreting the flawed, loving nature of the man who almost unwittingly betrays her.

Cassavetes has said of *Woman* that he found it "the first picture I've had anything to do with that wasn't made out of plain simple feelings, but out of a real desire to do something in my profession. It was extremely frightening for me not to come to work out of enthusiasm and instead put myself up as something of a craftsman."[1] The craftsmanship paid off, and *Woman* is the least indulgent of Cassavetes's works. Briefly, the story revolves around a housewife and mother, deeply in love with her husband, fiercely attached to their brood of children; and yet disturbed and incapable of functioning. She is "different" from everyone else: she dwells on the problems of self-expression, encourages her children to dance nude, vents physically the frustrations she is incapable of articulating. Mabel is not a victim of Women's Lib: she behaves the way she thinks is right. A simple guy, her husband (Nick) loves, but scarcely understands his wife and finally heeds his blustering mother and commits Mabel to an institution. When she returns months later, unsteady, but determined to succeed, the situation is just as hopeless and as loving as it was on the traumatic day of her departure.

Cassavetes's canvas is broader, his camera more flamboyant in *Woman.* The outside world assumes a validity of sorts— if only as a means of contrast; and we watch Nick in his truck, fixing a water pipe, at the beach. Even Mabel gets out of the house in *Woman,* and there is a marvellous sequence where Cassavetes stresses her eccentricity by portraying her inability to communicate with passers-by on the sidewalk. *Woman* is also the first film since *Shadows* in which a significant number of outsiders encroach upon the family domain: Mabel's one-night-stand, Nick's co-workers, the various parents, the doctor, neighbourhood children and their father.

On the surface, *Woman* is a study in betrayal — male betrayal in particular. In the beginning of the film Nick breaks their date, and Mabel retaliates by getting drunk and taking a stranger home to bed. When this stranger wakes up the following morning, she is gone. At first, he tries to locate her, and we fear (as he must) that she has attempted to harm herself. When his cajolery elicits no response, he

*Peter Falk and Gena Rowlands as Nick and Mabel in A WOMAN UNDER THE
INFLUENCE: a marriage at metaphysical crossroads*

begins to rationalise. "If you're in the shower, then you're all right."
In other words, "I cannot be bothered to take responsibility for
you."

This stranger's betrayal is harbinger of the events to follow, and
yet it is much too simplistic to view *Woman* as an indictment of male
complacency. Like Coppola's *Rain People* (which approaches the
problem a few rungs higher on the intellectual and social scale and
from the aspect of female rather than male betrayal), it is rather a
deliberation on how far one human being can be expected to put
himself out for another. It is a query about the extent to which love
means responsibility and an exploration of the capacities of both
men and women for self-abnegation. Just before he allows Mabel to
be committed, Nick says, "I love you... I'd lay down on a railroad
track for you..." And so he might, but then that is not the issue.

Like the "husbands," Nick is very similar to Updike's Rabbit.
He is less astute than Gus, but equally "physical" in the sense that
his motivations are triggered by the body, rather than a transcendent
intellect or faith. Updike's characterisation of Rabbit's final sprint is
very similar to Cassavetes's depiction of Nick's betrayal. "It's like
when they heard you were great and put two men on you and no
matter which way you turned you bumped into one of them and the
only thing to do was pass. So you passed and the ball belonged to the
others and your hands were empty and the men on you looked
foolish because in effect there was nobody there."

Nick is unable to handle the myriad difficulties of Mabel; so he passes. Of all Cassavetes's males, he is the simplest, while Mabel is the most complex of his females. Like Natalie of *Rain People* she suffers the traumas of claustrophobia; but unlike Natalie she lacks the capacity to intellectualise or to seek alternatives. Mabel does not fear motherhood. "You know I never did anything in my life that was worthwhile except make you" she tells her children with conviction; and they reciprocate her affection. Like Maria in *Faces,* she is trying to "find" herself, but she lacks the equipment and the support. Nick tells his wife, "Be yourself" — the very words Dick uses with Jeannie. Like Lelia in *Shadows* and Jeannie in *Faces,* Mabel *is* being herself to the best of her ability; what she is not being is the wife Nick wants her to be.

Woman is certainly Cassavetes's most complex exploration of the family, and his conclusions are far from unilateral. While the children serve as a bond between their parents the in-laws are more often than not impediments. At first fulsome, Nick's mother ultimately evolves as more misguided than intentionally cruel. While she is instrumental in sending Mabel away, she has no ideas whatsoever about rehabilitation. Nor does Mabel's own father comprehend what she wants when Mabel asks him to stand up for her.

Of all Cassavetes's characters, Nick and Mabel are least likely to change. The betrayal and the months at the institution will affect Mabel only as London did Gus of *Husbands:* as an intimation of complexities ordinary people cannot or are unwilling to handle. Her psychic demands for individuality and fulfilment will be overridden time and again by the demands of love and circumstance.

Mabel and Nick do achieve a specious kind of redemption. Not only do they love their children, but they love each other — very imperfectly, but very passionately. While the modern woman's stomach may sink for a moment as Mabel slips quickly back under the influence not only of her husband but of a lifetime's conditioning, the upbeat syncopation of the final chords ·of music are not totally unfounded. Their lives are no less "wonderful" than those of Capra's couple in *It's a Wonderful Life* or Cukor's in *The Marrying Kind* — or many of Chaplin's and Griffith's and De Sica's and Fellini's survivors, for that matter. What they possess — on an earthy level, granted — is that very passionate love that sent decades of Hollywood stars toward sunsets. While Cassavetes's films, like Le Nain's paintings, are divested of glitter, and while he has turned the romantic ellipsis inside out, he has not denied its power.

Robert Altman directing McCABE AND MRS. MILLER

Robert Altman

In "The Crack-Up," F. Scott Fitzgerald observed that "the test of a first-rate intelligence is the ability to hold two opposed ideas in the mind and still retain the ability to function." Fitzgerald was not the first to express the dilemma of the modern intellect, but his criterion is, nonetheless, peculiarly apt when applied to the contemporary film-maker *cum* artist — the creative temperament rejecting both the financial-political roots that nourish it and the viability of alternatives. It is a first-rate intellectual ambivalence (not to be confused with Fitzgerald's own "cynical idealism") which imbues *Nashville's* vapid "You may say that I ain't free, but it don't worry me" with reverberations of pathos and tenacity: a different species of moral elasticity, indeed, than that which generated Octave's philosophic, "You see, in this world there is one awful thing, and that is that everyone has his reasons," in *La règle du jeu.* If I am more predisposed to Renoir's humanistic yearning (and Fitzgerald's failed romanticism) than to Robert Altman's tougher brand of actualism, it is not to deny the formidable intelligence of the latter.

Altman is the "new" Hollywood's prodigal son: the most prolific (between 1970 and 1975, he made nearly two films a year) and, many claim, the most talented of its scions. Born in Kansas City, Missouri in 1925, son of a successful insurance salesman (an inveterate gambler on the side), Altman was raised a Roman Catholic and college-educated in mathematics. Returning from military service as a Second World War bomber pilot, Altman took a job directing industrial films for the Calvin Company in Kansas City, a position that eventually led to directing and producing *The Delinquents* in 1957 and co-directing and co-producing *The James Dean Story* a year later. Altman then spent most of the next decade working in television — directing episodes of *Alfred Hitchcock Presents* (after rejecting his third script, he was not invited back), *Bonanza,* and *Whirlibirds.* In 1967 he made a science fiction feature — *Countdown* — for Warner Brothers and in 1969 the technically deft, but only marginally effective *That Cold Day in the Park* (Ingo Preminger claims that had he seen this film, he would never have offered Altman *M*A*S*H*.) In 1970 he was anywhere from the fourteenth to the sixteenth director — depending on whose version one subscribes to — to be offered Ring Lardner Jr.'s script of *M*A*S*H*, and the rest, as they say, is legend. Asked about his twenty-odd years in industrial films and television, Altman usually shrugs that besides furnishing a technical dexterity, they taught him precisely what he *didn't* want to do.

Whatever their fringe benefits, Altman's films aspire first and foremost, to be entertaining. While his improvisational techniques and gifted repertoire of actors have prompted comparisons with such European surrealists as Jacques Rivette, Altman is the first to declare himself a commercial film-maker. He makes his films for a general public and trusts the reactions of the average moviegoer: that amorphous mass he has spent half a decade winking and throwing celluloid darts at. Despite his commercial intentions Altman's films are by no means easy to digest: the congratulatory nihilism of *M*A*S*H* and *The Long Goodbye* is abrasive (albeit intentionally so), while *McCabe and Mrs. Miller* has often been dismissed as pretentious and *California Split* as untowardly sanguine.

Altman has spent the first five years of his Hollywood career shaping a series of *genre* pictures (an anti-war film, a caper, a psychological thriller, a shamus, a cops and robbers, a gambling film, and a musical) to his idiosyncratic sensibility. *Brewster McCloud* was not the penultimate caper, any more than *Breathless* signalled the death of the narrative feature. What Altman has appended to the *genre* film is a contemporary dimension and he has evolved a style attuned to his own unromantic, dislodged vision of the universe.

Superimpositions, overlapping dialogue, and scrambled soundtracks are as endemic to the Altman style as camera angles and cameos are to Hitchcock. Even the casual viewer is likely to connect the loud-speaker system in *M*A*S*H*, for instance, with Hal Philip Walker's mobile slogan van in *Nashville*. Similarly akin are René Auberjonois's bird lectures in *Brewster McCloud*, Leonard Cohen's ballads in *McCabe and Mrs. Miller*, Susannah York's unicorn readings in *Images*, the title song in *The Long Goodbye*, the radio broadcasts in *Thieves Like Us*, and the gambling announcements and Phyllis Shotwell routines in *California Split*. For convenience's sake, I will label these auxiliary *motifs* (many conceived after shooting) as superimpositions. As a rule, Altman uses the superimposition to inject an element of irony or self-consciousness, but if the device is recognisable in each successive film, its function is by no means predictable.

The title song in *The Long Goodbye,* for instance, is integral to the plot, amplifying the transience suggested by an ever-itinerant *mise-en-scène.* (A corollary aspect of "The Long Goodbye" is that it is never sung in full — thus never resolved, even after the apparent plot resolution and Marlowe's harmonica-tooting "Hurray For Hollywood" exit.) Sometimes ironic, sometimes uncannily appropriate, the Leonard Cohn songs have a parallel effect in *McCabe and Mrs. Miller.* Like "The Long Goodbye," they are songs of alienation, but their elegiac, moody timbre weaves the various gossamers of plot together.

The radio broadcasts in *Thieves Like Us* produce precisely the opposite effect. Rather than confirming the tone of the *mise-en-scène,* they serve a contrapuntal role. The "Gangbusters" episodes, for instance, undermine the thematic salience of felony. Introduced as background for the bank robbing sequences, they tend to make the outlaw look childish, his vocation as American as Coca-Cola. The monotonous repetition of "And thus did Romeo and Juliet consummate their first interview by falling madly in love with each other" similarly works against the romance of Keechie and Boyie's first mating.

Altman's most effective use of the superimposition *motif* is in *Nashville,* where Hal Philip Walker's booming recording comes to define the film's major characters. While the P.A. announcements in *M*A*S*H* are gratuitous, figuring significantly in the plot only during Hot Lips's stereophonic debauchery, the Walker truck subtly insinuates itself into mainstream action. Like King Lear's fool, who disappears after the king has absorbed his message, the truck tends to recede once its ethos has been transfused into the foreground figures. It is also interesting that in the final scene at the Parthenon a national television broadcast, rather than the local truck, poses the most absurd question of all: "Has Christmas always smelled like oranges to you?"

Like the superimpositions, Altman's improvisational techniques are central to his style. Whether McCabe's mumblings and Barbara-Jean's breakdown are in fact spontaneous, actor-initiated, or only apparently so is almost impossible to detect. (Reputedly, Ronee Blakeley *did* write her own breakdown scene, while many of Warren Beatty's haphazard wise-cracks are scripted.) The end product, as with *Shadows* (unscripted) versus *Faces* (scripted) is virtually the same. Altman told "Sight and Sound": "According to me it's a collaborative art...If I tried to put in the middle of it everything that was in my imagination, it would be simply that. It would be a very sterile work."[22] But he has also said of improvisation on the set,

"It's fairly controlled. The improvisation usually comes out in rehearsals."

Both Altman's improvisational look and his uncannily appropriate atmospheres underscore the thin line between actualism — which I'll loosely define as suggesting authenticity — and realism, suggesting veracity. Once again turning to the wisdom of André Bazin: "Realism in art can only be achieved in one way — through artifice."[4] Thus, there is a plausibility to the comfortable values in Howard Hawks's *The Big Sleep* that is intentionally dispelled in the more authentic ambience of *The Long Goodbye*. The town Altman constructed for *McCabe and Mrs. Miller* suggests authenticity, but the "flashing," the cross-cutting, the sardonic humour, undermine emotional realism. Similarly, Altman's famous garbled dialogues (he boasts of throwing most of his best lines away) do not so much suggest casual conversations as an ailing soundtrack. This disruption of the narrative is Altman's way of underlining the function of artifice and at the same time commenting on the arbitrary nature of his story. "I'm trying to reach toward a picture," says Altman. "I don't think I'll ever succeed but somebody will, a picture that's totally emotional — not narrative or intellectual — where the audience walks out and can't tell anything about it except what they feel . . ."[3]

To undermine the plot further, Altman approaches his story at oblique angles. Brewster's flight comes as *dénouement* rather than climax; Bowie's death is experienced not through his own blood bath, but in a slow-motion close-up of Keechie's scream (an effective foil for Arthur Penn's slow-motion bludgeoning in *Bonnie and Clyde*). Explicit violence, like verbal fluency, is reserved for the minor character. Fast-talking gangster Marty Augustine unleashes a Pandora's boxful of virulence in *The Long Goodbye* when he precipitately slashes his girlfriend's nose. Similarly, it is the "glib" personalities like Dr. Verringer *(Long Goodbye)*, the lawyer *(McCabe)*, and the campaign manager *(Nashville)*, who speak fluently, while their betters are either laconic (Lydia and Haven in *Nashville*, Bill in *California Split*) or discursive (Wade in *Long Goodbye*, Warren Beatty as McCabe, Elliott Gould in all roles, and nine out of ten of the *Nashville* singers).

Not all of Altman's thematic concerns can be so neatly aligned with his style. To invoke Fitzgerald once again, there is an interesting line in *Gatsby*, where that romantic *ego* turns to the narrator and protests of Daisy's love for her husband, "In any case, it was only personal." For the romantic, there is a vast difference between the personal and the vital. Max Ophuls's Madame de . . .is permitted designless flirtations and sex with a husband she loves at best in desultory fashion, but only as prelude to the love of her life: the baron who will redeem her and for whose love she will (beautifully) die. Even the heroine of *Letter from an Unknown Woman* is allotted an interlude of security with a wealthy husband before the tumultuous rekindling of the passion of her youth. Similarly, Paul Mazursky's Blume of *Blume in Love* commits *physical* adultery, but such infidelity in no way mitigates his intense emotional monogamy.

For the unromantic (Gatsby's Daisy, for instance), the "personal" becomes more complex, less generic. Love is not an abstract whole, but rather an aggregation of particulars — lust, loneliness, boredom, impossibility. Valid one minute, these factors are subject to revision the next. This is the passion of Altman's world. Keechie outlives love through expedience; Mrs. Miller opts for opium over McCabe. One might make a case for Elliott Gould's Marlowe as the sole Altman character to pursue romanticism to its logical conclusion — death; but the details of *The Long Goodbye* mitigate against so atavistic an interpretation. Marlowe's killing, like the "Hurray for Hollywood" finale is merely a contemporary outlet for shaking off bad vibes. "If the world's crazy, why not enlist?" he seems to be saying as he dispenses with Lennox.

An article in "Sight and Sound" quotes Altman as saying that the only thematic continuity in his films is a "preoccupation with the flexible boundary between sanity and insanity." This precarious balance can be traced to every film from *That Cold Day in the Park,* where the frustrated virgin proves both docile and psychotic, right through to *Nashville,* where a self-important king of Country Music ultimately places the good of his Nashville Kingdom above his personal welfare. Yet, Altman's definition of sanity is itself in a state of flux, as no one who looks carefully at the discrepancy between *M*A*S*H,* the quintessential anti-war film of the Sixties, and *Nashville,* the anti-*hommage* to the bicentennial, can fail to note.

In *M*A*S*H* we are presented with recognisable heroes — heroes without a cause, but heroes nonetheless. Hawkeye, Trapper John, and their coterie of easy riding elitists are the scruffy, non-verbal heroes of Woodstock transplanted into the Korean war zone. They confound the military Establishment at every juncture, ridicule nationalism, religion, lofty ideals; but they stick by each other like Kesey's Merry Pranksters. (Note the disappointment when their Korean orderly is drafted.) Most important, they are excellent doctors. In *M*A*S*H,* Altman constructs a functioning anti-Establishment that confirms the peace marcher's hypothesis: if *we* ran the world, not only would it be a lot more amusing, but a good deal more efficient as well. "I'm for anybody who bucks the establishment, who goes counter to this mediocrity, this insanity," said Altman. "My pictures are sane. There is sanity when the heroes go against the insanity of the outside world; and the audience can feel it. So I'm not without hope." [18]

The 1970 counter-culture audiences (and who in 1970 didn't envision himself as counter-culture?) immortalised *M*A*S*H,* with its soothing correlatives (cool equals sane, square equals crazy) and its complacent, often cruel wit directed at cartoon ministers of organised religion, government, war. *Nashville* is quite a different story. There are no Hawkeyes in the Country Music capital — not even a bungling McCabe, with poetry in his soul. The only thoroughly sympathetic character is Lydia, also not so coincidentally the most inward of the personalities. Bucking the Establishment is *passé;* the Replacement Party is a bad joke: Connie (her own "replacement" party) is more venal and devious than the simple-minded Barbara Jean she'd love to outsing. Even the anti-politics so smugly championed in *M*A*S*H* is derided in *Nashvile.* "I don't vote for anybody for President," boasts vain rock singer Tom. "Hey, sergeant: kill anybody this week?" he taunts a docile soldier standing nearby.

America's strengths as evinced in *Nashville* are traditional: emerging unexpectedly in unlikely situations and people. The buffoon-like Barnett loves his wife (albeit an extension of himself) so unshakably that he humiliates himself for her sake. Lydia appears to love Tom, but "for the sake of the children," she remains with her unappealing husband. Most significant, it is Haven, bastion of the Country Music Establishment, who places the "people" above himself in the midst of the assassination, concentrating on keeping the music "a-going" rather than exploring his private wounds. The wheel has come full-circle, so to speak: the anti-heroes have grown up; the children no longer promise to overthrow and ameliorate. America turns for direction to the heritage of a cultural system that has survived two hundred traumatic years.

Altman's women survive to procreate, and his families stay together to regenerate their ethos. Although most of Altman's characters are loners or drifters, there is an almost Catholic reverence for family where it does exist. Altman does not allow Eileen to kill Wade, for instance, as she does in the Chandler book: he commits suicide instead. Particularly illustrative of the Altman (and American) vision of family is the ending of *Nashville,* where the various spouses pair off, like passengers on Noah's Ark, in the face of calamity. They may have been unfaithful, but they are spontaneously loyal. Bill runs from his date L.A. Joan to his wife Mary; the lawyer grabs Lydia from her gospel singing post; Barnett cradles the wounded Barbara Jean, shrieking, "I can't stop that blood," convinced it is his obligation to do so.

In one respect or another, Altman's films — with *Images* the exception — probe the American spirit. Wisely, he rarely tackles America head-on. In *The Long Goodbye,* homely populist values are parodied, in *California Split,* the conceit of infinite possibility. (What do you do once you've hit the jackpot, or the Pacific Coast?) Altman said: *"McCabe* is the genesis of what our values are today in America. We started with behind every fortune there is a crime. We'll carry it a generation further in *Thieves* . . . It's not about robbing banks. It's about what we condone." [6]

Altman's America is the Dr. Eckelberg billboard of *Gatsby* without the green light — it's *All the King's Men* without Jack Burden and *The Sound and the Fury* without Quentin and Dilsey. Though *genre* pictures, Altman's films are only deceptively nostalgic: their judgements are contemporary, now and then quaintly displaced by time. Altman said, "Like a lot of Americans I'm ambivalent about America. I like it and I hate it." At the end of *The Razor's Edge,* Somerset Maugham articulates a peculiarly apt definition of Altman's American: "so wistful of good, so cocksure on the outside, so diffident within, so kind, so hard, so trustful and so cagey, so mean and so generous." Altman might well have added — so giving and so selfish, so vital and so static, so translucent and so inaccessible.

M*A*S*H

While orthodox auteurists have gone to great lengths to defend *That Cold Day in the Park* as part of the Altman *oeuvre,* I find it a rather mediocre film, "Altmanesque" only in so far as it suggests a brilliant surface—in this case too stylish for its subject. Altman's evocation of the stolid Canadian life rhythm is admirable as are Kovacs's visual details. There is lovely footage in the opening sequences, for instance, where the pluvious outdoors, replete with dripping verdure and a smothered, isolated park bench, are nicely foiled by the warmth and desultory conversation inside the apartment. However, the film falls apart — even visually — as it attempts to weave the erotic tenderness and frustrations of its mild-mannered heroine into a classical psychodrama. Altman makes a never-to-be-repeated mistake of confronting his schizophrenic heroine (Sandy

Trouble   on   the   touchline   in   M*A*S*H

Dennis playing a typical Sandy Dennis role) head-on, and thus what comes across in *Images* as ellipsis (albeit abstruse) is here merely uninteresting. The film itself is of interest only as the skeleton of Altman's obsession with the proximity of sanity and insanity, a theme which emerges much more tenably in *M*A*S*H*.

M*A*S*H (Mobile Army Surgical Hospital) is a ribald comedy, and there is no aspect of the film, blood and gore included, that does not work on a comic level. Concerned with the unpatriotic activities of a doctor's unit in Korea, *M*A*S*H* is primarily interested in two officers: Hawkeye (Donald Sutherland) and Trapper John (Elliott Gould), a couple of the Army's least reverent servants. Their friends are characters like Painless — the dentist who loses his desire to live and play poker when he suffers a case of twenty-four hour impotence; and their nemeses are officers like Major Burns, who believes in God, and Major Hot Lips, who believes in the Army. The movie, like the television series that followed, never goes anywhere, but moves quickly from one comic episode to the next.

The devices in *M*A*S*H* are marvellously effective. The Public

Address System spews forth a ceaseless series of outrageous noises
from a Japanese "My Blue Heaven", to a stuttered re-rescheduling of
Yom Kippur services, to the music of Hot Lips and Major Burns
copulating. In *M*A*S*H*, Altman's lines are pithier and his editing
more directive than in the later films. Never is a word or the
opportunity for a laugh thrown away. For instance, while Hawkeye
is interrogating Major Burns on Hot Lips's dexterity in the bedroom
("Is she better than self-abuse?"), Altman cuts back and forth to
Trapper John's side-line extrapolations. ("Watch out for your
goodies, Hawkeye — that guy's a sex maniac. Hot Lips didn't satisfy
him . . . ").

Even in the overlapping dialogues, Altman creates a mood of
authenticity without ever allowing us to miss a vital word. A typical
situation is the juxtaposition of Hawkeye and Duke plotting to
seduce the nurses with the nurses themselves, chatting excitedly —
unaware of the men's presence. We seem to be missing something in
both conversations through hearing them simultaneously; but if one
listens carefully, it becomes apparent that both are merely babbling
about nothing (the women their finger nails, the men their lust).
Placed together, the dialogues are funny — separately, they're
expendable. Altman's camera is very clever in *M*A*S*H* holding
little back in the way of virtuosity. Painless's Last Supper is made a
big deal of, for instance, shot wide angle through a tent screen and
dressed in the manneristic effects of Tintoretto's painting. In the
football sequence, we are treated to T.V. coverage; and there are lots
of pannings, cross-editings, and close-ups during the Hot Lips
debauchery and the Tokyo trip. But the director is already
sufficiently adept to avoid "showing off," and there are many
sequences where the scope lens is docile, leaving the *mise-en-scène* to
the characters. *M*A*S*H* also introduces Altman's ironic use of
music, with playful, banal songs like "Suicide Is Painless" foreshadowing the upbeat, vapid tunes of *Brewster, Nashville,* etc.

While it plays to anti-war sentiment, *M*A*S*H* is no more a
rhetorical anti-war film than Joseph Heller's *Catch-22. Catch-22* has
an anti-institutional message, which fits very well with the use of
the military establishment as looming microcosm of Big Business.
Altman's film has similar overtones, but it is primarily black comedy.
Its humour is more smug than daring. For instance, asked where she
hails from, Hot Lips replies, "I like to think of the Army as my
home," and a "hip" audience is guaranteed to laugh or at least groan
at her sincerity. In a similar fashion, Altman sets the ever-vulnerable
Hot Lips up for perpetual put-downs. "How could a person like that
(Trapper) have reached a position of authority in the U.S. Army?"
she inquires incredulously. "He was drafted," is the reply.

But Altman's humour is often very tough, like Lina Wert-müller's. The surgery scenes are unremittingly lurid, and their coupling with mess room banter ("It's like the Mississippi River down here"; "I gotta scratch my nose"; etc.) is distinctly sinister or "anal" in a psychological context. A bomber pilot during the second World War, Altman probably viewed the war with the psychic distance he accords his characters. He has said that he didn't think about killing people during the war, but that if he had he doesn't know that it would have disturbed him. What is sinister in Altman's film is not that bloody death should flourish, but that even the good, "hip" doctors should laugh in its face. The fact that we as an audience experience complicity through laughter takes this "anal" ambivalence a step beyond comfort.

In the *New York Times* review, Roger Greenspun points out several of the abrasive elements to Altman's humour that lurk beneath surface smugness. "To my knowledge," writes Greenspun, "*M*A*S*H* is the first American movie to openly ridicule belief in God — not phoney belief, real belief."[14] He's right. Although the religion aspect is slipped in under a lot of jargon, it is irreverent to say the least. In discussing Frank Burns's religious zeal, Hawkeye asks Duke in front of the Bible-reading major, "Have you caught this syndrome before?" "Not in anyone over eight years old," he replies.

M*A*S*H makes no claims to subtlety, nor to humanitarian values. Clan loyalty (the "saving" of the suicidal Painless, the attempt to keep a Korean orderly out of the draft) and efficiency (they are by far the best doctors) are Hawkeye and Trapper's claim to fame. Expedience is not far behind as a priority. In "Catch-22" (book, not movie), Yossarian speaks of thinking of himself rather than the war effort to the idealistic Major Danby, who reprimands, "But Yossarian, suppose everyone felt that way?" "Then I'd certainly be a damn fool to feel any other way, wouldn't I?" This is the dialectic of *M*A*S*H*.

The plot slows down a bit and sags at places. The Tokyo trip, for instance, is rather attenuated. But as a rule the film is glibly funny with an easier humour than Altman will apply in any of his later works.

BREWSTER McCLOUD

Altman has indicated *Brewster McCloud* as his personal favour-ite of his films, adding that perhaps this predilection has something to do with loving your unsuccessful children most. Shot in Houston,

Texas, *Brewster* is among the most saturated — and, I agree, one of the best — of Altman's features: touching on everything from the Icarus myth to the red shoes that Margaret Hamilton never got to wear in *The Wizard of Oz*. (She gets to wear them here and in the first scene — unhappily for her, her last as well.) *Brewster* is the story of a boy preparing for bird flight in the depths of the Houston Astrodome, with the assistance of a bird-woman, mentor Louise. Brewster constructs wings, exercises potential flying muscles, steers clear of sex, and knocks off nasty, unliberal characters — like the niggardly, rich old age home owner he chauffeurs and the off-duty cop who whips his stolen camera. As his personal seal, he leaves victims coated in bird-droppings. The Houston authorities, totally baffled by these killings, call in a San Francisco private detective (a *Bullitt* spoof), who takes the case very seriously, but makes little headway. Brewster falls for an apparently innocent tour guide, becomes sexually involved, and is eventually betrayed by the girl's personal ambitions.

Like *Nashville, Brewster* manages to satirise just about everything. Andrew Sarris called it "the first American film to apply an appropriate tone and style to the absurdist follies of our time."[26] Others were less generous, and it was generally poorly received. While *M*A*S*H*'s follies were limited to the war or some aspect of military/institutional absurdity, *Brewster's* extend to all facets of Americana. We have cars that fly while wings sag; an *M-G-M* lion that forgets to roar; ominous bird shit that portends death. Although Altman has constructed two basic plots: Brewster's preparation for flight and the *Bullitt*-mocking detective's pursuit of his killer prey, the narrative is further distended by a politician's ambitions (Haskel Weeks is an interesting precursor of Hal Philip Walker's campaign manager), a nymphomaniac's frustrations, the police department's earnest inefficiency, and a plethora of *genre* details. Although I have no first-hand knowledge of Houston, Altman's florid surfaces and omnipresent freeways are generally considered extraordinarily appropriate. René Auberjonois plays an increasingly bird-like bird lecturer whose interjections further splinter the narrative; and in one of his hilarious discourses he expresses the aspiration (surely Altman's own) "that we draw no conclusions, else the subject would cease to fascinate us."

Altman's supremely talented repertoire of actors begins to take shape in *Brewster*. John Schuck (Painless in *M*A*S*H* and Chicamaw in *Thieves*) makes a brief, but memorable appearance as Johnson, the cop who reads "Captain America" while chasing murderers and insists on calling the imported detective Shaft, "Frank

— Sir." Sally Kellerman also gives a fine performance as Brewster's mysterious teacher, foiling her *protégé's* enemies at every turn. *Brewster* also stars Bud Cort as the contemporary Icarus preparing for flight in the bowels of the Astrodome and introduces Shelley Duvall as a variation on the "eccentric innocent" role she is to play in almost all of Altman's subsequent works.

While the *Bullitt* spoof is obvious, it is nonetheless hysterically funny. The Steve McQueen-like detective, brought in to assist a befuddled local police brigade, is described by a radio announcer: "His eyes are extraordinary — they're the most vivid blue I've ever seen." His efficiency reaches sublime absurdity when he insists on analysing the bird droppings for clues; and throughout the pseudo-caper he continues to drone, "Please call me Frank, Johnson," at the least appropriate moments. Shaft's suicide is ineffective, however, for the same reason that the thrust of *M*A*S*H* dissipates after the first hour or so: the detective plot is tenable only on a unilateral, sardonic level, and therefore whatever happens to Shaft, like the fate of Hawkeye or Trapper, is gratuitous.

What is less gratuitous is the fate of the quite lovable Brewster and the arcane Louise. While *M*A*S*H*'s heroes played at an illusory freedom (stealing trucks, taking off for golf in Tokyo), *Brewster* introduces the half-serious idea of freedom through flight. Brewster's flight is condemned to failure, but it is not without appeal. At several points during the film, we are presented with images of undulating clouds swerving like whipped cream through the atmosphere and painting a very alluring picture of flight. (They are counterbalanced, however, by the accompanying tunes which sport such banal lyrics as: "How the bird sings when he is flying/How the bee stings when he knows he's dying.")

The exit of Louise and her raven after Brewster's sexual entanglement with Suzanne is also quite moving, portrayed with a lovely wide-angle zoom that bleaches her bird-like figure nearly white against the black of the receding Astrodome. (The effect is almost like that of a photographic negative). Brewster's abortive flight is equally attractive viscerally, and Altman allows his camera to be seduced by the elegiac, buoyant rhythm of the soaring boy. While Brewster *looks* ludicrous (particularly as his limbs begin to give way), his flight nonetheless *appears* exhilarating..

Brewster also introduces the "eccentric innocent" and the betrayal *motif* — here one and the same, as portrayed by Shelley Duvall's Suzanne. Louise cautions Brewster that it is sexuality that will bind him to the earth. Discussing Brewster's nymphomaniacal grocery shopper, Hope, Louise cautions: "People like Hope accept

Bert Remsen and Bud Cort in BREWSTER McCLOUD

what's been told them . . . their sex is the closest thing they have to flying." Thus, Altman prepares us for Mrs. Miller and Eileen Wade and Keechie in the later films: the women whose sexuality binds their men to the earth or at least distracts them from loftier purposes.

Suzanne in *Brewster* has been compared with Patricia in Godard's *Breathless,* but the similarities are superficial. While Patricia is presented as being aware of her moral options, Suzanne is a shadowy figure, whose betrayal, like Daisy's betrayal of Gatsby, lacks the dimension afforded by understanding. Patricia betrays Belmondo, *knowing* both his charisma and his threat to her emotional equanimity. Not understanding Brewster, Suzanne betrays him because it seems pragmatic. After all, why would she want to fly out of Houston when all her friends, especially her old boyfriend, are there? When Suzanne tells Weeks about Brewster, thus swapping her new love interest for her old, her actions are devoid of moral significance. On an allegorical level, she is merely another Eve tempting Adam out of the Garden.

Suzanne's "eccentric innocence" implies intelligence only on the basest, most materialistic level (she immediately thinks of patenting Brewster's wings, for instance); and her appeal, unlike that of Keechie and Mrs. Miller, is minimal. Altman overdoes several of her sequences to the point where her childish prattle becomes inconceivable in light of her ghoulish behaviour. For instance, she demands to be kissed immediately after vomiting, purportedly in horror at Weeks's death.

Nevertheless, some of her actions ring peculiarly true on an absurdist level. There is, for example, the classic irony of beginner's luck, where she outfoxes the police at their own game and then sighs, "That was some race, huh? Those cops really hung in there." A similar use of contrapuntal humour can be found in *Nashville* where the Barbara Harris character walks just feet in front of a dramatic car collision and, totally oblivious to the incident, continues to fuss with her handbag and scamper across the street.

There are precursors of *Nashville* in other aspects of *Brewster* as well. The scrupulous attention accorded the atmosphere of Houston — and particularly the Astrodome and the freeways — will be lavished on an evocation of Nashville and particularly the country music haunts in the later film. Altman also begins to pay attention to insignificant characters in *Brewster,* a habit which becomes increasingly vital to the themes of his later works. We have a brief glimpse of Johnson's large family, for instance, and of the twittering old residents of the nursing home. While Suzanne and Brewster ride a miniature train, attention is suddenly drawn to a man who begins to rant: "You know when I think of all those years you spent with that monster . . ." While this incident is used primarily for comic irony, it — like the banal song lyrics — can also be applied to Brewster's predicament, in this case to his revised view of his relationship with Louise.

Brewster is almost divested of the communal social consciousness that suffuses *M*A*S*H*, but there are a few atavistic remnants of the earlier smug liberalism. For instance, all the murder victims are reactionary: the marijuana-disparaging cop, the penny-counting nursing home owner (coincidentally, a descendant of Orville and Wilbur Wright), the bigoted Astrodome song leader, etc. Even the bird droppings chose to fall on such fitting headlines as "AGNEW: /SOCIETY SHOULD DISCARD SOME U.S. PEOPLE." Altman has not yet brought absurdity to the point where no explanation is necessary, where insanity is displayed as the norm. In fact, it is not until *Nashville* that Altman presents the enigma of vicious murder with no tenable explanation.

That *Brewster* is replete with vitality as well as intricate plots and satire is one of its most attractive virtues. Many have disparaged its ending as a copy of *8½*, but to me it is more compatible with the

conclusion of Ophuls's *Lola Montès*. Like the Pirandellian end of
M*A*S*H it is of no overwhelming significance, but its allusion to
Lola Montès is interesting in that it underlines the freakish outcomes
of lofty ambitions, meeting their end on the floor of a circus or an
Astrodome, respectively.

McCABE AND MRS. MILLER

Where *Brewster McCloud* is garish and disjointed, sated with
absurdist humour, imbricate satire, and preposterous allegory,
McCabe and Mrs. Miller is tender and lavish and remote. Mesmeric-
ally elegiac, *McCabe's* muted, lapidary surface — like the pastel
chimera of Monet's *Water Lilies* — creates an intimation of lost
possibilities and an aching that Altman has not since equalled.
Pauline Kael aptly called *McCabe* "a beautiful pipe dream of a movie
— a fleeting, almost diaphanous vision of what frontier life might
have been." While *McCabe* is seductively "pretty," its washed-out
cinematography is not purely aesthetic. Altman said, "I was trying to
get the feeling of antiquity, like the photographs of the time. And
since there was not colour in photographs in 1901, we had to
suppose what it might have looked like. That's why the flashing."[20]
Simply, *McCabe* is the story of a man who builds a town,
watches it begin to thrive —with the help of a dexterous Madame
named Mrs. Miller, and then loses it and his life, to a mightier, better
organised battery of outlaws. The first quarter of the movie is
concerned with atmosphere, "collateral," as Altman phrases it, for
the audience to draw upon later. Like McCabe himself, the opening
sequences are bluster: conjuring up an image of a west and a western
hero which, or so Altman postulates, never really existed at all. In
the first scene we see McCabe as he would like to be seen — a burly,
furry mass of man, slow of tongue and deliberate. We watch the
shadow of his feet trample the moist grey of the bridge planks
leading to the saloon. We see the white of the puddles in the rain and
feel McCabe's menacing presence (like that of Slim in *California
Split*) at the poker table. The mystique of a tough, disarming nomad
— a charmer, a womaniser, lurks between the bars of the Leonard
Cohen "I Told You When I Came I Was a Stranger," Altman zeroes
in on an egg (an interesting harbinger of the film's final image — Mrs.
Miller's dilating, egg-shaped eye); and we watch McCabe crack it,
drop it in his whisky, and consume the bizarre concoction with
aplomb.
McCabe is about a lot of things. It's about the limitations of
bravura and how cunning, rather than pluck, is our national heritage.

It's about how the cards are stacked against the dream and how the pioneers were not very bright fellows. Like Bill and Charlie of *California Split,* McCabe is an inveterate gambler. He is also a cock-eyed optimist, a dreamer, and a born loser. Altman says of McCabe: "He keeps winning — but always he knows he's going to lose in the end because it's built into his character. It's a character I know. The gambler who never expects to win. I've been there a lot of the time."[3] All the false intimations of the exposition are slowly contradicted as the film progresses — like McCabe's nickname (Pudgy), they are peculiarly inappropriate. "Why the hell would they call him Pudgy McCabe?" one gambler asks another in the opening scene; the topic — like McCabe's purported killing of Bill Roundtree — is repeatedly brought up, but never resolved.

McCabe's dream is that of every *entrepreneur,* every poor and yearning dumb high school dropout. It's the inchoate freedom *motif* wedded to a time when empirical freedom actually seemed within grasp. McCabe is a take-off on the John Ford, Raoul Walsh, Howard Hawks prototypical American individualist, but he is at the same

"The snowy outdoors" of McCABE AND MRS. MILLER (with Warren Beatty)

time an individualist himself. When Sheehan suggests a partnership, for instance, McCabe snaps, "Partners is what I came up here to get away from." In *Thieves* Bowie, T-Dub, and Chicamaw have learned McCabe's lesson: they realise that there is strength in partnership. Thus Bowie's promises that he will strike off on his own are never tenable, and Keechie knows it. But *McCabe* is still hopeful that an individual can succeed on his own, and all the energy expended in constructing Presbyterian Church suggests the tenacity of this optimism.

The woman as inspiration (Louise) and betrayer (Suzanne) *motifs* of *Brewster,* are here meshed in the figure of Mrs. Miller, beautifully portrayed by Julie Christie. The chemistry of the ethereal pragmatist and the hard-nosed bluffer works marvellously, surpassed only by the idiosyncratic rapport between the gangly Shelley Duvall (Keechie) and the spindle-shanked Keith Carradine (Bowie) in *Thieves Like Us.*

It is upon Mrs. Miller's arrival that we begin to notice the "loser" element in McCabe's make-up, the chinks in his polish and the limitations of his acumen. "Hey, you know if you wanta make out you're such a fancy dude, you might wear something besides that cheap jockey club cologne," she tells him straight off. "You think small," she expostulates later, "because you're afraid of thinking big." Ironically, it is she rather than he who is afraid of *dreaming* big. McCabe's awkwardness is underscored during their initial prandial encounter. First, she eats voraciously and in silence; then she lectures him on his deficiencies as the camera strays to describe McCabe, fiddling with his drink, a perfect foil for his own suaveness in the opening sequences.

McCabe is the most appealing of Altman's heroes. Like Trapper and *The Long Goodbye*'s Marlowe, he mumbles and prevaricates, creating the impression that he throws away good lines. But Altman never discards lines (although his dialogues are rarely pungent); and by rendering them less accessible, he stresses their value. We have to strain a bit, for instance, to understand McCabe's love song: "Well, I tell you I got poetry in me," McCabe mutters, as if to Mrs. Miller; "you're just freezing my soul − that's what you're doin." Their love-making is tender, despite the money angle, and Mrs. Miller's tears are compelling when she begs McCabe to save himself by selling out Presbyterian Church.

The minor characters are also astutely and sympathetically defined. Shelley Duvall as Ida Coyle is a fine, unorthodox *ingénue:* widow turned career woman (whore), an interesting precursor of Keechie in *Thieves.* The whores themselves are portrayed with sympathy as well as humour. During the birthday party, for instance, candle light mellows their faces, rendering them ordinary, but clean and pink-cheeked. Sheehan works well as an American Judas; and the cold-blooded murder of the Keith Carradine character is memorable, one of the rare instances where Altman encourages complete audience identification. Keith Carradine's drifter is bovine, and his death is unanticipated and jarring.

The lawyer in *McCabe* serves as prototype for all the Catch-22-spouting villains of the Establishment in the later Altman works. (Altman even satirises his own use of the lawyer as rogue in Hal Philip Walker's tirade against lawyers in *Nashville*.) His rhetoric compiles all the American *clichés* and turns them back on themselves. He tells McCabe: "The law's here to protect the little guy like you, McCabe, and I tell you you don't have to pay me nothing." When McCabe protests that he just doesn't want to get killed, the lawyer replies wryly, "Until people stop dying for freedom, they aren't gonna be free."

McCabe's demise is inevitable: from the moment we see him buckling under at Constance Miller's disparagements, we know he will never survive venality and lust and the scheming dimension to other men's dreams. The ending of *McCabe,* with its lovely juxtaposition of snow and fire is foreshadowed visually, as well as thematically. As the murderers ride off the first time, for instance, we see domestic fires contrasted with the crisp, hard white of the landscape. Later still it is the yellow of Constance's candle (lit as she prepares her pipe) that foils the snowy outdoors where McCabe is stumbling up her steps with his offering of flowers.

Unlike *Brewster's* Suzanne, Constance is powerless to save or even assist her lover; and thus her option for survival (through a hazy opium stupor), like Keechie's refusal to mourn, is less a betrayal than many have suggested. What Altman evokes in the cross-cutting from burning church to the snow-enveloped pursuit of McCabe is the ultimate isolation of it all. In a curious fashion Altman elevates McCabe, who chooses to die for an ephemeral dream as he elevates none of his other characters. We actually ache at his poetically depicted death and are inclined to think much less of Constance, who turns in the end to the drugged euphoria of opium much as she had predicted that her "girls," given the option, would return to the Church. The fact that McCabe kills all his killers unethically (two are shot in the back, the other while he is feigning dead) provides an ironic twist on the traditional western's morality, but it does not undermine his own courage.

Critics have assailed the Leonard Cohen songs as banal, but

within the framework of the film they are extremely affecting. Are the whores the "Sisters of Mercy"? Is McCabe or Mrs. Miller —or perhaps both — the stranger of Cohen's song? Like the René Auberjonois lectures and "The Long Goodbye," the tunes start and stop inexplicably, asserting themselves as independent and refracting forces.

What McCabe leaves us with is the snow and the hearth — typical western *motifs*. Only here it is the hero who is bundled in the snow and the heroine solitary by the hearth. Like the beginning, the ending is a visual poem — a *mélange* of chimerical elements. While *McCabe* is perfectly able to stand by itself, it leaves reverberations that are caught and further elucidated in *Thieves Like Us*.

IMAGES

Opening at the 1972 New York Film Festival (though actually conceived in pre-*M*A*S*H* days), *Images* is Altman's poor little rich failure, disparaged almost universally by critic and public alike. Aptly titled, the film is constructed in the eclectic fashion of a photography exhibit, integrated by an unobtrusive theme and an auteurist stamp. Brandishing a plethora of stunning "images" offset by

Altman (right) discusses a sequence in IMAGES with Susannah York, Hugh Millais, and Cathryn Harrison

irrelevant or pretentious footage, the texture of *Images* would also prove more palatable in a collection of stills than in a pseudo-thriller. Starring Susannah York as Cathryn, a schizophrenic children's book writer, *Images* begins in London where we sense that Cathryn suspects her husband of infidelity. They then leave for a vacation in the countryside, where the situation grows worse instead of better. Wherever she is, Cathryn is haunted by her childhood or the memory of ex-lovers. The latter she proceeds to kill — whether in fantasy or reality we are never quite sure. Cathryn also befriends a young blonde child who looks suspiciously like her childhood self; and in an ironic twist kills her own husband rather than the nemesis of which she has wanted to rid herself.

Even Andrew Sarris, who values it more highly than most, wrote of *Images:* "Altman (like recent Bergman) becomes more pinched and more penurious with his audience as if he were afraid his own soul would be diminished in direct proportion to the pleasure he provided the spectator." [27] Distended, erratic, viscerally dense, psychologically untenable, *Images* seems to sweep together all of Altman's weaknesses. For instance, those who claim that Altman is not just disinclined, but unable to construct clever, cogent dialogue can point to the stilted conversations in *Images* for verification. Yet, while I would be the last to defend *Images* in its entirety, it is a tantalising, if extremely flawed work on several levels.

Historically, it is interesting to note that, with the exception of the science fiction *Countdown, Images* is the only "non" American Altman film. (Even *That Cold Day in the Park* was set in Canada.) It is also his first investigation of the upper middle-class, and he takes full cinematic advantage of the accessibility of lavish interiors and landscapes. Like Claude Chabrol and Alain Resnais, Altman has a marvellous flair for capturing the decadent detail: he fixes his camera on a lambent piece of glass, a bottle of wine, a windshield, and the object assumes ancillary dimension, like the layered contours of a Rembrandt costume. Unfortunately, Altman's style is not yet buttressed by a cohesive narrative or thematic structure and thus while Chabrol's camera meaningfully luxuriates in the hypocrisies of the bourgeoisie and Resnais's in the mysteries of time and memory, Altman's appears to oscillate to no apparent purpose. He is not willing to tell us a story, but neither will he commit himself to a subjective analysis of Cathryn's mind.

Habitually, Altman's camera serves as thematic spinal tap for his film's nervous system: thus *The Long Goodbye* entails a series of agitated tracks, while McCabe pans lyrically. In *Images,* however, the *mise-en-scène,* like the thrust, is ambivalent: and thus both the limpid photography and the sparse montage add up to nothing exceptional. The elegant mansion and the dangling charms, for instance, are lovely to look at but ultimately prosaic – lacking even in irony. The evocation of the verdant countryside, on the other hand, is quite an effective metaphor for mystical isolation and might have proved illuminating if coupled with a viable psychic correlative. (In *Le Boucher,* for instance, Chabrol used the sleepy cavernous town of Trémolat as juxtaposition for the convoluted tenderness of his lethal central character.)

Like *That Cold Day in the Park, Images* couples homicide and schizophrenia: here the plot is chiselled, however, fitted together like fragments of glass with a twist inserted at the tale. (The metamorphosis of one face into another, so effective in *The Fox,* is rather gimmicky as a final image here.) Susannah York has been unjustly criticised for her performance as wife and author of books like *In Search of Unicorns* (she actually wrote the book), the text that serves as superimposition *motif.* The actress's superbly affected fragility coupled with the chatty rhythm of the books' words, insinuates a pleasant, Mad Hatterish dreaminess to the film – encouraging whatever sympathy the work is capable of eliciting.

The difficulties in *Images* arise not so much from the intentional plot confusions (the puzzle-like nature is more effective than the dogged straightforwardness of *That Cold Day in the Park*), as from Altman's resistance – be it endemic or purposeful – to complex character analysis. When dealing with multiple characters and abstract themes, as in *Nashville, The Long Goodbye,* and *Brewster,* lack of definition leads naturally to ellipsis. I was happy, for instance, with Altman's decision not to psychoanalyse his killer in *Nashville,* so dense was the web of the film already. *Images,* on the other hand, is concerned primarily with one character, and the refusal to analyse the nature of her schizophrenia is an unjustifiable evasion.

Altman's finest portraits have been of receding, non-verbal characters, with only idiosyncratic personality quirks to intimate inner complexities. McCabe is such a character, as is Louise in *Brewster,* Lydia in *Nashville,* and both Bowie and Keechie in *Thieves Like Us.* The complexities of these characters are suggested not in their mentalities, but in the fragmentation or disintegration of the worlds they inhabit. While the lush nature of the cinematography in *Images* suggests Altman's facility with fragile and lavish compositions, the paucity of content and shallow character studies bode poorly for future in-depth personality analysis.

THE LONG GOODBYE

Having indulged Altman through the debunking of Church, war, western, and caper, audience and critic alike finally baulked at the profanation of Philip Marlowe, attacking Altman for want of the least fashionable of virtues — sincerity. In *Time* Magazine, Jay Cocks complained that Altman was deriding "an achievement to which at his best he could only aspire." Charles Gregory approaches the film more thoughtfully in his excellent *Sight and Sound* piece, "Knight Without Meaning?" "Altman has survived the Sixties," writes Gregory, "by learning to distrust heroes and heroics. . .The overwhelming competence and control of Marlowe is too much for him, because his vision does not include the possibility of control."

The Altman film is an updated variation on the Chandler story. Late one night loner/private detective Philip Marlowe is visited by his good friend Terry Lennox, who requests that he take him to the airport and ask no questions. When he later refuses to *answer* any questions for the police, investigating the death of Lennox's wife Sylvia, Marlowe is thrown in jail. With insufficient evidence to keep him behind bars, Marlowe is released and soon after gets a call from Eileen Wade, a Lennox neighbour, ostensibly frantic at the disappearance of her neurotic, alcoholic writer husband. Marlowe locates the husband with a Dr. Verringer, falls for the glamorous blonde Eileen, and continues to tell everyone in sight that his friend Terry Lennox is innocent of his wife's murder. Eventually, Wade commits suicide, and Marlowe finds Lennox in Mexico, awaiting the arrival of none other than Eileen Wade. When he learns that a very healthy looking Lennox *has* knocked off his wife, Marlowe proceeds to kill him, and then skips down the road to the tune of "Hurray for Hollywood."

After several viewings of the film, my own feelings remain decidedly mixed. To give Altman credit, he and screenwriter Leigh Brackett had announced long before the film's release that their intention was not to update the Hawks-Chandler *vision* of Marlowe, but rather to obviate it, satirising Marlowe's atavistic presumptions *vis-à-vis* contemporary *mores*. Marlowe's adherence to friendship, honour, etc. obtrude as incongruously upon Altman's 1973 Malibu as Bruno's solitary unswerving head during the tennis match in Hitchcock's *Strangers on a Train;* and the effect is comparably ironic.

As Gregory points out, Elliott Gould's Marlowe has less in common with the hard-nosed vulnerability of Bogart in *The Big Sleep* than with Fred MacMurray in *Double Indemnity* or Edward G.

Robinson in *Scarlet Street*. Altman's vision is actually quite compatible with Lang's — the difference being that while Lang's dialectic renders his *mise-en-scène* lugubrious, Altman's — like his protagonist ("It's O.K. with me. . ," says Marlowe repeatedly) — rolls imperviously along.

Each of the characters in *The Long Good-bye* — even Gould/Marlowe himself — could be summed up in Chandler/Marlowe's fine assessment of Terry Lennox in the book: "He was like somebody you meet on board ship," writes Chandler, "and get to know very well and never really know at all." Altman's camera is most effective at foiling the Hawksian "myth," not only of control, but of autonomy. The film opens magnificently on a contemporary Marlowe struggling with his finicky cat rather than the Chandler chess board; but soon after the cat is gone, and so is the illusion of Marlowe's independence.

Altman's style is particularly deft in *The Long Goodbye*. In the memorable sequence where the Wades bicker (about impotence, among other things) by the house, both Marlowe and the ocean are implicated in their conversation through a canny reflection in the glass door. When Marlowe moves to join them, the ocean continues to insist its presence through mirror image — serving both as prescient of Wade's suicide and underminer of the closure of the given relationships. Zsigmond's camera reverses the Emerson assertion that should the universe crumble, narcissistic man would seek to create a universe around himself. In Altman's world, it is the universe that shuffles and sculpts its malleable characters, and the ones that get on best are those that don't protest.

Even suicide is a communal affair in *The Long Goodbye*, and it is interesting to compair Wade's death with Cukor's portrayal of the James Mason character's suicide in *A Star is Born*. While Cukor intimates Mason's suicide through cuts, dissolves, and ellipsis, Altman sends Wade to his death in the same frame with Eileen and Marlowe. As bystanders chat at the cocktail party, Altman's lens dilates, pushing Marlowe and Eileen to either side of the frame and centring Wade. Then the image of Wade continues to expand, and as Eileen and Marlowe disappear entirely, we watch Wade approach the ocean.

Altman's camera has implicated Marlowe and Eileen, but that does not mean that it holds them guilty in any existential sense. With the death of morality and God, only perpetual flux remains a constant; and thus responsibility, like loyalty, is an anachronism. In the Chandler version Eileen kills her husband and *is* guilty, technically as well as ethically; in the Altman she is an accomplice who is virtually innocent. Even the violence in *The Long Goodbye* is of a

Sterling Hayden and Nina van Pallandt in THE LONG GOODBYE

desultory nature. In *Chinatown* Polanski wounds his principal character at a pivotal moment in the drama; and through his pain we identify with the dangers of involvement. Altman, on the other hand, uses the coke bottle incident as atmosphere "collateral" (the petty gangster Marty Augustine wounds his girlfriend, a very minor character, viciously and with no apparent motive) for us to draw upon, like the initial section of *McCabe*. The gangster's fulsome behaviour prepares us for Marlowe's precipitate violence in the end: it is there not as litmus paper, judging our hero's courage and dedication, but as an irrational undercurrent.

On a surface level, *The Long Goodbye* is very entertaining. Its "long goodbye" to the Hollywood dream factory with the "Hooray for Hollywood" opening and conclusion, the star-miming gatekeeper, the glistening surfaces, the homages to *A Star is Born, The Third Man*, etc. are successful, if far from innovative. Altman's sardonic humour is in fine form here, and his casting is idiosyncratic, but accurate. Nina Van Pallandt may not be Chandler's blonde, but the tanned refinement of her almost, but not quite fragile features works well with Altman's reconstruction. My one complaint as far as characterisation goes is that the Hemingway caricature has been slightly overdone; but the theme song, with its abrupt starts and stops, works superbly with the nomadic relationships and the ambulatory camera—and the decision not to develop the Terry Lennox character is unquestionably a sound one.

I admit freely that the part of me that loves *The Big Sleep* and *Only Angels Have Wings* and *Red River* as well as Chandler's *The Big Sleep,* resents the smugness of *The Long Goodbye* and its sardonic *adieu* to the gnarled poetry of Hawks and Chandler. Nevertheless, my quarrels with Altman are not so much a matter of approach (who can demand that he parallel his source or reference material?) as of structure. "It's okay with me," is Gould/Marlowe's *leitmotif,* and he's such an easy-going shamus, we never have any reason to suspect otherwise. The ending is a disappointment *not* because Chandler's Marlowe could never kill, but because Altman's Marlowe appears to kill just as easily as he does everything else. So vibrant on a visceral level, Altman's *Long Goodbye* lacks tension, and I suspect that it is this omission rather than the distortion of Chandler that audiences and critics alike find abrasive. "Although [Chandler's] Marlowe may well look as ludicrous as the knight of La Mancha," writes Gregory, "the need and the longing remain." Had Altman re-created the anti-heroes of *M*A*S*H* on the beaches of Malibu, his *Long Goodbye* would have been more palatable. With neither moral nor narrative tension, it stands as an enjoyable, but flawed satire. Flawed because it proposes to give us substantiation for the death of the hoopla and leaves us instead with a languid Hooray!

THIEVES LIKE US

The 1974 opening of *Thieves Like Us* was almost simultaneous with that of Terrence Malick's *Badlands* and Steven Spielberg's *Sugarland Express;* so comparisons were inevitable. *Thieves* lies somewhere between the cloying sanguinity of *Sugarland* and the brittle objectivity of *Badlands.* Concerned with the various aspects of crime and parochialism, Malick adheres to a scrupulously laconic montage, while Spielberg displays a range of virtuoso tricks in his florid, claustrophobic admixture of zooms, slow motions, and close-ups. *Thieves,* on the other hand, is a subtly variegated work. Even its hues fluctuate, from the washed-out autumnal tones of the opening pan to the contrasty darks and lights of the car crash sequence, to the warm earth colours in the domestic interludes.

The second adaptation of Edward Anderson's novel (Nicholas Ray also based a very dissimilar *They Lived by Night* on this book), it is Altman's most narrative work, true to its source in atmosphere as well as word. It is not, like *Badlands,* an oblique study of heroism gone awry; but neither does it attempt to extol the humanity of its protagonists beyond their vocation. *Thieves* begins as T-Dub, Chicamaw, and Bowie escape from a prison farm and set off to hide with various relatives. While the older crooks — T-Dub and an irascible Chicamaw — intend to continue making a living through bank robbing, the young Bowie plans to set off on his own once the coast is clear. For the time being, he robs with his friends in order to procure enough money to escape to a new life in Mexico with the girl he has fallen in love with, Keechie. The trio becomes increasingly notorious, and the law begins closing in. T-Dub is killed, Chicamaw jailed; and Bowie and Keechie hide out with T-Dub's sister-in-law Mattie. Bowie employs a ruse to get Chicamaw released, but they fight, and Bowie ends up leaving him on the road. When he returns home, he is greeted by the now pregnant Keechie and what appears to be the entire police force. He is killed; Keechie has her baby and leaves town to start a new life.

While Altman has said that *McCabe* was the father of *Thieves,* the later film is about a far less stable universe. McCabe had to die defending his property — the "thieves" merely pick up and leave. Much of the tension in *Thieves* arises from a pull for and against roots, rather than liberty. (Rootlessness will eaily triumph in Altman's next film, *California Split.*) Crouched by the railroad tracks, waiting for his buddies, Bowie fondles a stray dog. Lanky man and scrawny dog make a lovely pair (so do Bowie and Keechie later on), and Bowie mutters protectively, "You belong to someone?—or you just a thief like me?" Later, Keechie informs Bowie that his look-alike has run off with some stranger in a pick-up truck. So much for loyalty or permanence.

Like Bowie and his stray dog, Bowie and Keechie are doomed from the start, but not in the schematic sense of Eileen and Marlowe in *The Long Goodbye.* There is real tenderness between the homely, gum-faced girl and her stick of a man, more effective than the elegant bravado of Bonnie and Clyde. While their naivety is overdone (the dumbest of McCabe's whores would realise that Keechie's nausea might possibly be morning sickness), their innocence is beguiling. Here is a classic example of Atlman's genius with actors. Keechie's and Bowie's limbs seem destined for one another, just as surely as destiny is bound to disentangle them. The *Romeo and Juliet* radio superimposition is annoying, but it cannot destroy the youthful vitality of their first matings; and if Keechie's leaving her eggs on the fire to rejoin her lover is a bit coy, it is also a compassionate means of displaying her unromantic tenderness and desire.

"Their innocence is beguiling": Shelley Duvall and Keith Carradine as the lovers in THIEVES LIKE US

Felony as such is mitigated in the first half of the film. When Bowie asks the dog if he too is a "thief," we are meant to equate thief with tramp or homeless one. The coupling of robberies with "Gangbuster" broadcasts also tends to undermine the noxious implications of the game they're playing. As in *Brewster,* we don't see, but hear second-hand of most of the killings. For instance, even T-Dub's death is brought to us courtesy of the radio.

However, as the film progresses, both Bowie and the audience are forced to come to terms with the less seemly aspect of thieving. The precipitate transition from gameplaying (Bowie and Chicamaw, two oversized kids racing cars) to brutality in the head-on car collision and subsequent killings is viscerally jolting. This scene is our initiation to violence, and although Bowie is shortly to establish a conjugal relationship with Keechie; it is this incident that binds him inexorably to his male allies. It is also after this episode that Bowie begins to drink with the others.

Although the female betrayal *motif* is most extensively developed in *Thieves,* Keechie is far from an unsympathetic character. Like Mrs. Miller, she is full of spunk: she badgers children and whines for a coke when out of sorts. Despite her eccentric looks, she's vain and selfish, and still loves Bowie completely. She sets her hair, luxuriates in a middle-of-the-room bath, but sticks with her man. Altman also underscores Keechie's horror rather than Bowie's slaughter in the end by focusing on a close-up of her scream.

Yet, both Keechie and Mattie are Altman's most typical female pragmatists; and their capacity for betrayal is set up from the start. When Bowie arrives at Mattie's lodge, "The Heart of Gold" series is beginning on the radio — an obvious foil for Mattie's reluctance to shield her brother-in-law's friend and his girl. When she does agree to keep them, they are given cabin no. 13 — hardly a good omen.

There are sexual ties between Mattie and Keechie. While Mattie turns Bowie in so as to facilitate the release of her own husband, she sympathises with the pregnant girl. There is an almost maternal aspect to Mattie's attention to Keechie in the end and to her frenzied grip on the younger woman during the shooting. Like Mattie, Keechie will survive, procreate, and look after her own. She tells a stranger in the station, with obvious relish, that her husband died of consumption, adding (almost as a snide wink to a knowing universe), "He crossed me up one time too many lyin'."

A certain pathetic yearning for inaccessible roots suffuses *Thieves*, just as the desire for independence redeems McCabe and binds the disparate elements of *Nashville*. *Thieves* begins with a muted, wistful moan of a cry from a bird — the precise sound that Claude Chabrol accompanied with the death of his heroine in *Les bonnes femmes*. The squeal is repeated unobtrusively at strategic points throughout the film — for instance, at the point where Chicamaw kills the sheriff. At the end of the film, it reappears as a louder, more full-bodied yelp that bridges Keechie's own scream and the following cut to the waiting room. The point is admittedly abstruse, but there is an implication that the wistful yearning has metamorphosised into a child and, as such, its well-being will preclude any extraneous yearnings on the part of its mother.

The film could well have ended without the radio show with its references to the New Deal, which, for Altman, is, of course, only a variation on a pretty rotten Old Deal.

CALIFORNIA SPLIT

Where *The Long Goodbye* oscillates between episodic and classical plot thrust, *California Split* comes as close as any Altman film to the loose-ended structure he claims to be aiming for. The story of two gambling fanatics who meet casually, hit it off, and finally make a big killing, *California Split* is also a very benign film, with the more lethal aspects of gambling craftfully sublimated. Bill (George Segal), for instance, has lost a wife and is on his way to losing a job when the film begins; but Altman approaches these inconveniences as disarmingly as the mutterings of McCabe and Marlowe. Altman said, "This picture is a celebration of gambling. Not the traditional gambling film with the Mafia and the guy losing his shirt at the track or breaking the bank at Monte Carlo. This is a couple of guys who have a lot of fun gambling and playing around."

Structurally, *California Split* resembles a road picture: with Gould as Charlie and Segal as Bill playing buddies whose paths swerve and come together at various points on the road to nowhere. Essentially low-keyed, it is also one of Altman's funniest films. Ann Prentiss and Gwen Welles give superb renditions of antic call girls, and John Schuck makes a brief, but hilarious appearance as a transvestite.

What the Altman film underscores is not so much the obsessive nature of gambling — that is taken for granted and dropped — as its idiosyncrasies. Like Barbara and Susan (Prentiss and Welles), luck is a "travelling lady," and her arrival can be as traumatic as her departure. The insanity of gambling is no less "real" than the insanity of war or traditional virtues or assassination: it is only that Altman paints it with a bit more indulgence, and it is obviously close to home.

The humour in *California Split* is the whiter aspect of *M*A*S*H*. The "Fruit Loops" episode, where a frazzled Barbara listlessly offers cereal to whomever passes her portals is hilarious, but then so are any number of episodes. There is one totally extraneous scene in a bar which sticks in the mind. A woman, half-drunk, begins to rant and rave about how much better the bar was that she frequented the night before. "Any chance of your going back?" asks a suddenly hopeful bartender. Like most of Altman's humorous sequences, this one fades quickly into the next.

Altman never goes so far as to capsulise or recreate the exuberance of gambling, and gamblers who know the feeling are probably his most enthusiastic audiences. As can be anticipated, he gives us the resonances and the "actuality" of atmosphere, and the audience is left on its own from there. The gambling parlours are evoked with scrupulous detail. Asked what his specific responsibilities as director are, Altman once replied: "To set the arena. To set up the stimuli to which the actor will respond." Thus, in the crap game Altman uses real gamblers and dealers; and he imports the champion poker player, Amarillo Slim, for the poker scene. The gambling announcements and Phyllis Shotwell songs, which serve as superimpositions, also contribute to the credibility of the setting.

Like *M*A*S*H, California Split* is so thoroughly entertaining that one hesitates to pry for deeper significance. The one truly "sexual" scene between Bill and Susan is as "anal" as any sequence I've ever seen in a film; and Altman encourages us to share Bill's revulsion at the idea of making love with a mechanism that talks very placidly while efficiently removing her underwear. In its own way, this scene is as revealing of the innate tensions between the sexes as the one-night courtships of Cassavetes's "husbands." The transience of relationships (Charlie disappears, Bill approaches a long-lost friend for a loan); the fickle nature of Chance; the *ennui* of stability (Bill's routine office life): all these are present in *California Split,* as is the underlying notion that the gambler is not much better off than Sisyphus — forever destined to push his burden of feckless daring up the hill of risk. But this is not really what *California Split* is about, and thus the ending, once again, is little more than a dissolve. A tallying up of the parts of *California Split* is disappointing, and it is more profitable to see it as successful segments.

Elliott Gould and George Segal (right) at the track in CALIFORNIA SPLIT

NASHVILLE

In reference to *M*A*S*H*, Altman said that his ambition was to create an atmosphere of arbitrariness, to convince audiences that what they were seeing was "just the window they were stuck at. That if they'd looked out another window, they'd have seen a different movie, though with the same atmosphere." Reviewing some of the critical and popular reaction to *Nashville*, one gets the notion that Altman's wish may, indeed, have come true. Pauline Kael, and John Malone (whose controversial "Let Us Not Praise *Nashville's* Faults" appeared in the *New York Times*) must have been seated at different windows. While I am more inclined to agree with the initial raves than the often thoughtful reappraisals, the latter were both healthy and inevitable, because *Nashville* is not and should not be an easy film to stomach. Abrasive and controversial, it is a "film orgy," as Kael termed it, only on a visceral level.

To my mind, *Nashville* is Altman's consummate achievement thus far, which is not to say that it is my personal favourite. *Nashville* is masterful in that it manages to beguile twenty-four characters to life – from an ailing country music star to an ambitious campaign manager – with apparently no effort at all. They pulsate with the fugitive glitter of the ocean surface on a sunny day, and while their aspirations are as easily capsulised as the limericks of a Coca Cola ad, no character is without resonances of untapped depth. In the country music industry Altman has finally discovered a perfect vehicle for his ambivalent views of Americana. His characters are venal and loyal and transparent and reticent and provincial and, above all, resilent. They are unremittingly unromantic, and the dream for them is the Sunday ice cream soda of cardboard celebrity.

As many have pointed out, that dream is harsh because it denies the heritage of the pseudo-populist Sixties – the morality, the yearning, the camaraderie, but mostly what Dos Passos once called "the crazy need for change." The smug anti-war heroes of *M*A*S*H* have vanished, and what we have left is the closure of the Establishment. Liberals are made to look either foolish or hypocritical. I previously mentioned Tom's harassment of a docile young soldier. Altman also pokes fun at the possibility of political change when Walker's reactionaries call themselves the "Replacement Party" and Mary protests that she and Bill can't vote for Walker simply because they are registered Democrats. (Bill takes the absurdity a point further by revealing that they are only registered Democrats because of her father.)

Altman is not concerned with the diurnal and eternal

predicaments of individuals like Cassavetes's Mabel *(Woman Under the Influence)* or Scorsese's Alice *(Alice Doesn't Live Here Anymore):* he gives us History, and his oscillating focus is always set on stasis. One senses at the end, for instance, that not only is one star dead and another born, but that a whole culture would like to set its own lands in order. But his characters do not harbour the grand, if futile, illusions of Fitzgerald, conjuring boats, beating on "against the current, borne ceaselessly into the past." They want a reaffirmation of a comfortable stability that Robert Mazzocco describes as "so bereft of ideas, of any inner life"; but which is both just that — banal, vapid — and then something else again.

Nashville is Altman at his densest and his most laconic. It is here that his *mélange* of actualism and realism, substance and superimposition are both most compatible and most effective. Transience plays very little part in *Nashville:* as in McCabe, individuals may come and go (the characters possess vitality, but are shallow); the land and the ethos remain. Thus, the function of Hal Philip Walker's speaker is assumed by the television programme just as naturally as Tom switches bed partners. The rhetoric remains the same, just as the song ("It Don't Worry Me") is constant in each of Tom's successive conquests.

One has only to compare the car crash sequence in the beginning of the film with the classically edited finale to appreciate the awesome complexities of Altman's dexterity. The magnificent climax-*dénouement* of *Nashville* is eminently Hollywood — employing directive, tension-building editing (cuts to slow-motion cars, the billowing flag, the Walker party, Barnett, Barbara Jean, the assassin, the flag, etc.) to set us up for the kill. His style is every bit as salient and as terse as Cukor's in anticipating James Mason's suicide in *A Star is Born* or Hitchcock's in foreshadowing Ingrid Bergman's poisoning in *Notorious.* Thus, emotionally the assassination is realistic as well as mythic. The car crash sequence, on the other hand, is intentionally both myth and reality deflating. In keeping with the discarded lines in *McCabe and Mrs. Miller* and the mumblings in *The Long Goodbye,* its formal elusiveness is self-dissecting, like the false perspective of cubistic angles or the incongruous matings of surrealism.

Wallace Stevens once offered a very interesting comment on surrealism. "The fault of surrealism," he wrote," is that it invents without discovering: to make a clam play an accordion is to invent, not to discover." The same criticism could be levelled against certain Altman films — *Images,* for instance, which is lavish and intricate and shallow. It is not true of *Nashville.* Take, for instance, the issue of the assassin. Many have protested the incredibility of a likeable young man turned inexplicably irascible; but they have obviously ignored the ever-deranged eyes of the character as well as Altman's assiduous preparation for the assassination. Whenever violence or death are alluded to, Altman will almost invariably cut to Henry: in the hospital when there is a discussion of guns, for instance, and later after Opal from the BBC has discussed violence with Madame Pearl.

One can discover any number of justifications for the killing (the unhappy family Henry comes from, for instance), which is another tribute to Altman's many dimensions. Luckily, he does not attempt to analyse the assassin's gratuitous violence, which, like Marty Augustine's in *The Long Goodbye,* is essentially irrational. The Oswalds and Manson acolytes of the world may be harbingers of a Neronic age, agents of foreign ideologies, or more likely psychotics — the term we use, for lack of deeper insight, to conjoin the lethal and arcane mutations in our human and cultural heritage. Because the subject of *Nashville* is not the assassin, but the survivors, the former is most provocative in obscurity: defined merely as a predictable, if deviant growth in a country which has managed to last two hundred years.

Nashville is Altman's finest evocation of the freedom motif: uniting twenty-four skeletal characters and an audience of their peers

Ronee Blakley, Barbara Baxley, and Henry Gibson in NASHVILLE

in a hymn to lost freedom. The words the survivors chant are irrelevant: it is the ritual that is moving. These people, so transparent in their everyday idiosyncrasies, are lent stature in collective confusion. It is the American people who sing together in the finale, and Altman accords their mass hymn of jumbled truth and *cliché* — their stance of resilience and complacence — ample respect.

Francis Ford Coppola being dusted off by Shirley Knight while filming THE RAIN PEOPLE

Francis Ford Coppola

CREATIVE OVER COMPANY MAN, reads the oversized headline of "Variety," August 21, 1974: an epithet that would fit well in a Francis ford Coppola film. (PERSONAL OVER BUSINESS would work even better.) In large extra-black type the article continues to speculate on Coppola's purchasing of 72,000 shares of Cinema 5 stock. "Consider the implications: has Coppola fired the opening round in the so-called 'Hollywood revolution?' Or as the executives of the major distribution companies are apt to phrase it 'are the lunatics (meaning the filmmakers) really attempting to take over the asylum (meaning the distribution companies)?' " A little of both, one suspects.

Of all the new directors, Coppola's talent has thus far proved the most protean — and the least distinctive. *Enfant terrible,* he stormed through UCLA Film School, cashing in on porn films, playing jack-of-all-trades for Roger Corman, directing a major (albeit, from all reports, major in name alone) motion picture at the age of twenty-two and winning an Academy Award for his screenplay of *Patton* at thirty-one. The schizophrenic nature of Coppola's precocious success is reflected both in his films and in the manner in which he chooses to make them. Like Harry Caul of *The Conversation,* he has scrupulously divided personal from business: *Rain People,* for instance, was personal — *The Godfather,* business; Cinema 5 is business, Zoetrope was personal. Critically speaking, the discrepancy between Coppola's business and personal ventures is less rigid, the tensions of a commercial venture more often than not proving artistically salutary.

Coppola was born into an Italian family on April 7, 1939. The son of a concert flautist (Carmine Coppola was first flute under Toscanini in the NBC Symphony Orchestra) and a film actress, Coppola spent most of his youth in the suburbs of New York. As a child he was an expert tuba player and a fanatical gadget *aficionado.*

97

At ten, he was already experimenting with sound in home movies. The two distinguishing occurrences of his childhood were the development of polio in the late Forties (Harry Caul also suffered from polio) and his enrolment in a military academy for his early high school years. Apparently, both highlights were almost equally deplorable to the young Coppola, who amused himself at the Academy by writing love letters for his fellow cadets at the price of a dollar per page.

In 1959 Coppola graduated from Hofstra University with a B.A. in theatre (he had already written the book and lyrics for "The Delicate Touch") and entered UCLA Film School, where he began his film-making career with a passion. *Pilma, Pilma,* a screenplay which was never produced, won him the Samuel Goldwyn Award in 1962; and "nudie" films (porn's forefathers) like *The Peeper* and *The Belt Girls and The Playboy* provided him with cash as well as some rudimentary experience. Coppola then worked for Corman, whose fatherly example he would later follow in setting up his own company, Zoetrope. While on location in Ireland, Coppola convinced Corman to allow him to make the horror film *Dementia-13,* of which he has said "It was the only film I ever enjoyed working on." Critical reaction was less than hyperbolic. The *Post*'s position, for instance, was the following: "The photography's better than the plot, the plot better than the dialogue, and the dialogue better than the recording. The latter is something very hard to distinguish, which may be a mercy."

On the strength of the Samuel Goldwyn Award, Seven Arts Studio hired Coppola to adapt Carson McCullers's "Reflections in a Golden Eye," and he continued to write or collaborate on nearly a dozen Seven Arts projects in the following years. Coppola's script for *Patton,* initially tabled as too controversial an approach to a war hero, but resurrected at George C. Scott's insistence, was his first big success. At that point he had already directed *You're a Big Boy Now,* which I will discuss later, and *Finian's Rainbow,* the only of Coppola's major works that I have been unable to see.

As Coppola's dual role as director/artist and tycoon has evolved, he has continued not only his writing, but opera and theatre work as well. In 1969, while making his first "personal" film *The Rain People,* Coppola began American Zoetrope (the name pays tribute to Pierre Desvignes's primitive circular drum for demonstrating persistence of vision) on $300,000 of his own money and backing from Warner Brothers. Designed to assist new talent, Zoetrope was short-lived, but during its life span launched several careers — most notably that of George Lucas, whose *THX 1138* was its inaugural production. In 1972 Coppola directed a revival of Noël Coward's *Private Lives* for the American Conservatory Theatre in San Francisco and in 1974 created *City Magazine* – also San Francisco-based.

Those who characterise the "new" Hollywood as diffuse and actor-oriented would have a difficult time explaining Coppola's literary sensibility. Coppola says, "I feel that I'm basically a writer who directs. . .When people go to see a movie, eighty percent of the effect it has on them was preconceived and precalculated by the writer. . .A good script has preimagined exactly what the movie is going to do on a story level, on an emotional level, on all these levels. So to me, that's the primary act of creation. "It is not that Coppola is less visually oriented than many of his peers. but rather that he is more classical: his style rarely serving as counterpoint to substance. To give an example: both Scorsese and De Palma create visceral tension with antic, unsteadied cameras, often at odds with the rhythm of the plot or a deceptively benign *mise-en-scène.* Coppola maintains a steadied camera, and his mood-establishing images tend to have both narrative and thematic correlatives. The Lang-like chiaroscuro lighting in *Godfather II,* for instance, grows increasingly lugubrious as Michael Corleone becomes more ruthless and irredeemable. *The Godfather* itself opens with a very clear-cut visual exposition of the dual nature of the Corleones: cutting from the bright, florid frivolity of the outdoors wedding to the barely visible interior of the Don's study.

Coppola has become increasingly effulgent in his later films, often a bit conscientiously so. He has expressed awe for the weird, intuitive configurations created by Italian directors like Antonioni (whose *Blow-Up* he payed tribute to in *The Conversation*) and particularly Bertolucci. Of the latter, he's said, "He's an extraordinary talent. I look at two reels of *The Conformist* every day. He's my freedom therapy." Yet even at their most brilliant, Coppola's images are never gratuitous, any more than his actors' superb performances are improvisational. *The Conversation,* for instance, is cerebrally constructed around the primary metaphor of a camera (an artist) snooping on life and the secondary metaphor of a wiretapper's invasion of privacy; and the brooding, Baroque images of *Godfather II* are the filmic equivalents of Wilde's closeted portrait of Dorian Gray.

Coppola's strengths are closer to those of Hitchcock, whom he grossly underestimates as a craftsman "almost entirely interested in the design of his films";[2 1] and it is in his development of ambivalent character and complex plot that he proves most interesting. While

John Marley awakes to find his prize stallion's head in the bedclothes, in THE GODFATHER

Coppola has as yet to create a thriller as psychologically and narratively compelling as *Vertigo* or *Psycho,* he has succeeded in evoking suspense and character nuance within a cogent framework, and this is no mean accomplishment.

Like Hitchcock's characters, Coppola's are functioning members of society — rankled by inner contradictions, but nonetheless "normal" by world standards. Even Harry, the most introvert of Coppola's personalities, manages (until the end) to keep the lid on his seething libido. More than *The Conversation, The Godfather*(s) very subtly present us with good and evil impulses thriving simultaneously within the same characters and ethos. Like Hitchcock, Coppola coaxes us to identify with his sympathetic villains and then demands that we pay the psychic price of guilt. In *The Godfather*, for instance, we are confronted with the dilemma of *viscerally* wanting to see the Corleone enemies killed off, while intellectually realising that we're encouraging homicide. *The Godfather* is much more insidious emotionally than its "arty" sequel, because it plays with the exhilarating phenomenon of audience identification. By the middle of *Godfather II,* Coppola has distanced us from his increasingly fulsome characters (the portrait has come out of the closet) and is preparing us for the more stringent, voyeuristic approach of *The Conversation.*

The dichotomies that are the basis for Coppola's style are similarly the foundations for his themes. In all his films, Coppola is interested in freedom versus privacy. In the jejune *You're a Big Boy Now,* "Big Boy" is squelched by a self-serving maternal devotion, and in both *The Godfather*(s) and *The Conversation* business conspires to devour a man's private life. The most subtle form of invasion of privacy is elicited in *The Rain People,* where Coppola debates the extent to which responsibility to others precludes individual growth and freedom, through the drama of a suburban housewife unable to decide between flight or security, motherhood or abortion, etc.

Business and personal, societal and existential are juxtaposed throughout all Coppola's films, and a healthy balance is never fully realised. Don Vito touches on the crucial Coppola dilemma when he warns his son never to take his business more seriously than his family (personal) life. Unfortunately, Michael Corleone is no more deft at juggling the two than Harry Caul. Both Michael and Harry suppose that they can run their private affairs like a business. Harry tells his landlady boastfully, "I don't have anything personal. . .except my keys." Similarly, Michael kills his brother-in-law (and later his brother) as if he were balancing his budget.

There are few signposts in Coppola's world. The law and the Church are little better than "the Red and the Black." Government not only condones the Corleone empire (pusillanimous judges and politicians arrive or send presents for every conceivable occasion), but it encourages wiretappers to hold conventions. Coppola goes out of his way to underscore the hypocrisy of the Church by showing the priest blessing Michael (at his nephew's baptism) while the new Don's missive of revenge is being simultaneously delivered to unsuspecting victims throughout the country.

Individuals who presume to take sole charge of their own

psychic or business well-being do not flourish; and yet a social paranoia suffuses all of Coppola's *oeuvre.* The multifarious possibilities of Manhattan gleam in the seductive blinking lights and the lurid posters of Times Square, but they are too much for young Bernard of *Big Boy.* A nymphomaniacal actress of his dreams brings him only misery on her terms, and Bernard must look for shelter in his happy ending of a childhood fantasy, replete with pretzels and the girl next door. Similarly, America bludgeons its once hopeful Italian immigrants, and we easily comprehend the logic of an alternative "family" network as protection. When you've been kicked around enough, you kick back, is the lesson of Don Vito Corleone, who understandably found little attraction in dangling "like a puppet on a string" before the whims of powerful men. In the end of *The Rain People,* one senses too that the only answer — imperfect though it may be — to the crippling existential demands of freedom (Killer's helpless retardation, Gordon the policeman's claustrophobic trailer-ridden existence) is to confront life within the supportive microcosm of the family. Vinny will take care of you, Natalie assures Killer before he dies; but what she means is he will take care of *me.*

Coppola's characters possess an illusion of the control so conspicuously missing from Altman's universe, but guilt and/or violence are destined to thwart them. Michael Corleone constructs a complex business network founded on the inevitability of violence, and it is this violence that weds his otherwise "normal" ambitions to their fetid means. As in Hitchcock's (and Shakespeare's) cosmos, order, specious though its moral implications may be, must win out in the end; and Michael Corleone, like Bruno of *Strangers on a Train* and Macbeth, must suffer. (Interestingly, in *The Godfather,* Michael temporarily triumphs because he provides the means of reinstating a tribal order.)

In *The Conversation* guilt (precipitated by an intimation of violence to come) sunders Harry's carefully constructed barricade of indifference. He falls for a sweet, vulnerable voice on a tape — a voice which, ironically, is more than capable (not to mention culpable) of taking care of itself, and loses his objectivity and thereby his autonomy. But violence and guilt are far from purely cerebral devices for Coppola. The latter is used very subtly in his profound character explorations in *Rain People,* while violence for its own sake is indulged as an increasingly perverse affair in *The Godfather*(s). Similarly, little in cinematic history can compare with the galvanising effect of blood and guts spewing forth from Room 773's toilet in *The Conversation.*

Coppola has thus far proved himself less an innovator than an experimenter, and his style is still in a state of flux. Coppola told Brian De Palma after *The Conversation:* "*The Conversation* and *Rain People* were started almost as dares to myself. . .But from now on I don't think I will do it as a puzzle or a dare. It's like the difference between seducing a woman just to see if you can seduce her, or seducing her because you really want to."9

While I respect *The Conversation* enormously, I find it too effete and skeletal to stand up as a major work: a promising mosaic, it lacks Antonioni's visual majesty and the character depth which distinguished Coppola's own earlier screenplays and films. To my mind, *The Godfather*(s) and *The Rain People* are both his most "felt" and his best articulated works thus far: his undeniable talent lying in story-telling and characterisation.

YOU'RE A BIG BOY NOW

When *You're a Big Boy Now* was released in 1967 Coppola (then 28) was hailed as the Orson Welles of Great Neck. The film itself is something of an energetic *potpourri,* brandishing exuberance, prodigy, and a consummate mastery of craft — but little that could be construed as innovative or profound. *Big Boy* takes place in *Shadows* territory, but Coppola's camera is as little inclined toward *vérité* as his literary mind is suited to the anarchic syncopations of such early De Palmas as *Hi Mom!* and *Greetings!* What it demonstrates instead is a poised camera, nicely wielded by Andrew Laszlo, and the capacity to fashion a series of congruent story lines. (While the various plots are skeletal in *Big Boy,* the same skill permits Coppola to weave the dense web of *The Godfather (s).)*

The story is a simple one: young, over-protected son moves to the city (in the book, London; in the film, New York), where his appetites are whetted by a profusion of new posibilities — primarily sexual. Ignoring the advances of the "nice" girl from P.S. 109 (Karen Black), Bernard (Peter Kastner) falls for a schizoid actress who calls herself Barbara Darling, nicely played by Elizabeth Hartman. Bernard then proceeds to find himself impotent, homeless, and ultimately in jail. Life, with a little help from his ever-bizarre and unhandily available parents, quickly opens his eyes to the inadvisability of tampering with the unknown; and the film ends as Bernard skates off into a pretzel factory paradise with his beloved "Dog" and the "good" girl by his side.

Molly Haskell said of *Big Boy* that it "used every trick in the New Wave repertory to simulate the insanity of modern urbanity";

and so it does. The basic assumptions of *Big Boy* are not unlike those of Chabrol's *Les Cousins*. Bernard is very much the bungling younger cousin figure, while Tony Bill as Raef (Bernard's poetic fellow librarian) even bears a striking physical resemblance to Jean-Claude Brialy, the worldly cousin in the Chabrol. The situations are also predictable: the jealous, coddling Long Island mother; the guilt-riddled, but nonetheless prurient son; the goodie-goodie "nice" girl; the beautiful Charybdis of a love-object. As Andrew Sarris has pointed out, even the one-liners are derivative. For instance, Bernard's adherence to the name "Dog" (his mother insists on calling the animal Rover) is very much like Audrey Hepburn's christening of her cat, "Cat" in *Breakfast at Tiffany's*.

What is *not* derivative in *Big Boy* is Coppola's sensitive use of actors; his flair for the prurient; the suggestion of characters and themes to be filled out in maturer works. The cinematography is lovely — replete with bravado and buoyancy. The roller skating scenes in the New York Public Library (Mayor Lindsay gave Coppola unprecedented permission to film the library on Sundays) nicely conjure up the youthful exuberance of both character and director, as does the Lovin' Spoonful score (a rollicking "You're a Big Boy Now") that accompanies Bernard's elated skating in the sun routine after receiving a letter from his idol Barbara Darling.

Coppola is at his weakest in the areas of fantasy and anarchic humour. Bernard's mental elaborations on the graffiti "Niggers Go Home," for instance, is as gratuitous as most of the flashbacks in *Rain People*. Barbara Darling, on the other hand, is an interesting rehearsal for Coppola's treatment of the schizoid woman in later films. While Barbara is clinically "sick" and therefore absurd, many of her characteristics: vacillation between affection and repulsion, greed and generosity, are shared by the "normal" women in Coppola's subsequent works. Natalie in *Rain People* is loving and cruel; the Cindy Williams character in *The Conversation* is apparently helpless and actually cunning and ambitious. The world paranoia, just touched upon in the Times Square scenes and Bernard's misadventures, is also seminal to the Coppola *oeuvre*.

But the best parts of *Big Boy* entail the messy, naïve lustiness of its young hero; and Coppola nicely captures his erotic adoration of Barbara Darling and his itch for experience.

Elizabeth Hartman and Peter Kastner in YOU'RE A BIG BOY NOW

THE RAIN PEOPLE

Based on a story he'd written in college, *The Rain Poeple* is Coppola's favourite "personal" film. One of the first road pictures and a "woman's" vehicle in the best sense of the word, its ending in particular has proved somewhat controversial. Roger Greenspun concluded an essentially positive review in the *New York Times* by adding: "At the very last, Natalie's revolt is exposed as the retreat from responsibility any idiot might have thought it to be. The terms of her grand escape become counters in a psychological parlor game, and she, the audience, and the film itself are sold short in a frantic effort to make conventional amends."

To my mind, *The Rain People* is not just a lovely film to look at but one of the most thoughtful explorations of responsibility and independence, of the moral implications and ambiguities of love and guilt, ever documented on the screen. Despite the hysterical ending, overburdened, I'll concede, with extraneous flashbacks, the film comes to no conclusions. What it depicts with feeling and insight is an eternal existential dilemma filtered through the vague and primarily gut apprehensions of a Long Island housewife with a car.

Coppola's camera is self-conscious but never obtrusive — balancing an unwonted realism (we hear authentic traffic sounds on the highway outside Natalie's phone booth; sense actual time passing as she waits in the sterile numbness of the motel room) with close-ups of windshield and rain drops, pannings around landscapes and people that create a graceful, natural setting. The film opens in the languor of early morning, where garbage trucks pass almost noiselessly through the light rain of cloistered, suburban streets, not unlike those of *Our Town* or *Rabbit Run*. In bed, Vinny adjusts·a sleeping arm to embrace (and constrain) his very much awake wife, Natalie. This is the last we see of Vinny. Within minutes, Natalie has showered and taken off for her childhood home, a matter of blocks away. "I just said I wanted to be free for five minutes," she explains to the parents who spoiled her, "for half an hour, half a day. . ." Having discovered that she is pregnant, Natalie panics and leaves home to see if she might just possibly have made something different out of herself; if she can manage to unshackle her grocery list-worth of responsibilities that add up to life with a husband she loves. Thus far, the plot is somewhat routine, but Coppola beautifully evokes the tension that takes hold of a spoiled, pretty, bourgeois young woman caught between yearning for otherness and respect for experience. There is a marvellous sequence in a motel room, for instance, where Natalie stops to rest (and vomit) during the day. At one point, she sits motionless on the bed, and we share with her the exuberance of complete freedom (nobody knows where she is or can track her down) and the queasy feelings of new beginnings.

The film becomes polemically and chemically interesting when Natalie picks up a young hitch-hiker — Killer, an attractive brain-damaged football player (beautifully played by James Caan). It is through Killer that Coppola poses a more disturbing question than that of domestic responsibility. "I only picked you up in the first place because I thought I wanted to make it with someone new, and I end up with a freak!" Natalie moans as much to a disinterested universe as to her unruffled companion. How deeply are we wedded to chance meetings? Are we responsible for the crimes we witness? These are the very questions Coppola poses less persuasively in the more austere *The Conversation*. Natalie's own mixed feelings are reflected in the fact that she almost always refers to herself as "she" or "the woman," using the third person as a means of separating the kernel that is uniquely *her* from the confused mind and body that now enshroud it.

In *Rain People,* as in *The Conversation* and *The Godfather*(s), Coppola underscores the hypocrisy of the Catholic definition of repentence. After days of battling responsibility on a domestic and cosmic level, Natalie calls to admit to her husband that she's been a lousy wife. Coppola encapsulates his view of Catholic confession in Vinny's reply (interestingly, we hear his voice, but never see his face): "Look," he tells her, "you've just excused everything you've done by telling me how goddam guilty you feel."

Coppola is intrigued by character inter-relationships and unafraid of confronting moral and sentimental issues head-on. Unlike Altman's characters, Coppola's exert a degree of control, not just over each other, but over their own fates: thus Natalie is as responsible for never making it out West as Harry is responsible for his own isolation.

One of the most complex scenes in the film entails Killer's confrontation with the family of his ex-girl friend, whom he was intending to marry before his accident. The dynamics of obverse perspectives excites an ambivalence of sympathy and identification. Killer has come to the house to accept the job the girl's father offered him years before. To the father, Killer is still a champion athlete and a desirable candidate for son-in-law; to the daughter a buried, disquieting memory to be dismissed as quickly as possible; to Natalie a threat (if the family doesn't keep him, what will she do?). Most important, the scene forces Natalie to choose. Tentatively, she has embraced a solipsistic philosophy, refusing to take into consideration demands other than her own welfare. However, in the back of her mind is a lifetime's heritage of spontaneous moral responsibility. Belying her own flaunted amorality, she informs the callous ex-girlfriend, "I don't think it's right to talk like that to anyone." Later she will vacillate and end by abandoning Killer at the Reptile Zoo, informing him that he has to take care of himself. (In other words, "I'm trying not to be my brother's keeper.")

Greenspun's hypothesis that in the ending Natalie realises that her quest for freedom was merely a thwarting of responsibility is one aspect of a complex dilemma. What Coppola evokes through the introduction of a good-looking cop named Gordon (Robert Duvall) living a claustrophobic existence in a trailer with an unmanageable daughter, is less Natalie's own responsibility than the overwhelming burden of freedom. On the road, Natalie is "free" of her diurnal cares, the closure of a middle-class universe, in which daughter grows into mother into grandmother, never changing. But true freedom implies the embracing (or rejecting) of cosmic responsibility – a dilemma which has sent more courageous minds than Natalie's back to the womb of the microcosm (e.g. the family). Unable to divest herself of the instinctual pull toward responsibility (she cannot rationalise her abandonment of Killer), she is not mentally "free" of the precepts her life has embedded deep beneath the skin. She is not

Shirley Knight argues with Killer (James Caan) in THE RAIN PEOPLE

even "free" to enjoy sex without complications: not because she doesn't will it, but because life and personality keep getting in the way.

Natalie is a complex character, and our feelings toward her are always mixed, but sympathetic. Far from a purely conceptual personality, she is vain and idiosyncratic and sensually alive. Shirley Knight does a superb job of evoking that sensuality: her face lights up with pleasure as she watches herself administer mascara to long lashes, and her body relaxes with anticipation at the prospect of love-making.

Just how responsible is Natalie for Killer's death? This is a question Coppola is still asking in *The Conversation*. His title is actually misleading. In a rather forced expository statement, Killer tells Natalie, "The rain people are made of rain, and when they cry, they disappear altogether." Coppola's characters do not disappear — even Michael in *Godfather II* is not allotted the release of death. Natalie is forced to live with her responsibility of choice.

THE GODFATHER

The Godfather catapulted Coppola to overnight celebrity, earning three Academy Awards and a then record-breaking $142 million in world-wide sales. Vincent Canby of the *New York Times* described it as "the year's first really satisfying, big commercial American film;" and unlike *The Sting, The Exorcist,* and *Jaws* it was as well received in critical circles as by the public. Where *Nashville* is a pastiche of sugar-coated American viscera, *The Godfather* is a study of acumen as well as libido. In Puzo's novel, Coppola found built-in the schizophrenia he had imbued in *Patton,* and if commercial limits precluded the tumid, lugubrious embellishments of *Godfather II,* they are also most likely responsible for the flawless pacing and the laconic images.

The plot of *The Godfather* is so complex that it is impossible to give more than a brief and unsatisfactory description. Faithful to Mario Puzo's potboiling best seller, it is the story of a Mafia family (the term Mafia is scrupulously avoided in the movie), the Corleones, who behave in admirably humane fashion toward their loved ones, but make an honest living by bribing, stealing, and knocking off their enemies and acquaintances. The two main characters are Don Vito Corleone (Marlon Brando) — founder of the dynasty and already an old man when the film opens, and his youngest son Michael, an Ivy League scholar and war hero. Michael has been purposely excluded from the seamier aspects of his father's profession, but as the film progresses he becomes embroiled in Mafia dealings and eventually assumes the role of Don himself.

Like Hitchcock, whom Coppola does not much admire, Coppola here bids us to identify first and question later. (With its more extensive artistry and overt ambivalence, *Godfather II* will never so perfectly embody this first film's ambivalence nor render its audience so guilty through complicity.) Evil is an undercurrent, a reverberation here; and Coppola is anything but realistic in his sifting of information. For instance, during the opening wedding sequences, we are completely unaware of the presence of the groom — an odd omission, as it is, after all, his wedding. Or is it? In Michael's and, by implication, Coppola's eyes this wedding is violable; and thus in the final wedding shot we see the bride, Connie, dancing with her father and not her husband. Hence, Coppola very subtly maximises sympathy for the Don while precluding any potential identification with Carlo later on. As we never see Carlo treating Connie nicely — even on their wedding day — we are less sorry to see him mutilated.

Coppola is selective with his violence in *The Godfather.*

Compare Tessio's death, which is left almost totally to our imagination, with Carlo's, for instance. Tessio dies out of frame, while Carlo passes away with lurid explicitness, right down to the final shot of leg reflexes thrashing his feet through the windshield. The attenuation of Carlo's death and its flagrance serve two purposes: first, it balances the equally manifest murder of Sonny (visually and morally); second, it stresses Carlo's death as thematically important, introducing revenge within the family itself.

In the expository scenes where Coppola is intent on winning our sympathy, Don Vito is only very obliquely connected with unpleasant acts. For instance, when the producer awakens to find his prize horse's head deep beneath the covers, Coppola cuts to a pensive Don meditating in his study, thousands of miles from his writhing victim. Michael, on the other hand, is much more intimately aligned with his deeds: the baptism-purge scenes are schematically intercut, and, most important, we see him immediately after Carlo's death, just feet away from his brother-in-law and obviously the mind behind the crime.

Coppola's moral ambiguities are manifested in the recurring light versus dark motif — a device that is carried to an extreme in *Godfather II*. The most stunning examples of this manipulation of light occur in the opening scenes and later the juxtaposition of baptism and purge; and both sequences are less simplistic than they might at first appear. The film opens in a gloomy study, where the Don listens to the pleas of his vengeance-seeking godson Bonasera. Immediately, Coppola cuts to the florid outdoor colours and the wedding celebrations there transpiring. The montage will continue in this fashion (cut to study, cut to wedding) as the sequence progresses; but the study itself becomes lighter, the face of the Don more easily distinguishable as the editing accelerates. Finally, the two worlds merge with a sympathetic shot of the Don, now emerged from his cavernous chambers, dancing with the bride. While appearing to give good and evil, dark and light equal time, Coppola thus subtly sways the balance in favour of the Don's humanity.

The dovetailing of the baptism and the final purge is handled in similar fashion, although here the cuts are more abrupt and the lighting more erratic. In the sacred-secular contiguity, it is less ambivalence than moral hypocrisy (slyly generalising to incorporate Church as well as suppliants) that is underscored. Thus, the priest's voice intoning over the montage of the killings serves as blatant irony, as does the fact that every Corleone enemy is expunged between the priest's two questions (both answered by Michael in the

The alfresco wedding at the start of THE GODFATHER

affirmative): "Michael, do you renounce Satan?" And next: "And all his works?"

The lighting, on the other hand, is more enigmatic. The church itself is decidedly less tenebrous than the Don's study, with daylight filtering through the stained glass windows and the glow of the candles beguiling a kind of docility. Beams of light strike both the face of Michael and his godson; thus, one might infer that the Church does not regard practicing Catholic Michael any more blackly than the baby. And while Michael is linked with the murders through editing, it is only Carlo's death (which takes place after the baptism) for which he is held uniquely responsible morally and cinematically. (Don Vito was incapable of killing his daughter's husband; thus we know Michael alone plotted this revenge.)

As in *Rain People* and *You're a Big Boy Now,* the outside world of *The Godfather* is remote and gorgonian. Independence and privacy are to be cherished, and Sonny's smashing of the intruding photographer's camera at his sister's wedding is a precursor of Harry's tearing apart of his entire apartment in search of a wiretapper in *The Conversation.* The family is, of course, a buffer between the Italian and a chaotic, subjugating world. Don Vito has renounced American government, which views him as a mere "puppet." He tells

Michael shortly before his death: "I refused to be a fool, dancing on a string for all those big guys." (Significantly, he nonetheless hopes that his grandchildren might *become* those big guys.) He has created a microcosmic state, predicated on both secular and sacred law. Loyalty, for instance, is the highest virtue. Fear of the Don, like fear of the Lord, is the necessary key to the family kingdom. The analogous methods (violence, bribery) of the U.S. government and the Cosa Nostra are continually alluded to. Judges and politicians send telegrams to Connie's wedding; policemen are bought and sold by the various warring families; before the "Family Conference," the camera pans up the side of a New York building, fastening itself significantly on an American flag.

The Godfather introduces the discrepancy between "business" and "personal" that is to be more scrupulously dissected in *The Conversation*. Unlike Harry Caul, Don Vito judges the personal — in his case nuclear family — as every bit as important as business. He warns repeatedly that a man is not a man unless he spends time with his wife and children and is himself incapable of ordering the murder of his son-in-law, despite Carlo's responsibility for the death of Sonny. Like Harry, Sonny suffers from an inability to differentiate between business and personal; he is doomed to bring his personal emotions into business dealings and thus to be killed. Tessio, on the other hand, shows a perfect understanding of the division when he accepts his fate with equanimity. He has betrayed the family *business* and must therefore be eliminated. "Tell Michael," he says with no ironic intentions, "it was always business. I always like him."

The difference between men and women — not physically (Coppola's women are terribly erotic, as were Puzo's), but intellectually and politically — is underlined in *The Godfather*. The most priapic scenes are between Michael and a Sicilian wife he can barely converse with: thus undermining the necessity of mutual understanding in marriage. "Women and children can afford to be careless," the Don tells his youngest son; "men cannot."

The distancing between Michael and Kay (his New England girlfriend, then wife) as Michael grows closer to the Family is portrayed with consummate craftsmanship. It begins when Michael first learns that his father has been shot; and Coppola shows us a magnificent image of Michael bundled up in a phone booth (like the phone booths in *Rain People*, a striking metaphor for isolation), with Kay's head framed very much outside. The greater isolation comes when Michael has so effectively severed personal and business that he is able to lie to Kay about Carlo's death. The final image of a door obliterating Kay's face entirely is the perfect metaphor for Michael's isolation and his disentanglement of personal and business emotions — stress having been irrevocably placed on business.

Business is not without its own ethics, however. Like the wiretappers, who openly carry on conventions, the Family has a Ten Commandments of sorts. The Don, for instance, is opposed to exploiting the drug market, and he reprimands Sollozzo (who has come to foist the drug trade on him): "Your business is a little dangerous." In the book Puzo perfectly sums up the business relationship sealed through "personal manifestations" (protestations of loyalty, hand wringing, etc.): "It was not perhaps the warmest friendship in the world, but they would not murder each other. That was friendship enough in the world, all that was needed."

Coppola's *Godfather* figures are beautifully developed, and they are some of his most authentic characters to date. James Caan and Robert Duvall have been imported from *The Rain People*, and they make a fine Sonny and Hagen, respectively. It has been argued that Richard Castellano (Clemenza) or Abe Vigoda (Tessio) could have played Don Vito Corleone without giving a thought to the Method, and the point is well taken. But Marlon Brando lends a dignity to the role that transcends type, and his dying scene misconstrued by his grandson as play, can compete with any of Brando's former performances for poignancy and grace.

Al Pacino is also superb as Michael, and Coppola develops his gravitation toward the Family with utmost subtlety. In the movie, as in the book, it is the scene in the hospital that turns the tide; and Pacino skilfully displays how the yen for power and authority (like mother-love in *Rosemary's Baby*), more than loyalty, draws him magnetically into the clan.

THE CONVERSATION

Much to the chagrin of those who would like to see *The Conversation* as a timely or capricious work, Coppola was two-thirds through with the filming (he recalls that he was shooting the warehouse scene) at the time of the Watergate break-in. Too much stress has always been laid on the tenuous relationship between life and art. Simone de Beauvoir sums up my feelings in *Force of Circumstance:* "The extent and the manner of the fiction's dependence on real life is of small importance; the fiction is built only pulverizing all these sources and then allowing a new existence to be reborn from them." More interesting is the gratuitous stipend art may derive from history. Films like *The Graduate* and *Easy Rider* thrived on the malaise of the Sixties; and a thriller like *Three Days of the Condor* derived potency from the CIA investigations that were being conducted at the time of its release.

A similar phenomenon is at work in the case of *The Conversation,* which Coppola originally conceived during a "conversation" with Irvin Kershner in 1966. Kershner mentioned the existence of a microphone with gun-sights so precise they could pick up the dialogues of individuals within a large crowd. "From just a little curiosity like that," Coppola recalls, "I began to very informally put together a couple of thoughts about it, and came to the conclusion that the film would be about the eavesdropper rather than the people."[21] Thus began the story of Harry Caul, a professional wiretapper — best in the trade, who once uncovered information that led to several deaths. He fiercely guards his privacy: living alone, having an unlisted number, not even letting his girlfriend know his whereabouts or what he does. On a very special assignment, Harry traces two young people and comes to believe that his tapes might lead to their deaths. He insists on speaking with "the director," his boss, in person; and when refused he takes the tapes away. A woman, feigning romantic interest, steals the tapes from Harry, and the wiretapper grows increasingly sure that a crime is

Harry is forestalled in THE CONVERSATION

about to be committed. It is — but by the young people themselves, who in a plot twist are not the victims, but the ambitious murderers. Harry has allowed himself to lose all objectivity and is now being bugged himself. He dismantles his apartment, but is unable to locate the tapping device.

The Conversation begins high above Union Square in San Francisco and slowly zooms in (the camera serving the function of a gun sight on a microphone) on Harry Caul, professional wiretapper and personal cipher. Like Michael in *The Godfather* and Natalie in *Rain People,* Harry's tragic weakness is an inability to discover the balance between business and personal. Sensing that his client is planning to murder two young apparent innocents (played by Cindy Williams and Frederick Forrest), whose activities he is paid to record, Harry begins to take personal responsibility for the ultimate repercussions of his "business" activities. Like Hesse's Harry Haller of *Steppenwolf,* Harry Caul possesses a dual nature (Catholic/existential; business/private; animal/spiritual), and like Antonioni's *Blow-Up, The Conversation* pieces together the puzzle of a crime (here incorrectly) through editing. Coppola's irony derives from the final twist where Harry learns that the victims of his "private" melodrama were, indeed, themselves the plunderers in a real-life crime; and through his own abandonment of objectivity, Harry has left himself the prey of other wiretappers — his privacy, like his autonomy, violated.

Some of the best aspects of *The Conversation* arise from Coppola's life-long fascination with electronics. Both the magnificent sound effects (the most outstanding are in the hotel sequence where a crime is literally committed before our very ears) and the editing — itself very much like tape editing — were handled by Walter Murch, a sound expert and classmate of George Lucas's at USC. (Murch also handled the sound for *Rain People, American Graffiti,* and *The Godfather.*) Visually, Coppola has marvellously evoked the film within a film, eavesdropper eavesdropped back upon through an obtrusive camera. Like Orson Welles in *F for Fake,* Coppola is both wizard and accomplice in celluloid magic. Coppola said that he decided not to use a long lens to suggest directorial eavesdropping because it was hackneyed. "Then I thought of doing it with a static camera which gave the impression that it didn't have an operator at it." Thus, for example, the camera continues to focus on a particular sector of the apartment, while it allows Harry to walk in and out of frame. (Taken to a metaphysical extreme, this type of shot suggests the irony of free will.) The final and very effective panning shot, uneasily searching out the dismantled apartment, was also planned to act as a "supermarket TV camera."

The Conversation's style is not always so felicitous. The heavy-handed treatment of the Big Brother office building with a *Zabriskie Point*-like distortion of glass and exaggeration of its menacing anonymity is incompatible with the sombre texture and slumbrous rhythm of the film as a whole. The jazz music, on the other hand, is peculiarly apt, meshing both with the pacing and with Harry's love of the saxophone. My primary criticism concerns the dishonesty of the final switch in emphasis of Cindy Williams's "He'd kill us if he had the chance." Every time we hear the speech — and we hear it over and over — the emphasis is on *kill;* the final time we hear it the *us* is stressed. Up until this point, the plot has adhered to the stolid, reasoned impressions of guilt-obsessed Harry and what he at least thinks he sees and hears. Why all of a sudden do we hear the tape distorted?

Although *The Conversation* is far from my favourite Coppola, it is replete with fine touches. The use of Cindy Williams's "old/young" face, for instance, was very effective. "I wanted the audience to think that although she was young there was something troubling her or, in this case, someone oppressing her," said Coppola. "But at the end you see the real twist and realise her face is showing hardness and ambition."[9] Cindy's voice is also curiously sympathetic and evasive, vulnerable and cloying at the same time. While Harry is vicariously in love with her, the audience is more equivocal. Lines like "Whenever I see someone like that I always think the same thing — that he was once somebody's baby boy," for instance, become irritating with repetition, like Sissy's monologues in *Badlands.* Thus, Coppola cleverly differentiates his protagonist's perspective from our own — and at the same time exempts us from aspects of his guilt.

Coppola has said that he had trouble with Harry because he couldn't identify with him, and this is obvious. Unable to identify, Coppola decided to "enrich" his character, and it is therefore not surprising that Harry — despite the marvelous performance by Gene Hackman — is little more than an assemblage of incidents and quirks: Catholic guilt, unhappy childhood, etc. Coppola's skill is not yet commensurate to his design: he has decided to make a film about the autonomous prerogatives of gadgets and has thereby sacrificed the credibility of his characters. (Hesse's *Steppenwolf* suffers comparably from an unwieldy philosophical skeleton.) Coppola may give Harry his childhood polio, his interest in music (not only was his father a flautist, but Coppola himself was an expert tuba player), his

Catholicism; but these are merely finely woven garments with which to cloak a straw man.

While the characterisation is weak, the design of *The Conversation* allows Coppola the most expansive canvas for his themes thus far. The idea of privacy versus responsibility is explored through the perspective of the ultimate paradox: a man whose business is to vitiate other people's privacy, while his obsession is to safeguard his own. Coppola included Catholic confession not just as a metaphor for guilt, but because he views confession as "one of the earliest forms of invasion of privacy." Coppola also discusses the use of a building down the block from Harry and barely noticeable in the film, which is surreptitiously stripped down as the movie progresses. By the end, the rooms are entirely bare, which, says Coppola, "is to me an eavesdropping image — that is, seeing through the walls of the buildings."

There are subtler, more "human" instances of invasion of privacy. To assert his total indifference to material possessions, Harry tells his landlady that he has no personal belongings besides his keys. His relationship with his girlfriend, one of the nicest touches in the film, insinuates an almost mystical element. Like Natalie and Killer, these two connect on a subliminal level. When Harry arrives at her apartment, for instance, she just happens to be singing "Wake Up You Sleepy Head" — the very song that suffuses Harry's tapes of Union Square. Harry immediately blenches at yet another invasion of privacy — human intuition. Anxious to close off all unstipulated wave lengths, he attempts to attend to business, sex, and maybe even love (later, in an unconvincing confession to the planted siren at the wiretappers' party, he seems to intimate that he loves his girlfriend) without "personal" involvement. While Harry is far more successful at this game than Natalie, his fortress too is obviously pregnable, and he has no human resources to fall back upon once his mathematical defences cave in.

The tragedy of being unable to intermingle "business" and "personal" is most evident in *The Conversation.* As Peter Cowie has pointed out, Harry's dismantling of his apartment, Virgin Mary included, save his beloved personality extension — the saxophone — is comparable to Michael's isolation at the end of *Godfather II:* both fail to perceive the "seeds of nemesis"[8] within their own characters.

THE GODFATHER PART II

Godfather II is a voluptuous film, a brilliant failure as an entity, but successful on so many levels that it must be considered Coppola's

most ambitious work thus far. Like *Nashville,* it is a study in power
— and particularly American power (here represented by the Italian
rather than the hillbilly sector). Unlike *Nashville,* both the structure
and the images of *Godfather II* protest that there exists a difference
between the energy that struggles to attain power and that which
struggles to keep it. Frankie (played by Michael V. Gazzo) at one
point compares the Corleone *régime* to the Roman Empire, and
Coppola's crosscutting from pioneer Godfather Vito Corleone to
Michael's contemporary syndicate suggests that with the Cosa
Nostra, as with the Romans, decadence lies not so much in power
itself, as in the perpetuation of power. Opening with a dim shot of
Pacino's (Michael's) face, attenuated like a Mannerist portrait,
Godfather II proceeds to wallow in the very decadence that it
illustrates.

A comparison of *Godfather II* to *The Godfather* is rather like a
discussion of Tintoretto's "Last Supper" *vis-à-vis* Da Vinci's. The
basic elements of the earlier film have been uncannily reshaped,
almost, but not quite parodied. Michael is now established as
Godfather, with a somewhat dowdier Kay as wife and mother of his
two children. De Niro has replaced Brando as the young Vito
Corleone; and Connie, Fredo, and Tom Hagen (all played by the
same actors) seem pinched variations on their more vital counterparts
in the earlier work. Connie, for instance, has taken to picking up and
marrying fortune hunters, presumably as reaction to her first
husband's (Carlo's) infidelity and death. Fredo, married to a woman
he cannot handle, is more pitiful than ever, and it therefore comes as
little surprise when we learn that he has betrayed his powerful
younger brother. Later we find that even the circumspect Tom has
taken on a mistress. Like *The Godfather,* the sequel opens in the
sunlight of outdoor festivity — here the celebration of Michael's son's
communion; but the director is obviously no longer concerned with
audience identification. While the earlier film proceeded to play with
our sympathies, juxtaposing dark and light, *Godfather II* becomes
increasingly chiaroscuro and ultimately lugubrious as Michael's
tenuous objectivity capitulates to his passion.

Godfather II is both more visual and more literary than its
predecessor. The thrust of the film is deflected through the literary
device of flashbacks and forwards, lending a mythic and historical
dimension to the plot. Specific images, particularly regal or religious
references, also come to play a heightened symbolic role in the later
film. Michael's concern with the male child as successor borders on
fanaticism, and throughout the film children assume a pivotal role. For
instance, directly after Michael has been informed of Kay's "miscar-

GF-Ⅱ- 5524-28

THE GODFATHER PART II: Michael (Al Pacino) enters the courtroom

riage" (later revealed as an abortion) Coppola couples the sound of a child's cry with a fade-in on young Vito Corleone and his family. The first time we see Michael lose his temper is also in connection with Kay's loss of his child. "Was it a boy?" he shouts at Hagen, in an unprecedented breach of etiquette. Religious imagery is similarly prevalent. Fredo is killed while saying a "Hail Mary," and the water − instrument of baptism − serves as premonition of death. Frankie opens his veins in the bath tub; and it is in the boat house, overlooking the water and with snow falling about them, that Michael informs his brother, "Fredo − you're nothing to me now. You're not a brother; you're not a friend."

Family loyalty, the most sympathetic chord in *The Godfather,* is now more than a trifle off pitch. In the flashbacks to Vito's activities, we sense that intelligence as well as ruthlessness were at work in the genesis of the "Family" network. Vito grew up to avenge the deaths of his Sicilian parents and his older brother, but he also used his wits to devise a system that allowed fellow Italians to prosper in the New World. That a large chink has been struck from Vito's system can be detected at the beginning of *Godfather II,* where we see Michael contemplating serious business with an outsider − a Jew, Hyman Roth. Michael himself is aware that things will never be quite so straightforward for him as they were for his pioneer father. To begin with he is dealing with a business that has distended beyond his wildest dreams. Roth says gleefully, "Michael, we're bigger than U.S. Steel." But Michael is puzzled by the changing times and policies. To his mother, he poses the ultimate question of leadership: "But by being strong for his family, could he *lose* it?" Indeed, that is Coppola's theme.

The times alone cannot be held responsible for the discrepancy between Michael's "Family" and his father's. Vito arrived in America an orphan – God the Father, so to speak. Michael has sibling rivalry to contend with. Fredo and Connie freely admit that bitterness and jealousy mitigate the love as well as the respect they owe him. When Michael suggests that despite his personal disappointment in Fredo he will judiciously take care of him as a clan member, the gentle Fredo explodes. "You're my kid brother, and you'll take care of me?" After this outburst, only respect for his mother deters Michael from exterminating his brother immediately.

It is Coppola's contention that the tide cannot be stopped, that having reached a certain degree of power/madness Michael, like Macbeth, is incapable of turning back. When Kay first threatens to leave, he pleads with her to remain. "I've learned that I have the strength to change," he asserts, but this is the futile gesture of a lost soul. Rather than take the politic course of allowing Roth to live out a few more harmless years, Michael insists that he be killed at the airport, and even Frankie is forced to die for his temporary disloyalty. In the end, Michael is left alone: Kay gone, his son (Anthony) psychologically bruised, Fredo murdered. The final zoom-in sees Michael a gloomy fallen angel, ruler in his own purged hell.

Besides its more seductive visuals, *Godfather II* has several advantages over the first, more classical thriller. While Diane Keaton's role as Kay is dealt with very perfunctorily here, other characters – such as Hyman Roth, nicely portrayed by Lee Strasberg – are astutely conceived. The garish Cuban sequences also contribute a new angle to the dialectic, suggesting that a foreign ideology may supplant both the "Family" and the American capitalist system on which it is based. Michael marvels that the rebels are fighting for something other than money, and this fact correctly strikes him as ominous.

Godfather II is a broad film, too broad to explore fully any of its individual facets. The sequel therefore lacks both the satisfying cogency and the directness of the earlier work; but its density, visual as well as literary, bodes well for future projects.

THE GODFATHER PART II: Robert De Niro (above) as the youthful Don, who takes vengeance on a family foe (below)

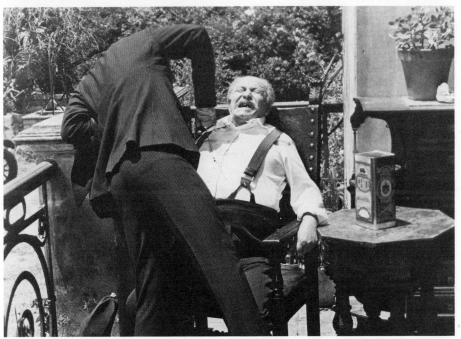

Martin Scorsese with Robert De Niro on the set of TAXI DRIVER. On a certain level both men identify with the main character

Martin Scorsese

As Scorsese has pointed out, it is somewhat premature to describe as an *oeuvre* what amounts to only five features – and one *(Boxcar Bertha)* an exploitation film at that. The most recently recognised of the new directors, Scorsese did not become commercially viable until *Mean Streets* created a sensation at the 1973 New York Film Festival; and frankly were it not for *Mean Streets* and *Taxi,* one would not consider Scorsese's eclectic body of prize-winning shorts and his initial "promising" longer works worthy of a chapter. It is in light of the superb *Mean Streets,* fit for comparison with Fellini's *I Vitelloni* or Truffaut's *Four Hundred Blows,* and the complex, maturely conceived and crafted *Taxi Driver,* that Scorsese renders himself a talent to be seriously dealt with, even so early in what promises to be a fecund career.

Scorsese's background has been vividly documented in his films. Born in 1943, he grew up, like Charlie of *Mean Streets* and J.R. of *Who's That Knocking?,* in New York's Little Italy. Scorsese's parents were devoutly Catholic blue collar workers; and at grade-school level Scorsese began preparation for the priesthood. Scorsese's health (he was asthmatic) precluded sports, and around the same time his father began taking him to New York equivalents of Langlois's Cinémathèque – the old Thalia movie theatre and the Museum Of Modern Art.

Scorsese claims that it was only because he failed the exams for Fordham College's divinity programme that he went to New York University, and although he is no longer a practising Catholic, the Church is still very much a working creative and emotional rescource. Scorsese began his college education in English, but soon transferred to the Film programme, where he remained as teacher and graduate student, making such shorts as: *What's a Nice Girl Like You Doing in a Place Like This?* and *It's Not Just You Murray.* The Belgian Cinémathèque sponsored his next award-winning short, *The Big*

Shave, described as "a brief (five minute) American nightmare." Scorsese's first feature began as *Bring on the Dancing Girls* in 1965 and emerged in final form as *Who's That Knocking?* in 1969. Then began a period of editing such films as *Woodstock* and *The Great Medicine Caravan,* leading to *Boxcar Bertha,* his first commercial directing assignment, commissioned by Roger Corman and released in 1972.

Following the Corman film, Scorsese finally managed to accrue financing for twenty-seven days of filming on the script he had conceived nearly seven years earlier, and which opened as *Mean Streets* at New York's 1973 Film Festival. The critical acclaim and "cult" following of *Mean Streets* facilitated other projects, and in 1974 he completed *Italianamerican,* an affecting documentary exploring the experience of Italian immigrants through informal talks with the Scorsese clan. (*Itanlianamerican* is part of a bicentennial series on immigrants entitled *A Storm of Strangers.*) In the same year he completed *Alice Doesn't Live Here Anymore* and picked up Ellen Burstyn's Best Actress Academy Award for that film the following Spring. *Taxi Driver,* from Paul Schrader's trenchant script, was released in February 1976.

Like the French *Nouvelle Vague* directors, Scorsese grew up at the movies, and his films are consciously derivative. One can't watch even the exploitation *Boxcar Bertha* without thinking of Arthur Penn, while the controversial beginning of *Alice Doesn't Live Here Anymore* is as much a tribute to William Cameron Menzies and *The Wizard of Oz* as Truffaut's *Day for Night* is to Orson Welles and the Gish sisters. *Who's That Knocking?,* with its abrupt cuts and movie talk, is as New Wave-ish as anything since *Shadows,* and *Mean Streets* is indebted both to the communal neo-realism of *Paisan* or *Shoeshine* and to the idiosyncratic subjective realism of Cassavetes.

While his preoccupations are by and large more mythical, less restrictive than those of *Shadows* or even *Woman Under the Influence* (to which *Alice Doesn't Live Here Anymore* has been justly compared), Scorsese is certainly a Cassavetes *protégé;* and Cassavetes (understandably impressed with *Who's That Knocking?*) supported him as Corman did Coppola, Coppola did Lucas, etc. Scorsese remembers Cassavetes's taking him out for a three hour heart-to-heart after a screening of *Boxcar Bertha,* when he urged him to abandon exploitation films and adhere to more personal works — a suggestion Scorsese took almost by accident. (Exploitation films were not thrown his way.)

The *cinéma-vérité* quality of *Who's That Knocking?* and *Mean Streets* is very much in the Cassavetes line, although, like the Italian neo-realists, Scorsese balances a facility with the human particular against the urgent evocation of place and time. At their best, *Mean Streets* and *Taxi Driver* have the same immediate quality that James Agee discusses in his review of *Open City*. If one supplants historical with personal immediacy, actual with autobiographical or mythical, Rome with New York, Agee's lines are peculiarly apt: "They [here, Rossellini and writer Sergio Amidei] understand the magnificence of their setting — the whole harrowed city of Rome — as well as the best artist might and perhaps better, for though their film bristles with aesthetic appreciation and eloquence, these are never dwelt on for their own sake: the urgency of human beings always dominates this architectural poetry . . ."[2]

Despite his facility with atmosphere, Scorsese prior to *Taxi* was more adept with interiors than with external phenomena, and even in *Taxi* New York comes to represent the claustrophobia and ready-to-explode Pandora's Box conveyed through the bars of Little Italy and the motels of the Southwest. Sequences such as the marvellous cemetery episode in *Mean Streets* and the driving interludes at the end of *Mean Streets* as well as on the freeways of *Alice* serve as foils for an oppressive myopia. It is interesting to note that the florid prologue to *Alice* is designed to look like a 1948 *interior* set. The brutal, confining hand-held documentation of confrontations between Charlie, Johnny Boy, and Theresa in *Mean Streets*; Alice, Tommy, and Ben in *Alice* are also reminiscent of scenes in *Faces* and *Shadows* and uncannily similar to Cassavetes's most recent *Woman Under the Influence*. While *Taxi* perpetuates Scorsese's concern with myopic relationships and interiors (Iris's hotel room and Travis's apartment are brilliantly isolated from the flux of the Manhattan streets), it is also concerned with an evocation of the sultry New York summer, both as actuality (filth on the streets, sweating bodies, fans swirling lethargically) and as counterpoint to the mythic imagination of Travis, so beautifully reflected in the soundtrack and the surrealistic interludes.

Like Cassavetes's characters, Scorsese's are uneasy within relationships, but hopeless without them. His characters *need* each other on very basic and profound levels. Alice says, "I can't live without a man"; and we realise that whether she can or cannot is irrelevant — she doesn't *want* to. Alice lacks the sophistication of *Rain People's* Natalie — had her husband not died on her, she would never have stirred from the kitchen. Unlike Altman's Brewster or Coppola's Harry Caul, neither Alice nor Travis envisions glory in solitary flight. "I can't live without a woman," admits Scorsese: "I say I should be able to — *we* should be able to, but I can't." While the tension between self-sufficiency and dependence is an undercurrent in his films, Scorsese is mostly concerned with the struggle for freedom within relationships and not at their expense. The bonds of tradition pull against contemporary *mores:* the rituals of Church and family mitigate against sexual and emotional fulfilment. Yet, Scorsese's characters are unable or disinclined to untangle themselves from the web of desire and responsibility: they fight their battles within the strictures of existing relationships or in the process of striving for new, more perfect commitments. Even cipher Travis is forever hopeful of connecting with the world through love and, finally, a convoluted altruism. Kris Kristofferson is eminently more appealing than Alice's wobbly voice, and Scorsese leaves little doubt in our minds which she should chose to follow, if, indeed, a choice must be made.

Scorsese's camera is not nearly so predictable as Cassavetes's or De Palma's: indeed, it has grown increasingly versatile and chamelion-like in his more recent films. The ambulatory, hand-held camera used for *cinéma-vérité* and rhythm effects, is most effective in *Mean Streets,* where it underscores both a youthful exhilaration and an insidious malevolence. In the bar-room scene a bibulous Charlie rocks by himself, and the camera's subjective tilting and swaying contributes a marvellous sensual energy to his dance. The hand-held treatment of the Church scenes also serves to integrate sacred ritual with the profane agitation of the streets. "You don't make up for your sins in Church — you do it in the streets," dictates the voice-over in the opening sequence; and a vertiginous camera links the sanctuary with the previous street montage.

In the nude scene between Theresa and Charlie, the camera serves very much the same purpose as Cassavetes's in *Husbands.* In both, the rough texture of the cinematography stresses the transitory nature of the tenderness it depicts, its relegation of loving to a few hours in capricious or sterile surroundings. Conversely, the exigency of the situation and its uneasiness, as reflected by the camera movement, also serves to heighten the sexual tension, undermining tenderness, but bolstering eroticism. In *Alice* and *Taxi* the generally ambulatory camera continues to stress an under-current of frustration and violence; but in these films the images are often lyrical or surrealistic as well as brusque and gritty. The panning around Alice as she sings portrays her as a good deal larger than life, for instance, and the blurry pastels of early Fall create a quality of luxury and ease in the final shot of Travis and Betsy in *Taxi.*

While Altman takes various autonomous elements and rounds them into an uneasy solution, Scorsese has tackled the art of fusion

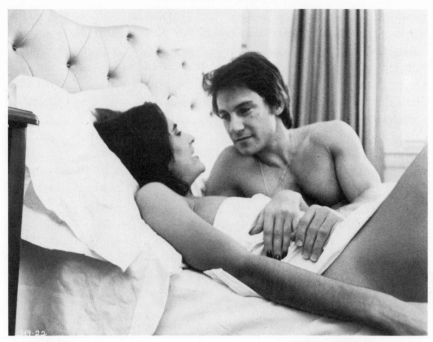

Charlie, the lover, in bed with a testy Theresa, in MEAN STREETS

and cinematic collage. In *Mean Streets,* juxtaposition of rock and Italian "Feast" music are meshed like the ingredients in Mama Scorsese's metaphorical spaghetti sauce in *Italianamerican.* Visually, the jump cuts and lack of establishing shots (this latter a matter of circumstance – they simply hadn't the time to shoot them) serve to mingle the Uncle's uptown restaurant with Johnny Boy's puckish stunting; "stolen minutes" between Charlie and Theresa and violent eruptions like the bathroom homicide. *Taxi Driver* fuses myth and reality, rich and poor, prominent and insignificant, stable and insane, through a moving metaphor of a cab, reiterated by the camera. The streets of New York are replete with dichotomy: trees garnishing one block, pimps patrolling the next. The people who ride with Travis are illicit lovers or Presidential candidates or prurient wife-watchers. Similarly, the Bellmore Cafeteria is actual blocks – but metaphorical worlds – from the torpid atmosphere of Travis's apartment, the busy Columbus Circle campaign headquarters, and the shadey residential block where Betsy lives.

Violence is endemic to Scorsese's world – not just in the eye-for-an-eye sense of Coppola's Sicilian justice, but as an expression of frustration and ultimately a perversion of the love impulse. For no "good" reason Johnny Boy blows up a mail box or shoots at the Empire State Building. Even the nice-guy bartender Tony takes pleasure in owning a caged tiger, and Michael has Johnny Boy killed for vengeance, yes, but also as a means of asserting a dignity frustrated by his sexual predilections. The frenetic energy of Scorsese's style is itself a visceral expression of frustration, of violence threatening to spill out into the plot. In *Alice Doesn't Live Here Anymore,* for instance, Scorsese uses the camera as a means of foreshadowing Ben's violent entrance into Alice's seemingly tranquil motel room. The camera tracks constantly throughout the film, not in the gluttinous, bludgeoning fashion of *Boxcar Bertha,* but with a subtle prescience, just visceral enough to undermine the deceptive calm of small town living. Violence as release of pent-up frustration is best explored in *Taxi Driver,* where love of Betsy is visually transmitted into love of weaponry. Travis's affection for guns, like Hedda Gabler's, borders on the pornographic, but it is significant that neither his interest in killing nor his potential for violence surfaced until after all hope of winning back Betsy was lost. (The first time we see him fight is in the campaign headquarters where Betsy refuses to speak with him.)

Even more than visceral violence, religion — in the sense both of ritual and of an Absolute power — is more vital to Scorsese than to any of his fellow directors. For Coppola, religion is essentially a negative or compensating force. In *The Conversation,* confession is

A sudden jolting moment as Ben (Harvey Keitel) lets out his frustrations in
ALICE DOESN'T LIVE HERE ANYMORE

yet another example of eavesdropping. In *Rain People,* Natalie seeks to appease her conscience by "confessing" her inadequacies as a wife to her husband through the confession booth anonymity of a phone. For Scorsese, the Church is unquestionably also a propagator and false appeaser of guilt. When I asked Scorsese what remained the strongest legacy of his strict Catholic upbringing, he replied unequivocably, "Guilt. A major helping of guilt, like a lot of garlic." Charlie feels guilty about everything: Johnny Boy, Theresa, his own procrastination; and he sees fit to conduct a continuing one-way dialogue with the Lord, in which he assures him that he's trying.

As with Coppola's Church, Scorsese's represents the fear of hell. Michael Corleone seeks to arrange matters in heaven by having his "family" properly baptised, presuming that He can be as easily bribed as secular officials. A more superstitious Neopolitan Charlie is forever holding his finger to a flame, trying to approximate a billionth of the pain of hell. (A priest once actually suggested this exercise to Scorsese.)

But the Church is more than guilt and pain to Scorsese; although he has technically renounced Catholicism, he is still friendly with several priests and maintains the warmest of ties with his religious family. As with Ingmar Bergman, T.S. Eliot, Simone de Beauvoir — a few other artists who grew up to reject a thoroughly ingrained dogma, the concept of an Absolute is difficult to purge. In Scorsese's case, it serves as much as inspiration as albatross. He has said, "The whole idea of faith fascinates me. I say, 'I have faith in this project; I have faith in this person.' Now, these are material matters, and you could view them concretely; but I tend to feel they're spiritual. I've never gotten over the ritual of Catholicism, but I guess it's the same type of feeling someone else might get from taking an acid trip." Scorsese's characters thus far have not achieved the ecstasy of Anna Magnani in Rossellini's *The Miracle* or of the knight in Bergman's *Seventh Seal,* who looks at his clenched fist and proclaims that the sun is high in the sky and he is playing chess with Death.

Nevertheless, Scorsese's characters do long to be good, in the simple and exalted sense of the word. Charlie is trapped in the imbroglio of his own self-serving goodness, but his conversations with the Father (a little like the Jewish mother of Mazursky's *Next Stop, Greenwich Village,* talking to herself) do reflect a sincere desire to better the world as well as himself. Just before jumping a red light on the way to safety in Brooklyn, he confides, "I guess you could say that things haven't gone so well tonight, but I'm trying, Lord, I'm trying."

This concept of trying suffuses *Alice* as well. Like Mabel in *Woman Under the Influence,* Alice is of a breed that would never consider frustration, boredom, humiliation causes for leaving one's spouse. Unlike Mabel, she does allow herself the luxury of self-pity turned outward as well as in (she has soul mates Bea and her son to converse with) — and, most significant, her husband happens to pass away, giving her the opportunity to experiment with the fantasies gestating in her long suffering head. For Alice, the Absolute is self-fulfilment, which she initially defines in terms of getting to Monterey and becoming a singer: the implausibility of such a scheme, the obvious "return to the womb" psychological angle couldn't matter less. Monterey signifies all that is right to Alice: her Tara, and every bit as much a beacon to her lost star in the night as the Catholic God is to Charlie. Like Charlie, she's set out on the wrong trip — she can't embark like Dorothy for Kansas, anticipating that all the intervening years will disperse like a bad dream of Oz. But she too learns something and, perhaps, finds a better life; so the Absolute, while objectively foolish, has not been denigrated.

If *Mean Streets* is gritty realism, then *Alice* is a much-tampered-with myth. The obvious hand-held camera in the Ben (Harvey Keitel) sequence and the general cinematic apprehensiveness from beginning to end is reminiscent of the undercurrents of violence in Cassavetes's "Hollywood" *Minnie and Moskowitz.* But Scorsese takes myth a step further than Cassavetes, past the realm of the absurd (no one could truly hold up the marriage between Minnie and the car-parking Moskowitz as tenable) and into the wish-fulfilment arena of the studio Hollywood that Mazursky has so deftly updated. *Alice* is myth just real enough to believe, not quite the romance of Doris Day's *My Dream is Yours,* but not the glossy cynicism of *Carnal Knowledge* or *Five Easy Pieces* either.

Even Alice's happily-ever-after ending pales in comparison with the limitless pink horizons of her embarkation; a comment, perhaps, on the expectations of Hollywood-weaned children, but also a nice compromise between dream and inevitability, Absolute and diurnal. Certainly, it is a bit implausible that the singing waitress with the bratty son should reel in a ranch owner as attractive as Kris Kristofferson — and rich to boot. But in the light of the foggy red dream of fame and Alice Faye, Kris Kristofferson is not all that much to ask for. It's myth, certainly, but on a scale we're permitted to feel comfortable with.

Taxi Driver is also mythically handled, with an even more insidious camera (the cab often assumes the tracking function), which now pans over the explicit mutilations of Travis's victims rather than jumping helter-skelter from TV coverage, to accident to parallel events, as it did in *Mean Streets*. But here the religious angle is most fully exploited in its potential for evil. Of Travis, Scorsese said, "There's the whole false saint idea I tried to develop in *Mean Streets:* the guy who set out to save people who don't want to be saved and ends up hurting them. In the end the prostitute is safely ensconced in the bosom of her family and miserable, thanks to our hero, and a lot of people are dead."

It is interesting to note that while Scorsese's works have become increasingly mythic in style, more comprehensive in subject matter, they have thus far remained true to the impulses of little men and women. His messages and his character perversions are political or metaphorical only in the broadest contexts. *Taxi Driver*, for instance, can be viewed as a sly political statement on "the candidate," so completely out of touch with the people he goes overboard to cajole and mingle with. But the political ironies are incidental to the thrust of the film. Travis is not the outgrowth of anything so hackneyed as "our way of life" or "our political system" except insofar as it sent him to Vietnam. He is a loner, no more afflicted by the candidate (whose views he could not care less about) than by the pimp, and much more sensitive to the vibrations of a stifling New York summer than to any other exterior influence. He is the victim of anonymity and despair; and two hundred years ago he might have turned religious fanatic — today he becomes an assassin and unintentional cultural hero.

While the themes of guilt, loneliness, innate violence, and frustration crop up again and again in Scorsese's work, the director has demonstrated an admirable versatility of mood and style, the ability to find humour and compassion as well as tragedy or melodrama or irony in human behaviour. Alice, like Tony the bartender in *Mean Streets*, is capable of sublimating her libidinal tensions and living a "normal" life — that is a life with compromise and satisfaction. If Scorsese's characters are always on the brink of disaster (like candidate Palantine in the wonderful scene where Scorsese portrays him as almost killed), they are also on the brink of happiness.

WHO'S THAT KNOCKING AT MY DOOR?

Who's That Knocking? is Scorsese's first and, some will argue, his best feature. I much prefer the feverish *Mean Streets*, but there is a lot to recommend this story of a younger and less involuted Charlie

– J.R., torn between his Twentieth-century American desires and a tenacious Italian heritage. The plot takes place in the early Sixties and consists of a series of sometimes garbled flashes from present to past and back again. Like Coppola's *You're a Big Boy Now,* it is essentially concerned with a pubescent's view of sex, and because J.R. is a Catholic Italian, sex inevitably means guilt and tension between emotion and ritual. "Broads" are non-virgins, and although J.R. loves his blonde non-Catholic girl friend, he is convinced that he will dishonour them both by making love to her out of wedlock: thus rendering her a broad. "If you love me, you'll understand," he stammers. When he later learns that she has already lost her virginity (the fact that she was raped does little to redeem her virtue), he is outraged.

Who's That Knocking? is replete with *Nouvelle Vague* and Cassavetes influence. If the Italian "scumbags" have difficulties handling the outdoors (in one hilarious scene J.R.'s pal Joey moans that he can't believe he was crazy enough to climb the least menacing of mountains), they at least drive the obligatory New Wave cars and find headlights and skylines and old westerns dazzling. The energy of the film is also very *Nouvelle Vague:* lighter than *Mean Streets* in tone and theme, it is a buoyant film, with even the medley of rock tunes more lyrical than cacophanous. The love scenes are also particularly sensuous, with the initial rolling and licking and exploring on J.R.'s bed more erotic than almost any subsequent Scorsese love sequences. *Who's That Knocking?* is a self-conscious film, but like Cassavetes's *Shadows* it is more eager than intellectual; and the facetious tone and camera fluidity (marvellous pans and zoom-ins and montage shots) are more prescient of *Alice* than of the more brutal *Mean Streets.*

On the Staten Island Ferry, for instance, Scorsese zooms in on J.R. and then proceeds to pan around the girl and back to him in very tight close-up. The shot is both a rich stylistic device and a means of eliciting an undercurrent of uneasiness. It is at once lyrical and a bit unsteady, in much the same fashion as the pan around Alice as she sings and plays the piano. As in *Alice,* the camera is also eminently self-aware; we have lots of angled shots and moving for the sake of moving shots; but there is little of the abrasive tempo of *Bertha* or *Mean Streets* or *Taxi.*

The time is the early Sixties, slightly later than *Shadows* and in the same era that saw Lucas's teeny boppers cruising the Strip in Modesto, California. Like Benny in *Shadows,* J.R. hangs around with a gang of drifters (J.R. prefers to see them as "between positions"), but unlike the *Shadows* crowd, they have very definite roots to refer to. J.R.'s mother is never seen, but she is as real a presence as the priest behind the confessional door. The implications of Catholicism are introduced in the very first series of lovely superimpositions and dissolves, portraying an arbitrary mother making dinner, while in a nearby mirror we see both the mother and the Virgin Mary. Throughout the film, Scorsese returns to the pasta and the Virgin and the holy candle: at times a trifle ostentatiously (such as when J.R. refuses to make love and the camera makes a beeline for his icons), but never without conviction. Scorsese tells of how producers initially laughed at the film's premise of sexual inhibitions in the *Easy Rider* era of purported baccanals and nonexistent superegos. Today the feelings in this film hold up better than the "all-hanging-loose" bravura of many of the Sixties' youth films, serving both as a rites of passage statement and as faithful evocation of the *mores* of a particular sect and time. As with *American Graffiti* and Mazursky's *Next Stop, Greenwich Village, Who's That Knocking?* evokes a vulnerability both universal and timeless.

There is surprisingly little violence in *Who's That Knocking?* — quite a distinction as it falls between *The Big Shave* and *Boxcar Bertha* in Scorsese's *oeuvre.* The men look fragile and prove that they *are* so in the marvellous scene where the big city guys nearly die climbing a small mountain. As in Scorsese's later films, the men are much more at home with each other than with women — broads or virgins — and they spend a lot of time like all youths, seeking to alleviate boredom and to fulfill a vision of life as game. One of the nicest sequences entails a party of six guys and two whores. While the first two athletes begin their sessions in the same bedroom, the remaining four impatiently await their turn outside. The ribald wit is very much that of a younger *Husbands* — particularly when J.R. can no longer contain himself and leads the gang in to speed up the copulations.

Even more than *Mean Streets, Who's That Knocking?* is uncomfortable with its women. While Harvey Keitel is extraordinary in the role of J.R., Zina Bethune is embarrassing as "the girl" — significantly nameless. She is not an icy bitch like Betsy in *Taxi Driver,* but neither does she have any dimension. Like Coppola, Scorsese is uneasy with the concept of woman. He has knocked her off the pedestal, but is still wary of playing around with her. (In *Alice Doesn't Live Here Anymore* he has an easier time with an older woman, herself forced to play the male role of provider.) "The girl" is the least palatable of Scorsese's women. We know nothing about her — age, profession, or background (except that she was raped and isn't Catholic); and the only chink in her armour of femininity is her love of westerns. (One senses that this love is more a function of Scorsese's inability to conceive of anyone, male or female, not loving westerns.) Lelia Goldoni, with her spunk and vulnerability, could have handled the part splendidly; as it is, the film falls down in the end because we are left untouched by this "girl's" refusal to marry J.R.

Scorsese's cuts are at times confusing, his pacing less proficient than in the later films; but as a whole the film works very well. Unlike the Charlie of *Mean Streets,* J.R. has no aspirations toward sainthood; but like Alice he wants to do the "right" thing, and he wants to find his place in the mainstream of America — without unsettling his fragile Virgin Mary or giving up his pasta dinner.

BOXCAR BERTHA

Scorsese made *Boxcar Bertha* in twenty-four days, which is about the nicest thing I can say about it — except that David Carradine gives a fine performance as Bill Shelley, union man who stoops to conquer (what I'm not sure) during the Depression and ends as a Christ figure swinging from a moving train. What is understated or incorporated into *Mean Streets* (namely, the violence) is underlined in *Bertha,* the story of a sensitive young girl (Bertha) who saw her father killed in a plane accident and later loved and luted with unionist-outlaw Bill Shelley, also accompanied by a black crony Von Morton (Bernie Casey) and a not-so-bright Yankee gambler Rake (Barry Primus). The film was adapted by Joyce and John Cornington from an autobiography by Boxcar Bertha Thompson. Although it received some favourable notices, *Variety* just about sums up my own opinion when it says, "Whatever its intentions, *Boxcar Bertha* is not much more than an excuse to slaughter a lot of people...There's hardly a pretense toward justifying the carnage."

It would be comforting to lay all the blame on a screen-play that snatches its characters willy-nilly from one *debacle* to the next with maddening regularity. But the plot, with its token *hommage* to *Bonnie and Clyde* and a profusion of sociological, political, and religious allusions is just a small part of the problem. It is a self-professing exploitation film in which potential for violence is gleefully mined with singular disregard for relevance. To add insult to injury, its hillbilly music is grating, and all the relationships — particularly those involving Barbara Hershey as Bertha — are cloying.

Where *It's Not Just You, Murray* (a tongue-in-cheek short about an Italian gangster) and *Who's That Knocking?* had demonstrated admirable sophistication and restraint, *Boxcar* tears into its plot with

a vengeance. There is scarcely a moment from the time of the
opening air crash that one form of carnage or another is not
occurring; and the film gyrates with the cadence of a shooting
gallery. Barbara Hershey plays Bertha like a cuddly mongrel or a
second-rate ballerina sinking into a Camille. Sex is Scorsese's coffee
break between bludgeonings, and Bertha is usually the willing
subject. Her little girl smile never fails to snare males of all
backgrounds — it even juices up an anthropologist, who comes to her
whore house to research, but stays to bed.

Scorsese says he could not have made *Mean Streets* without
Bertha, and it is possible to speculate on the lessons he learned from
this first commercial failure. Where the unflinching violence is
exploited in the earlier film, *Mean Streets* employs a modified, but
equally straight-forward approach to what the director obviously sees
as a "natural" outlet. The final shot of the film, with colt-like
Bertha, face vulnerable and resolute puffing along beside the train
taking a hanging Bill to glory or whatever, is oh-so-offensive plot-wise
(who cares about them anyway?), but interesting as visceral exercise.
We first have a shot of Bertha and her black buddy exchanging
despondent glances; and then Bertha moves out of frame. Next
moment we see the train is moving, and Bill is on it, with Bertha
below, holding onto his feet. As she squeals, "Don't take him," the

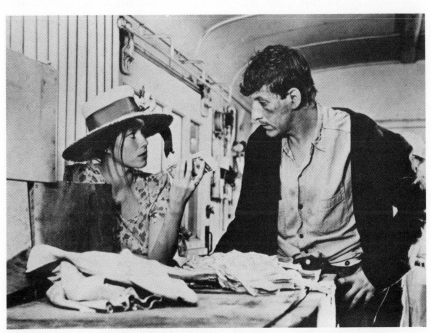

Barbara Hershey (left) in BOXCAR BERTHA

camera moves to a very pictorial overhead shot of train, man, and woman. Gradually, she falls behind, and the camera follows her man toward the hereafter.

Painstakingly elegant in this banal context, shots like this one prove effective not so much in the laconic *Mean Streets* as in *Taxi Driver* and *Alice*. The shot this immediately calls to mind is the quick juxtaposition of Alice and her waitress friend Flo sunning their faces and the following cut of the two in perspective — their small bodies set against a long, empty lot. Of course, it also prefigures the grim, surrealistic tracking through Iris's blood bath of a hotel room at the end of *Taxi.*

MEAN STREETS

Mean Streets is the story of a would-be saint, would-be *entrepreneur* on the streets of Little Italy, who attempts to solve the very real problems of his friends and satisfy his personal ambitions through the power of diligence and good intentions. Instead, he ends by causing the violent woundings (whether or not his childhood pal Johnny Boy is actually killed is left uncertain) of his epileptic girl friend and his irrepressible buddy, as they flee the vengeance of a small-time money shark — too late.

Whether or not *Mean Streets* is Scorsese's autobiographical film (many have protested that the asthmatic, academic Scorsese witnessed, but never experienced the brutalities of his film) is semantical: surely, *Mean Streets* is Scorsese's cathartic work. He himself sees it as something of an allegory. He says, "See, it's the idea of success — in fact, when I first wrote it, it was like an allegory for what was happening to me trying to make movies. Mardik and I were working together, writing scripts about ourselves at that time, trying to get things going...I drew from personal experiences about a guy trying to make it."[2 8]

Mean Streets is not the most perfectly crafted of Scorsese's films, but it is my personal favourite. It was made with *Bertha's* crew and on $350,000 in cash and $200,000 deferred. Scorsese and Martin Mardik wrote the first draft for *Mean Streets* in 1966 and spent several years unsuccessfully attempting to get backing. As he had just made *Who's That Knocking?,* Scorsese wrote the laterday sequel with Harvey Keitel (J.R. in the first film) in mind as the older Charlie. De Niro, who lived on 14th Street, was well acquainted with characters like Johnny Boy, the role he was to play; and Keitel, from Brooklyn, knew the neighbourhood from experience as well as his part in the earlier film. The shooting of *Mean Streets* took twenty- seven days, six in New York and the rest in Los Angeles. (They couldn't afford to shoot the entire film on location in New York.) They had time for a mere ten days of rehearsal, and some of the content emerges from improvisations along the lines of Cassavetes's — only three or four scenes that were on-camera improvisations, but several that materialised during rehearsal, were taped, and written into the script. "If *Mean Streets* looks frenzied," says Scorsese candidly today, "it's because we *were* frenzied."

The disjointed nature of *Mean Streets* is surely abetted by the manner in which it was shot. While the orderly, lulling, fantastical quality of late Fifties/early Sixties rock music is underscored in the stereophonic cruising radios of *American Graffiti,* it is pulsating cacophony that emerges in the over-loud pre-Beatles rhythm of *Mean Streets.* Scorsese shot the film during the Feast of San Gennaro, and the soundtrack reflects the tension between traditional Italian life styles (the Feast music) and contemporary New York ("Be My Baby" is a kind of theme song for the contemporary aspect of the film). It is a dark film (again, it had to be shot at night), about small-time Italian gangsters, for whom Brooklyn is the other side of the globe and the world of *The Godfather* is as foreign as the plantations of *Gone with the Wind.* Scorsese describes the street mentality, saying, "Somebody does something wrong, you've got to break his head or you shoot him." Charlie's girlfriend Theresa is striving to escape the strictures of this mentality: she's begging her parents to let her get an apartment uptown, and wants Charlie to come with her. Charlie, however, is not committed to escape, but to immanence. By transcending, he hopes to succeed in heavenly terms (in his private dialogues he continually reminds God that he's trying) and within the bounds of terrestrial Italian ambition (he wants to take over his uncle's restaurant).

Like *Who's That Knocking?* and *American Graffiti, Mean Streets* zeroes in on specific personalities whose existence is not just idiosyncratic, but also a reflection of group sensibility. The secondary characters are thus very important: Tony, the nice-guy bartender who sits caged with a lion and coaxes the beast to lick him; Michael, the fidgety homosexual who literally cringes when told his "girl" has kissed a "nigger"; Jerry, the apparently carefree veteran who explodes in the midst of his Welcome Home party. These are all foils for Johnny Boy, Theresa, and Charlie: insiders, like the *vitelloni* in Fellini's film, who through bravura, pluck, or enterprise hope to break out of the womb-prison of their apparent predestination.

Unlike the Fellini surrogate of *I vitelloni* or Curt of *American Graffiti,* Charlie never does succeed in either severing his bondage to

Charlie (Harvey Keitel), the aspiring saint, trying to approximate the pain of hell

childhood rituals and companions or in abrogating his own priorities in favour of unsullied altruism. Like a perversion of the prototypical Capra hero, he thrives parasitically on the dependence of those he is ostensibly helping. "Charlie likes everybody; everybody likes Charlie – fuckin' politician," croons Johnny Boy with the antic sagacity of Lear's fool. Leaving Johnny Boy to the gangster wolves would be too much for Charlie, who likes to view himself as a laterday St. Francis of Assisi, but neither is he willing to do the one thing that might save the boy: speak to his uncle about employing this slightly demented chum (and thereby risking his uncle's displeasure). Scorsese has compared Charlie to the Pharisees, a sect that gave money to the poor in order to solicit attention. "Christ said that they had already received their own reward because they had received reward on earth."[28]

What makes *Mean Streets* extraordinarily affecting (much more so than *Taxi,* for instance) is that Scorsese's characters are not purely emblematic. On the one hand, Charlie *is* an aspiring saint, forever holding his hand near a flame to try to approximate the pain of hell should he, God forbid, end up there; attempting to atone for his sins through a personal code of sacrifice. "Now when I do something wrong, I just want to make up for it my way... Now you just don't fuck around with the infinite," he mutters to an unseen Absolute. He is also an aspiring stud who gets drunk, dances, taunts pick-ups. The mercurial Johnny Boy and testy Theresa are also interesting characters, with their own whims and options; and it is interesting that ultimately Charlie chooses the pal over the lover, the man over the woman, filial over romantic responsibility. Little attention has been accorded to what I found to be a pivotal sequence, where Charlie races off in pursuit of Johnny Boy (in a sense, his salvation) while leaving the epileptic Theresa suffering on the staircase and in the hands of a neighbour. Granted, this is innate Italian sexism, but it is also indicative of a more profound irresponsibility, of a hunger for a specious kind of glory.

Although Scorsese does a splendid job of evoking the atmosphere of the Feast and of the crowded bar, the nicest scenes in *Mean Streets* are one-to-one. The sequence where Charlie and Johnny hide out in a familiar cemetery is immensely moving in its understated camaraderie, particularly as it follows the showy sniper episode where Johnny pretends to be shooting at windows. Wedged in the confines of the cemetery, both have returned to the world of childhood, where Charlie no longer has to play martial school master, Johnny the frantically obstinate dunce. At one point, we watch Charlie glance down on Johnny Boy, placid on a tomb stone, and it is as if both we and Charlie foresee his death. Just as the syncopated rhythm of *Mean Streets* is redolent of *Husbands*, this interlude is much like the mellow, morning after scene in *Shadows*, where the tension pauses for a minute, supplanted by a sadness and nostalgia usually precluded by the exigencies of life.

Like Alice in the later film and Natalie in *Rain People*, Charlie is very much at a metaphysical crossroads — unable to choose between the guilt-appeasing balm of self-negation and the give-and-take responsibility of secular freedom. The choice is not simple, and like Natalie, he never gets a chance to make it. The *deus ex machina* of Death precludes even tentative resolution, a possibility which Scorsese will explore in *Alice*.

ALICE DOESN'T LIVE HERE ANYMORE

Alice is not an easy film, but oddly enough — considering its vaudevillish mother-son routines and its Hollywood gloss — it is a film that improves with reviewings. On one level Robert Getchell's very literary script is an update of the old Doris Day *My Dream is Yours*, fulfilment through man or career dilemma, and Alice is a petulant, thirty-five-year-old housewife variation on the cloying

Warners spent $85,000 to recreate the look of a 1948 set, in homage to William Cameron Menzies and films like THE WIZARD OF OZ

Bertha. On another, it is the *Minnie and Moskowitz* ingesting of "realism" into myth in the form of its cast: Lelia Goldoni (playing Bea, Alice's best buddy and confidante); Diane Ladd (a garrulous waitress, Flo, whose vocabulary puts Alice's genteel bad-mouthing to shame); Harvey Keitel (Ben, Alice's psychotic married lover), and Ellen Burstyn as a widowed ex-singer on the road with an insufferable eleven-year-old son. *Alice* is, of course, also the claustrophobia of *Mean Streets* come to small town America, Catholic strictures wired around the Protestant ethic.

There are parts of *Alice* that simply don't work. Alice's truck driver husband (Billy Green Bush) is just too unlovable to accept (Scorsese attributes his fulsome image in the film to enforced cutting of his more sympathetic scenes); and the mother-son routines at times get out of hand. But as a film, *Alice* succeeds, not just on the merit of "privileged moments," but like *Mean Streets,* as a moving *collage.* By no means is *Alice* a feminist film — hyperboles to the contrary. It is a message comedy, employing a lot of women long unemployed and with reason for bitterness and anger; but their frustrations, along with Scorsese's own, are exorcised, rather than enumerated through the catharsis of art.

Alice opens with a marvellous *hommage* to William Cameron

Menzies and films like *Duel in the Sun, East of Eden,* and *The Wizard of Oz.* The shot of a child Alice Hyatt on a Monterey bridge beneath the pink-red hues of a studio Hollywood sunset cost Warner Brothers $85,000 for one day's shooting *(Who's That Knocking?* cost $35,000 *in toto*), but the effect is stunning. It is interesting too that in recreating a 1948 look, Scorsese takes his exterior indoors, creating both the blurry effect of wish-fulfilment and undermining the actual openness and freedom of the vast western outdoors.

From Monterey, Scorsese cuts abruptly to Socorro, New Mexico, where the bad-mouthed little girl Alice, who was going to out-sing Alice Faye, is presently married to a truck-driver and is mother of an eleven-year-old brat. The husband soon dies, ushering Alice and Tommy onto a road-trip "home" to the land of the pink sunset, where Alice foresees a return to the singing career she married out of a good fifteen years before. The fact that she no longer sings very well (it is doubtful she ever did) is one handicap, as is the fact that she hasn't the money to make it to Monterey without detours as bar singer or, when all else fails, waitress. After several tentative wrong steps and near explosions, Alice finds love with a rancher and the option to sing as well — if she still wants to.

It's difficult to relate the plot of *Alice* without making it sound trite. As I said earlier, the plot *is* essentially conventional with uneasy camera tracking and sudden jolting moments (the scene between Alice and the adulterous Ben, for instance) rendering it something more complicated than a buoyant comedy. Alice's wit is so quick that we expect more of her than of Cassavetes's Mabel; and at times she is infuriatingly disappointing. Despite her consciously un-glamorous *facade* (blue jeans and ten extra pounds), she gets what she wants through the wiles immortalised by Doris Day and Betty Grable (she tries the Betty Crocker trick with pies for her husband, but it doesn't work) and familiar to all liberated and unliberated women alive. Her tears con a soft-hearted bar-tender to hire her as singer, and a smile wins the day with Kris Kristofferson in the role of rancher of her dreams. Those who have protested have sought in *Alice* what neither Scorsese nor Getchell nor Burstyn herself (it was her property, and she had a lot to do with the development of the role) intended. "I never set out to make a feminist film," says Scorsese; and he hasn't. He has made a film about a conventional woman who, almost by chance, stumbles upon a relationship a little more fulfilling, a little more equitable than her first marriage. It is no step at all for sophisticated womankind, but it is a small step for Alice Hyatt.

The film is replete with fine moments. The relationship between

Alice and fellow housewife Bea is both understated and affecting — a kind of pre-Women's Lib companionship based on shared and unquestioned suffering. The scenes between Diane Ladd as Flo, the outrageous waitress, and Alice are also high points. In one scene they sit by the diner, sunning their faces and chatting of love and life and loneliness; and the camera pulls back to show them protruding in the midst of a flat, empty lot. It is not a breathtaking scene, but it touches the ironies of high hopes and low horizons without drilling the point in. The lyrical 360 degree pans around Alice as she plays the piano are also handled deftly, like the comparable scene of Jack Nicholson in *Five Easy Pieces:* on the one hand, a tribute to the pursuit of myth or art, on the other a comment on its ineffability. I am also partial to Tommy's wino girl friend Doris (Jody Foster, appearing as Iris in *Taxi Driver*), who may be "weird even for Tucson," but finally manages to slow the ever-abrasive tongue of "the kid" just when we begin to think that impossible.

Alice is an achievement for Scorsese, as it allows him to air his dirty linen in unfamiliar places. Like Charlie (and Scorsese), Alice wants to do both what's right and what's pragmatic; and is not quite sagacious enough to predict exactly what that might be. The relationship between Alice and Tommy also has parallels in the

The camera pans 360 degrees around Alice at the piano

Charlie-Johnny Boy alliance. Like Charlie, Alice depends on Tommy as someone who needs and, as such, may redeem her.

But the tone of *Alice* is far from that of the earlier work, and the Hollywood ending is not merely tacked on. Through the road scenes (accompanied by the bittersweet Elton John number, "Daniel, My Brother"), the cardboard motels, the hysterical waitress episodes, the thrust is away from pain. In the final car crash in *Mean Streets,* we see that everything beforehand — the tradition-asserting Feast, the small-time Mafioso uncle, the insistent rock — all were leading to ultimate collision and violence.

In *Alice,* just the opposite is true. The jokes, the tears, the routines, were leading to a transcendent comedy; and that is what the ending gives us — mother and son, arm in arm, walking toward a sign of Monterey in the heart of Tucson. But the *deus ex machina* of comedy is no more capricious than that of tragic death. "A lot of peoples' lives are soap operas," says Scorsese; "mine is anyway."

TAXI DRIVER

Scorsese has said, of *Taxi Driver,* "It's basically about loneliness and sexual frustration and restrained violence." Do he and Robert De Niro, who gives a flawless performance as taxi driver Travis, identify with this character on any level? "Well, I'm not homicidal," laughed Scorsese in reply, "but, yes, both Bob and I identify with the character. The guy is very quiet but intense."[1][7]

One's first reaction to *Taxi Driver* is to note the lacuna rather than the continuity between this and Scorsese's earlier works. Surely, this consummately crafted, sinewy, convulsive story is as far as one sensibility can travel from *Alice's* Southwest. While *Mean Streets* pulsates with its character's head and heart and visceral beat, *Taxi Driver* is often scrupulously contrapuntal, replete with Bresson *hommages* (screenwriter Paul Schrader had written a book on Bresson) and surrealistic colour and texture. The Bernard Herrmann score, for instance, intones mellifluously over garbage, past crime, through havoc, just as the initial shot of the slow motion steam and looming yellow cab tower over the anonymity of their paltry, real-life counterparts. Like Travis's first vision of Betsy (Cybill Shepherd), dressed in white and as unblemished as an all-American goddess, the music is "alone" and "untouchable." (Interestingly, it *is* touched and distorted when Travis himself begins committing violent acts.)

Paul Schrader, ex-film critic and author of *Transcendental Style In Film,* wrote *Taxi,* and while the script is highly personal, it also follows the formula Schrader has noted in the films of Bresson, Ozu, and Dreyer. *Taxi* begins with the everyday, insinuates the character's own passionate and irrational commitment, brings this passion to its climax, and then returns to the diurnal. Schrader has suggested that the difference between his character and the European or Japanese counterpart lies in the American's (coming from a still adolescent culture) predilection for thrusting his aggressions outwards, thus killing others, as opposed to the old world character who turns inwards and kills himself.

Paul Schrader's screenplay is much more dichotomous than Scorsese's earlier sources: like Scorsese and De Niro, we are encouraged to have mixed feelings about Travis right from the beginning. An ex-marine, Travis first is spotted signing up as cab driver as an anodyne for insomnia. We note immediately that he is somewhat out of touch with reality: his eyes wander; his laugh is strained; and he blanches at reference to moonlighting − obviously unaware of the word's connotation. Cab driving fails to alleviate his sleeping problem (after driving all night, he checks in at early morning Broadway peep shows), but it brings him closer to the fetid aspects of New York life. The passengers in his cab lower an already sceptical opinion of human nature, and he shows no indication of setting even his own lands in order (or "organizising" as his sign playfully admonishes). He confides in a diary and leads a mass consumption existence (eating MacDonald Quarter Pounders, watching television, observing rather than participating in sex), making no contact with individuals. He spots the beautiful blonde Betsy who works for candidate Charles Palantine and for a short period intrigues her with his "contradictions," being so unlike any of the college and business types she's accustomed to. When he takes her to a very explicit porn film fear and disgust override her curiosity about this strange man, and she quickly drops the cabbie, sending back his flowers and refusing to talk to him.

Travis's frustration becomes menacing. He makes one last effort toward human intercourse by confiding in fellow cabbie Wizard, "I got some bad ideas in my head." But Wizard does not succeed in convincing him that "comme on fait son lit, on se couche"; and Travis goes ahead to buy guns in preparation for assassinating Palantine, a mission he grows to feel is his destiny. He has no choice. In the meantime, he meets twelve-year-old Iris, a prostitute, and also takes it upon himself to save her from her foul-mouthed pimp, Sport. When Travis is diverted from killing the candidate, he kills Sport instead and then proceeds to knock off all the men gathered around Iris's hotel room. Inadvertently hailed as a hero (it seems one of the

TAXI DRIVER: De Niro (left) as cabbie Travis, quiet, but intense, and Jodie Foster as twelve-year-old Iris, the prostitute Travis takes it upon himself to save

victims was a wanted gangster and none was unduly mourned by the police), Travis is now looked up to by everyone, even Betsy, but he is no longer interested.

On a stylistic level, *Taxi Driver* is the densest of Scorsese's projects. Its evocation of the squalid, teeming New York summer, in the steam rising from blistering pavements, the unplugged fire pumps, the sweat pouring off a musician's brow, is as pungent as it is myopic. The nuances of character and relationships, so effectively drawn in *Mean Streets* and *Alice* are here sacrificed to a rigorous dissection of a psychotic's vision. "Loneliness has followed me my whole life everywhere," says Travis, and we sense that it is this solitude, rather than the actual violence and torpor, that allows destiny and dissatisfaction to loom so large in Travis's disconnected eyes. While the candidate, for instance, is caricatured (as "out of touch" with the people as Travis himself), nothing he or any of the other characters do, merits the justice Travis has in mind for them. Even Sport, the pimp character we should ostensibly hate most (after all, he's exploiting a child), is portrayed as not all that loathesome for his trade.

Scorsese chronicles Travis's dissipation with consummate

finesse. In the beginning Travis is trying to connect. He attempts to strike up a conversation with a girl at the candy stand of the peep show; he addresses the candidate; he courts Betsy. As his chances with Betsy dwindle, he feeds more on himself. He doesn't even bother to answer the demented passenger (played by Scorsese himself) who speaks of shooting off his wife's head and bosoms with a .44 magnum gun — but he does go out and purchase one himself. He also becomes narcissistically preoccupied with his own body, and the camera dwells on his muscles (looking a bit like a Giacometti statue) as he flexes, does push-ups, practises his shooting for the big day.

In Travis's scenes with Iris, as in his preparation for assassinating the candidate, we become increasingly aware of his "failed saint" psychosis. With Iris, he is arguably doing the right thing in trying to send her home or to a commune, but his reasons are undoubtedly self-serving. Scorsese cunningly portrays Travis's approach to the admittedly unappealing pimp as merely a variation on his equally vociferous denunciation of Betsy's rather amusing fellow worker. Of Betsy's friend, he said, "I don't like him — not that I don't like him; I think he's silly...he doesn't respect you..." Iris is more perceptive than Betsy. When Travis begins denigrating Sport, she counters, "What makes you so high and mighty? Didn't you ever try looking at your own eyeballs in the mirror?"

While the camera's pacing accelerates as the film progresses (at one point it cuts brutally from Sport seducing Iris to Travis shooting at a target), it is as restless as its character's mind from the very start. At times, it assumes the pace of the cab; at others it explores rooms (particularly the Bellmore Cafeteria) like a soul in limbo, condemned to roam, to be ceaselessly moving, never· fastening on anything permanent or balancing. Like Travis it is unable to cencentrate: when the cab drivers converse, it shuffles back and forth, peering at opaque faces or carelessly deposited trash. Like Travis's cab — vulnerable to the blood left in the back seat or the eggs slung at it, the camera appears helpless to avert its gaze from the horrors that walk in its path. And like Travis, who chooses *not* to limit his anguish by steering clear of notoriously "bad" areas, it revels secretly in the filth and the suffocation.

Only occasionally does the camera assert itself as an objective entity. The panning of the mutilated bodies and the marvellous evocation of Palantine's near-assassination are the most obvious cases in point. This latter is handled in the supermarket method of Coppola's *The Conversation.* Scorsese begins by cutting from Palantine in Columbus Circle, speaking about "crossroads" to a pan of the melting pot watching him, past the "No Pedestrians" sign to Travis dressed for the kill. He then cuts back to Palantine, to a pan of the supporters including Betsy, back to Travis. Then, subtly, the shots begin to change, and we watch Palantine as though through the eye of a gun. Sometimes his whole body appears in a frame; sometimes merely flailing arms. This device very effectively sets up tension. We worry about the would-be victim subliminally, rejoice when he does *not* appear in a certain shot.

This studied camera work pays off at the climax of the film, undermining whatever sympathy remains for Travis, who after all kills the pimp and gangsters as second fiddles. His initial plan was to kill a candidate of whose views, we are continually reminded, he is abjectly ignorant. Travis's behaviour from the moment he kills the robber in the delicatessen has been potentially violent; and violence has been amply foreshadowed in the street scenes as well as in the shopkeeper's bludgeoning of his would-be predator. But nothing prepares us for the delight in violence for its own sake (that "real"

Scorsese directs Cybill Shepherd and Robert De Niro in the porno theatre foyer sequence

rain Travis speaks of earlier, cleansing not the city but his own frustrated psyche), shared by character and director alike in the virtuoso climax. Scorsese's handling of the killings (no holds barred) is similar to if more surrealistic than the butchery in *Boxcar Bertha,* and even the Christ imagery in the overhead panning is comparable. Until this point the duality of the character – so pitiable when he is walked out on by Betsy, so potentially lethal when he shoots at the gallery (significantly, Scorsese has him point his gun at us) – has been handled with the utmost intuition and control. Physically and intellectually we have been distanced from an increasingly deranged protagonist. But in this final scene we are not observers in his last hurrah; no, we are unwitting *accomplices* mercilessly subjected to his cathartic shock therapy. We are not estranged, but implicated – and unjustly so. Here a pictoral affection for violent death gets out of control and dulls the impact of a still extraordinarily forceful psychological study.

The final reunion of Travis and Betsy is beautifully shot, but gratuitously misogynic. Betsy, who initially appeared potentially complex (she responds to Travis as someone less banal than her co-workers) is now presented in just the way Travis has come to view her. She's like all the others ("cold and distant – women in particular; they're like a union"). Her belated interest is merely self-serving: she wants to be associated with a hero. However, the finale, where Travis drives off into the night and the surrealistic images of white cab light and neon signs flood the screen, is Scorsese's most perfect melding of myth and reality. (Ironically, it is Broadway – with its theatres, its movies, its porn houses, its slimey streets.) Despite the apocalyptic climax that momentarily slipped out of the control of his accomplished hands, *Taxi* establishes beyond question that Scorsese is one of the finest American directors working today.

Paul Mazursky

"I think the hardest thing," said Mazursky of his craft, "is to find that fine grey line which is the distance between sentiment and sentimentality." It is Mazursky's greatest triumph thus far that with a few glaring exceptions (moments, not whole films), he has succeeded. His career would seem to substantiate an equation of sentimentality plus humour (catalyst) equals sentiment plus catalyst. Seen from another angle, Mazursky's update of the traditional Hollywood comedy is absurdism humanised with a generous helping of personal implication.

Like Mel Brooks and Woody Allen, Mazursky began his career as a comedian; and like Altman, he came to film through television. Born Irwin Mazursky in Brooklyn in 1930, Mazursky's early life is much like that of Larry Lapinsky in *Next Stop, Greenwich Village.* Like Larry, Mazursky graduated from Brooklyn College and set off for New York's Greenwich Village, where he remained from 1951 through 1956 as stage actor, night-club comic, and teacher. As he remembers it, he also spent a lot of time unemployed. In 1959 he went to San Francisco to play at a night-club called "Hungry Dog" and never came home. In 1961 he and Larry Tucker were hired to write for the Danny Kaye show, a position he maintained for four years. During summer vacations Mazursky and Tucker wrote a film script called *H-Bomb Beach Party,* which was sold but never produced and created a pilot for the Monkees' television show. In 1968 their script of *I Love You Alice B. Toklas* was produced, and in 1970 Mazursky himself directed their next collaboration—*Bob and Carol and Ted and Alice*—the antic spoof of Los Angeles life styles from inside and out that brought Mazursky a good deal of acclaim in Hollywood.

Mazursky is anomalous precisely because, like Preston Sturges, Leo McCarey, George Axelrod, and Blake Edwards before him, he is deceptively accessible. Richard Corliss has said of Mazursky that he

149

"has become that contradiction in terms, the liberal satirist: closer to an indulgent Horace than to a bitter Juvenal."[7] In approach, Mazursky has more in common with McCarey (indeed, *Blume in Love* is very much a Sixties update of *The Awful Truth*) than Sturges, whose ironies are heavier with pessimism than compassion. Mazursky may underscore the outrageous duplicities of his bourgeois half-truth seekers, but he is none too sure that Truth, in one form or another, does not exist; and if it does, who is he not to be looking?

Visually, Mazursky is more or less straightforward. His canvas is wide, particularly in the California films, but he has thus far evinced little interest in either Coppola's chiaroscuro effulgence or the contrapuntal cinematography of Cassavetes and Scorsese. The texture of his films is by no means unilateral, however. A film like *Bob and Carol and Ted and Alice* for instance is conspicuously smooth, while *Alex in Wonderland* and *Blume in Love* are disjointed and dreamy. As with Coppola, it is the story and not the camera whose rhythm determines the look of the film. In the final scene of *Blume,* for instance, the image never tells us for sure whether what George Segal's Blume is witnessing is really his pregnant wife in the Piazza St. Marco, or a vision of the same. The camera is ambivalent because the story would have the same effect either way: it is important only that Blume *appears* to have his happy ending.

While a film like *Alex* is replete with subjective *tableaux* ("Hooray For Hollywood" versus the Revolution; black nudes gambolling on the beach); Mazursky is equally adept at evoking an objective authenticity. In *Next Stop, Greenwich Village,* for instance, he carefully reconstructs the streets with yellow and red cabs, old cars, old signs, period costumes and attitudes. Like Michael Ritchie, Mazursky offsets absurd behaviour patterns with a tenable backdrop. Thus, our attention is never deployed from the action (as it is with Brooks, Allen, De Palma) to question the autonomous fantasies of the camera itself. If we see fantasies, they are the character's fantasies (and more often than not, surprisingly lifelike).

Stylistically, Mazursky's films reflect the paradoxes that beset his characters: based on an existing reality, they are subsumed with the myths of the possible. The myth of *Bob and Carol* is the most convoluted of all, as it entails the paradox of the Esalen mystique, of radical life styles bought on Establishment expense accounts, which was itself a reality in California when Mazursky made the film. *Bob and Carol* is not, as many have claimed, a film about California as a suburb of Hollywood, but rather about Hollywood dangling its toes in California proper, which was then the gold mine of counter-culture mythology. Mazursky's subsequent films have also been shot through with literal (often literary) mythic references: Alex seen as Hamlet or Fellini; Blume as an ironic variation on James Joyce's Bloom; Harry as an Upper West Side Lear; Larry Lapinsky as Marlon Brando with the face of a Jewish tramp.

Mazursky's tributes to Hollywood or to European auteurs are more viably compared with those of Bogdanovich or Scorsese than Altman. The actor-miming guard in Altman's *The Long Goodbye,* for instance, is a scabrous comment on the atavism of a dead myth: a put-down of men looking for models in outdated codes. Mazursky's references to Godard, Doris Day, Jeanne Moreau, Marlon Brando, Judy Garland, etc., are upbeat, like J.R.'s western talk in Scorsese's *Who's That Knocking?* He's ironic, but never sinister. The critical decrying of Alex, for instance, arose from a misunderstanding of a very broad, but intelligent irony. *Alex in Wonderland* is not Mazursky pretending to Fellini, any more than *Blume* attempts to be

Paul Mazursky coaches Ellen Greene on the set of NEXT STOP, GREENWICH VILLAGE (photo: Adger Cowans)

Visconti: it is Mazursky yearning toward Fellini, laughing at himself, and continuing to yearn. His approach is triple-edged, where a director like Michael Ritchie, for instance, takes his ironies only so far as the second level. Even in *Smile,* Ritchie's best film, he stops with a view of small town California as nimble and constricted: Mazursky has never failed to take his uptight, pretentious *bourgeoisie* one step further. They *want* to be better (be that more open, more knowledgeable, more famous, more loved, more loving) than they are. The boomerang is forever landing right back in their laps — and they are forever thrusting it out again.

Of all the "new" directors, Mazursky alone is portraying the real dilemmas — political, sociological — of the present with success. Why? Comedy is part of the answer. In this respect, it is interesting to compare a film like the dated *Five Easy Pieces* with *Bob and Carol* and *Blume in Love.* Mazursky's perspective as comedian, quasi-tourist in the land of the swingers, lends his films a certain objectivity. Half-in, half-out, part of Mazursky is always the uprooted New Yorker as bemused spectator in a maybe charmed but certainly strange land. The *clichés* that Rafelson assumes — like commitment and cop-out and revelance and generation gap — are always a bit coy for the Mazursky sensibility. California itself, something of a myth to the world at large, provides a further distancing angle to these films. In speaking of *Bob and Carol* Mazursky has said, "What struck me then — and as a native New Yorker I feel qualified to say this — is that the Eastern heavyweights so to speak, didn't understand that what I was portraying was *real.*" This dichotomy was probably responsible in large measure for the film's success. "I think that if Solzhenitsyn moved to L.A. he'd be doing three *Kojaks,*" Mazursky continued. "He'd do a *Hawaii Five-O.* If Olivier actually settled down there, he'd do *Father Knows Best.* He'd do a series. It gets to you."

The paradox of a real culture that appears unreal to so many people is an interesting buffer between myth and reality. Unlike Cassavetes, whose tough realism divests its characters of every ounce of pretence and dignity, every suggestion of sustaining environment or cultural complicity; Mazursky has wound his personalities in a cultural womb that looks like the Emperor's New Clothes to the majority of filmgoers. Interestingly, when Mazursky comes back to New York with *Greenwich Village,* he is not dealing in the present, but sifting his own past experiences though the greatest myth-maker of all: time.

Mazursky's stylistic admixture of myth and reality is beautifully paralleled in his themes, which invariably deal with the struggle between impulse and intellect, will and desire, ambition and possibility. Mazursky himself preserves his equilibrium and his humour — even in such potentially bathetic films as *Harry and Tonto* — through a phenomenon Leonard Woolf best describes in *Beginning Again*. Woolf writes that "the man or woman who is by nature addicted to introspection gets into the habit, after the age of fifteen or sixteen of feeling himself, often intensely, as 'I' and yet at the same time of seeing himself out of the corner of his eye as a 'not I,' a stranger acting a part upon a stage . . . It has a curious psychological effect; it helps one, I think, to bear with some equanimity both the ills one has and the ills one knows not of. If you begin to regard yourself, you begin to find that what matters so violently to you subjectively hardly matters at all to the objective you."

In *Next Stop, Greenwich Village,* Larry says approximately the same thing to his girlfriend Sarah following Mrs. Lapinsky's catastrophic visit: "The crazy thing is while it's happening, I still see the humour." In a description of his earlier films Mazursky says, "These films were about people who didn't know whether to have an orgy or become grandparents." Cassavetes's characters are also troubled by a discrepancy between instinct and intellect, but while the Cassavetes character broods, Mazursky's experiment; while the pies hit Cassavetes's little men square in the face, Mazursky's duck.

The discrepancy between Cassavetes and Mazursky can best be demonstrated in a comparison between Harry and his daughter Shirley in *Harry and Tonto* and Mabel and Nick in *Woman Under the Influence.* Both love each other; neither are capable of living together. Cassavetes shows us a plebean tragedy — a *"huis clos"* from which neither party can escape. It is the subject of an entire movie. The sequence between Harry and the four-time divorced Shirley, on the other hand, takes up only minutes by the shore of Lake Michigan. They love each other; they even like each other; but it's immediately obvious that they will never be able to get along. She is a spunky, modern Cordelia, the one member of the family really capable of understanding Harry, but she would throw him out just as heartlessly as a Goneril or Reagan. But Harry doesn't give her the chance, and neither does Mazursky. She says, "Come on, kid; I'll buy you a drink," and in that minute we realise that they'll go on sublimating their pain and enjoying life as best they can. This detachment — their unspoken agreement to see life as a stage production they can always abandon — is their calling card to dignity, and it is one rarely possessed by the Cassavetes victim.

In the rites-of-passage *Greenwich Village* Mazursky takes his characters closer to the breaking point than in any of his earlier films. Anita actually commits suicide because she doesn't like life (on the other hand Bernstein, initially devastated, recovers sufficiently to take himself to Mexico). Larry loses the girl he loves. Shelley Winters's Mrs. Lapinsky comes very close to a raw *Faces*-like revelation. Before Larry leaves for Hollywood, he tells his mother offhandedly, "You're a funny lady." "My life has not been very funny," she replies precipitously, all bravura drained from her voice. At this point Cassavetes or Scorsese might have closed in on the sorrow that has eaten out this woman's life. Instead, Mazursky and Larry veer away, and Mrs. Lapinsky takes the hint. Minutes later she is telling Larry to inform Clark Gable that she's loved him all her life, and she's crossed the barrier back to the sublimation and humour which have made life palatable thus far. We sense the frustration that marriage to a stolid, unimaginative man and poverty must have brought this woman; but we also leave the theatre assured that she can carry her own burden and give life back some of its own hot air.

A similar dynamic is at work in *Alex,* where the serious young director quotes Hamlet's "To Be or Not To Be" — in the bathtub, and ponders whether to make a political film while he drives his kid to school singing, "Somewhere over the rainbow, I'll get high." *Bob and Carol* and *Blume* are equally preoccupied with this discrepancy between intellect and instinct and the absurdity of it all. Intellectually, Mazursky's characters agree, more or less, that sexual fidelity and taboos are outdated, unhip, constricting. Blume can enjoy sex with his secretary and still love his wife.

This is all very fine, says Mazursky, but emotions are ticklish vibrations. In this sense he is very close to the Truffaut of *Stolen Kisses, Bed and Board,* and *Day For Night.* Alice is never going to enjoy communal sex — much as her intellect may signal that it's O.K. Blume *knows* that there are millions of other women as desirable as his wife, but his heart protests obsessively that he'll never love anyone but Nina and will die if he can't get her back. Esalen feels good to the epidermis, but monogamy is also relaxing; and love may be irrational, but it's every bit as consuming as ambition.

Much of the humour in Mazursky arises as a conflict between *id* and *ego:* phenomena that directors like Hitchcock use as grist for suspense. In *Blume,* Mazursky's devices are anything but subtle. Blume, incapable of accepting the loss of his wife, resorts to listening in at her psychiatrist's key hole, hanging around her now lover (whom, Mazursky-style, he comes to like), even raping her when all else fails. In one of the funniest scenes in *Bob and Carol* Alice is burdened with a disinclination to make love and the conviction that her husband should not get up to take a walk under any

George Segal comes to visit his ex-wife, played by Susan Anspach, and finds Kris Kristofferson in residence (from BLUME IN LOVE)

circumstances. The vision of an uptight Alice confronted by a searing psychiatrist pinching his cheek is equally uproarious: particularly when Mazursky goes on to satirise psychiatry by having the analyst (played by his *own* shrink) push her out just as she begins to loosen up.

In *Greenwich Village,* Larry's mother coaxes Sarah to admit she's slept with Larry, reassuring her that she's an intelligent, balanced woman, inured to shock. When Sarah proceeds to confess in the spirit of things, "We've had sex," Mrs. Lapinsky goes wild. Like Blume, she is an exaggerated externalisation of a deep-rooted emotional ambivalence toward the "new morality."

None of Mazursky's scripts are strictly autobiographical, although *Alex* and *Greenwich Village* come pretty close; but they are all based on personal experiences or feelings. He wrote *Harry and Tonto* — the odyssey of a 72-year-old man, when he turned forty. Suddenly, he said, he could project to what it might feel like to be 70. Of *Blume,* Mazursky says, "It was based on real feelings and problems I'd had with my wife in Rome. We were unhappy, we were arguing a lot. I had strange feelings. Nothing in the movie ever took place, but I guess what I wanted to write was 'What if this woman that I love so much said, Get out!'"

Mazursky's themes are fairly congruent from *Bob and Carol* through *Harry and Tonto.* What feels good, *is* good, he seems to be

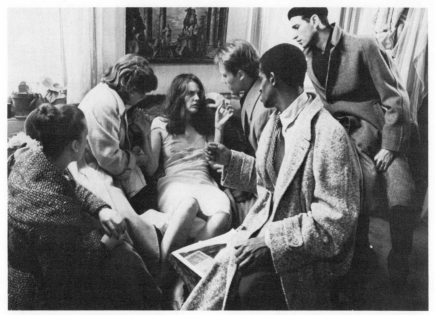

Larry (Lenny Baker) with his coterie of friends: Sarah (Ellen Greene), Connie (Dori Brenner), Robert (Christopher Walken), Bernstein (Antonio Fargas), and the suicidal Anita (Lois Smith)

saying; but here's the rub — what is it that feels best? The endings of *Alex, Blume,* and *Harry and Tonto* are rather like filmic Grecian urns, turning to art as reference book. *Alex* gives us *8½; Blume,* Venice and fertility; *Harry,* the ocean and youth. Truth is beauty and fantasy. In *Bob and Carol* there is a somewhat more ironic ending with "What the World Needs Now is Love, Sweet Love"; a pop, flower child variation on the general theme.

 Next Stop, Greenwich Village has taken Mazursky in a slightly different direction. A "coming of age" film, it seems to imply that experience and not aesthetic or natural beauty equals Truth. At the end, we watch Larry take out his apple strudel — his Jewish madeleine — and stay a moment to fix the image of his boyhood home in mind. And then he, the artist, walks out of this frame (which continues on without him for several seconds) and into the future. He is not a *voyeur* like the characters of *Bob and Carol* and *Blume.* He is very young, and experience is the mystery that will determine not only his perception, but the very course of his existence — whether or not he will be fulfilled.

 The sentiment in Mazursky's films arises primarily from their very serious attitude toward love: whether it's invested in a dead-serious Welfare working liberal like Blume's Nina or in Harry's first girlfriend, now living (with dignity, mind you) in a nursing home. Blume shows his love by raping Nina; Sarah won't tell Larry she loves him, but she'll get a diaphragm. All of Mazursky's characters are searchers: Alex and Larry, like Mazursky, are looking for success (quality as well as quantity) in Hollywood; but in their own ways Bob and Harry and Blume are also in search of tangible and intangible rewards — for fulfilment and acknowledgement.

Often his characters have difficulty in communicating. But while lust and ambition and awe of the impossible are present in almost all of Mazursky's works, it is always love — of a cat or a child or, usually, the romantic kind that is ultimately important; and in this respect Mazursky admits to being square, indeed. His films remind one of Browning's lovely poem about a rendezvous in an ancient city, "Love Among the Ruins," whose ending reads like the conclusion of a Mazursky film:

> "In one year they sent a million fighters forth, South and
> North,
> And they built their gods a brazen pillar high As the sky,
> Yet reserved a thousand chariots in full force — Gold, of course.
> Oh, heart! oh blood that freezes, blood that burns! Earth's
> returns
> For whole centuries of folly, noise and sin! Shut them in,
> With their triumphs and their glories and the rest! Love is best.

Chariots are conspicuously passed over, along with most conventional behaviour, in Mazursky's *oeuvre*. But it is in his exultation at all sorts of disorderly love and beauty that Mazursky brings a final ironic, romantic *hommage* to his idiosyncratic tales. He at times goes overboard, but rarely does he lose touch with innate compassion and intelligence.

BOB AND CAROL AND TED AND ALICE

Unlike many of the fledgling works I've discussed, *Bob and Carol and Ted and Alice* is a full-bodied film, introducing almost all of Mazursky's preoccupations and uproariouly successful on its own account. It is the good-natured story of two wealthy, successful couples, one a little "straighter" than the other, confronting the burgeoning of the Esalen culture in the California of the late Sixties. As is the case with most well-fed bodies and amply cloaked libidos, these couples deal with radical life styles and change through a nimbus of play. They don't consider peace marching with Berkeley students or sponsoring rehabilitation centers: it's the symptoms that fascinate them — the pot and (maybe) the sexual musical chairs. It all begins when couple one (Bob and Carol) return from a week-end of "heavy" group encounter, resolved to be more "open" with one another, to find uncharted means of expressing affection — like confiding in one's best friends that one's husband has had an affair. Wow, that's beautiful! Ted and Alice are at first hostile or inclined to take a somewhat irreverent attitude towards the ethos: Ted, for instance, demonstrates his idea of frankness by confessing that he *feels* Bob should pick up the tab for dinner. Cool, groovy.

Alice is so upset when she hears of Bob's one-night fling that she forswears sex with her husband and in due course ends up on the psychiatrist's couch, where she learns that she loves her son, but only likes Ted. Ted fantasises an affair, and then actually has one; Bob proves a bit less open-minded than he had presumed when he discovers his wife sleeping with the tennis pro. Both couples put their "openness" to the final test when they agree to switch partners and swing, but emerge Fellini style, arm-in-arm, to the pop tune "What The World Needs Now is Love, Sweet Love," suggesting that little has occurred in the way of erotica or final solutions, but that they're all reasonably content with their carnival of a life.

The tentative radical gestures of *Bob and Carol* all take place around swimming pools and in sprawling Beverly Hills abodes, where those with lots of time on their hands worry ponderously about where their heads are and ought to be. They smoke pot and consume large, expensive dinners. They wonder if they oughtn't approach the servants more intimately, and in doing so make them very nervous. Unlike the troubled *bourgeois* couple of Claude Chabrol's *Partie de Plaisir,* who similarly decide to swing, these Californians are well-cushioned against disaster by Victorian inhibitions. Mazursky said of California at that time: "It just so happens that in L.A. — maybe it's the weather — the things you wouldn't dream of doing in other places you start to take seriously . . . I mean, it's the only place in the world where serious people go to the houses of serious people who answer the door, 'Come in — Harri Krishna, Harri, Harri, Krishna — how are you? Oh, my wife? She'll be with you in about an hour. She's meditating in the other room.' It's the only place I've been where children of the middle class complain about their parents' being too far out."

Bob and Carol is the most expressly comic of Mazursky's films, and it is replete with hysterical sequences and one-liners. Dyan Cannon gives her finest performance as an uptight sex object, with a lip that tends to twitter and slump at the mere thought of infidelity. Disinclined to make love, she at one point tries the new openness on

A toast for BOB & CAROL & TED & ALICE

her frustrated husband. "Now you wouldn't want to do it just like
that, with no feeling on my part?" she parries. Yes, as a matter of
fact he would.

Part of *Bob and Carol*'s humour stems from a foiling of Bob and
Carol, who see themselves as serious searchers on the brink of
consciousness, with Ted and Alice, lagging a few crucial steps behind.
Part arises from the couples' shared disinclination to swing and the
ticklish nature of their queasy *bourgeois* stomachs, marvellously
epitomised by Ted, who orders a glass of water at a tacco stand. The
humanity of the film is insinuated through the director's complicity:
he sees them as the fools they are, but is right there sweating with
them. With the money accrued from the film, he went out and
bought a house with a swimming pool and began fretting about the
pros and cons of radical causes. Bob and Carol and Ted and Alice
have a bad case of unliberated emotions, and they're desperately
hoping that a joint or some anything-goes rhetoric will fill out their
lives.

"They were afraid," says Mazursky of his couples. "We're all afraid. We walk around in terror every day of our deepest feelings." While the characters, save Alice, are never developed much beyond caricature, it is this sublimated terror that renders them quite a bit more than buffoons. A crucial one step further and they might have been the victims of melodrama. Because they never take that step, we are free to enjoy Mazursky's smooth cinematography, his lush verdure and limpid images. The camera very subtly underscores the proximity of fantasy and reality by making the dream sequence of Ted's infidelity (imagined on a plane) stand for the actual infidelity that ensues. The only erotic scene — somewhat out of place here — is between Bob and Carol, whose love-making on a bathroom floor is shot in an exaggerated overhead. Mazursky also gives us one slow-take of Bob and Carol and Alice in the bedroom awaiting Ted for their orgy. Ted, on the other hand, is seen frantically administering mouth wash, deodorant — anything in order to delay this ultimate moment of Truth.

Bob and Carol works as an enjoyable, semi-loving spoof with few searing undertones. Of all the characters, Mazursky seems to identify most closely with Ted — played superbly by Elliott Gould, who has his toes in something to which he would prefer the rest of his body were not exposed. He is very happy not to be in the eye of this drama, but to let Bob and Carol and his increasingly neurotic wife assume centre stage.

ALEX IN WONDERLAND

Alex in Wonderland opens with little zooms in and out on Alex (Donald Sutherland), seated in the bathtub with his daughter, miming/parodying a cosmic dilemma he shares with Hamlet, "To be or not to be . . ." Alex approaches his own incongruities with a degree of comic appreciation, but not quite so much irony as Mazursky accords him. In this second film (also co-written with Tucker), Mazursky assumes centre stage, imbuing Alex with his own direct experiences as well as sympathies. Director of an extraordinarily successful first feature film (suspiciously like *Bob and Carol),* Alex finds himself plagued with limitless freedom of choice. Most of this very amusing film he spends boring his friends, family, and sometimes us with the ineluctable fate of the talented and the appreciated; although to give him credit, he does take time out for short trips, getting stoned, and house shopping.

As I described earlier, *Alex* has been criticised for trying to be *8½.* To my mind, it goes somewhat too far proving that it is *not*

Fellini. Mazursky says in his own defence: "I was trying to say that in Hollywood, in this coconut palm tree, lotus, dopey place, one could still want to be an artist. That doesn't mean one is an artist, but I was trying to say that a human being can have that dream, that passion, in that crazy place. Now, that is not necessarily the heaviest statement of all time, but it is a real comment." Essentially, I'll agree with Mazursky rather than with his tar-and-featherers. *Alex* was a victim of too high hopes (primarily commercial as far as M-G-M was concerned) set in motion by *Bob and Carol.* It is a dreamier, less accessible, though no more profound film than the first; and despite occasionally tedious references to old films and Europe as a better *milieu* for artists, Mazursky's sensibility is as buoyant as ever, his sympathies as compassionately ambivalent. *Alex* is also very amusing, particularly in the scenes where Alex converses with himself. Mazursky nicely reverses the cliche of the misunderstood artist by rendering Alex incapable of communicating or even *listening* to anything but his ever-ticking psyche. He is the perennial calculator of his own creative temperature.

Like *Bob and Carol, Alex* spoofs the characters that Mazursky knows best: the fortunate few burdened not with the world's problems, but with the problem of how best to approach these problems. Like the Truffaut character in *Day for Night, Alex* is plagued by his possibilities to do good: should he make a film about blacks, about pollution, about revolution? "Do a film about us," his kids, exasperated, advise him. "That's *8½*," he sighs. Simultaneously, and as though this were not enough, Alex is beset by the life style dilemma: to move or not to move into a magnificent new house (actually portrayed by his own house). These are more problems than a man of Alex's sensitive nature can handle. His is like the oft-quoted Cybill Shepherd complaint: "It's not easy being the prettiest girl in Memphis."

No authority figure is of any assistance to Alex. A producer (played by Mazursky himself) is dying for him to make none other than the film of his choice — money is no issue. The producer thrusts a Chagall painting in his direction, offers him a trip to Europe with no strings attached. By the way, he wonders if Alex would like to make a musical of *Huck Finn.*

As Mazursky evokes Alex, he is not much fun to live with at this time. The least suggestive comment or image can call to mind a movie possibility and unearth a Pandora's boxful of dreams. Alex sees both "Hooray for Hollywood" and the revolution taking over Hollywood Boulevard. Jeanne Moreau emerges to console him with her mystery and Fellini with his ineffable genius. Giraffes also approach him, and his wife looks good and ready to leave him.

As Mazursky has pointed out, *Alex* is not a particularly profound comment, but it is "relevant," to borrow a favourite criterion of the time. On the one hand, it is a documentary satire of days of wine and roses — few and far between, as Mazursky was soon to learn — experienced by a man who suddenly makes it big and has no idea how to handle it. Like Bill and Charlie in *California Split*, Alex is less delighted than worried about his next step. Alex is also a reflection of the campus unrest at the time: a film about a character dissatisfied with his good fortune and seriously in search of new gods and viable roots.

Alex is less accessible than Mazursky's other works because the personal chemistry is missing. Ellen Burstyn is fine as the wife, and the children and friends are all very tenable and refreshing, but they are dwarfed by the broodings of Alex's prodigious imagination. *Alex's* failure to become a great film is also a function of the ingenuousness that renders it so winsome. While he asserts scrupulous objectivity in the development of his character, Mazursky has little objectivity about the character's predicament *vis-à-vis* the rest of Hollywood. In this respect, it might have been more effective to show us Orson Welles than Fellini. Mazursky realises that Alex is living in a privileged state, but he gives us no idea of the alternatives or of the everyday routines of Hollywood proper — some of which will be nicely intimated in the later *Next Stop, Greenwich Village.*

There is a nice irony to the story of *Alex,* with a very Mazursky-like touch. Unable to handle the initial critical and box-office failure of the film, on top of M-G-M's all but non-existent publicity campaign, Mazursky and his wife left for Rome. While there, he received a call informing him that the New York Film Critics had voted him runner-up for Best Supporting Actor of the year for his three-minute role as the producer in *Alex.* The film had won no other accolades.

BLUME IN LOVE

Many consider *Blume in Love* Mazursky's best film. Having seen it just once, I feel better qualified to analyse than to judge *Blume,* Mazursky's first screenplay without Tucker and his most unabashedly romantic work. The story reads like an update of Leo McCarey's *The Awful Truth,* with Cary Grant and Irene Dunne supplanted by George Segal, a successful liberal divorce lawyer, and Susan Anspach as his sexy, humourless, bleeding heart Welfare worker of an ex-wife.

George Segal and Susan Anspach in BLUME IN LOVE

The film takes place in California, with a series of flashbacks and forward to Venice, scene of their honeymoon and symbol of romance and beauty. As Blume remembers it, everything was fine with a love affair that began at a fund-raising party for lettuce pickers and soon culminated in marriage: fine, that is, until the day his beautiful wife Nina caught a cold and came home early to discover Blume in bed with his secretary. Despite endless protests of monogamous love, if not lust, Nina kicks Blume out and, like Irene Dunne's equally inclement, wrong-done wife in the McCarey film, refuses so much as to listen to his entreaties.

At her welfare office Nina meets Elmo: an out-of-work musician, who soon moves in to share her life and render Blume's increasingly fervent contrition even less alluring. Thus, Blume is forced to resort to all kinds of ungainly stunts to get her attention and ferret out her innermost feelings: listening at the keyhole during her sessions with their shared psychiatrist, befriending Elmo, raping her. In the final scene, we see Nina, pregnant with Blume's child, walking toward her incredulous lover on the Piazza San Marco: fulfilling his fantasies, or a function of them — depending on one's interpretation. (Like the dream sequences in *Bob and Carol* and *Alex,* one may view this one either as prescient of reality or true to the spirit, if not the fact of the image. In other words, Blume *does* get her back.)

As in *Alex,* Mazursky turns to Europe to find roots for the yearning and confused souls of his over-analysed, under-reconciled California dreamers. Mazursky seems to empathise with the bungling, priapic, romantic Blume even more than with the technically more autobiographical Alex. The film is premised on Blume's conviction that he will never love another woman but Nina and will perish if he can't win her back. From here, Mazursky proceeds to spoof all the elements of courtship (or, in this case, re-courtship) without ever questioning the sacred nature of that love itself. "Love is blind" is nicely evoked by Nina, who, while certainly voluptuous and self-righteous, never seems worthy of a fraction of the idolatry Blume accords her. She is stoically humourless, intractable as far as her ex-husband is concerned, and as politically committed as a Daughter of the American Revolution — albeit to the opposite camp. Unlike the equally undeserving concert pianist/love object of Max Ophuls' *Letter from an Unknown Woman,* Nina is seen not through the blur of the lover's eyes, but in all her prosaic splendour. As such, she is a nice variation not only on the "love is blind" adage, but on the concept of the love object as "special" — her qualities appealing to a particular man and not being accessible to the masses.

Blume writes his own romantic conventions. For instance, he takes his secretary to bed in order to break the news that he has to fire her because he's taken her to bed. Rather than detesting Elmo, his hippie competition, Blume grows rather fond of him. When the venerable seduction routine fails to bear fruit, Blume is forced to improvise: he rapes Nina. A twist on the sex-softened female, Nina is just tough enough to deprive Blume of the satisfaction of seeing her move so much as a big toe in response.

Like *Bob and Carol, Blume* is concerned with the discrepancy between thoroughly modern life styles, primitive instincts, and Victorian emotions. Blume's *élan* is contemporary, and he performs all the modern rites: analysis, social consciousness, adultery; but like the Woody Allen character in *Love and Death,* he would act essentially the same if deported to Tolstoy's Russia.

There are several nice small bits in *Blume.* Shelley Winters, so excellent in the subsequent *Next Stop, Greenwich Village,* has a minor role as a Beverly Hills housewife who vacillates between rage and magnanimity in respect to a youth-oriented wolf of a middle-aged husband. Kris Kristofferson is also an attractive Elmo, although his part is the least convincing. With Elmo Mazursky has wisely created Nina's antithesis: a phlegmatic charmer to her uptight didactic. While their chemistry is amusing, Elmo as guitar-sporting hippie is too much the caricature. One senses that Elmo is to

Mazursky what Nina is to Blume: a personality he yearns toward (the calm artist, the unruffled "liver") and thereby finds difficult to view with objectivity.

The Venice ending of *Blume,* like the country ending of *The Awful Truth* — is at once lovely and satisfying. One sense that both parties — and Blume in particular — have suffered enough. Just as Cary Grant's eccentric charmer deserves a Swiss Cuckoo clock of an ending, so Blume's baroque passion merits a fertile, happy-ever-after by the quays of Venice.

Art Carney (left) proudly presents his cat in HARRY AND TONTO

HARRY AND TONTO

"I got the idea for *Harry and Tonto* when I was forty," Mazursky told me. "When I became forty, I began seriously to think about the fact that I would one day be seventy. When you're twenty, you'll never be seventy, but at forty, you're half-way there. What the movie was probably about was loneliness, and loneliness is the same at any age." The prospect of a lonely old man posing as Lear/Odysseus, crossing the country with cat in tow, did not thrill Warners, who had just produced *Blume;* and it is not difficult to understand their scepticism. Harry had built-in potential for unbearable pathos or sagacity, and could easily have been developed as

Art Carney in HARRY AND TONTO

modern Job or Isaiah. Instead, in the film eventually produced by Fox, Mazursky and old friend Josh Greenfeld (co-writer) turned him into a sympathetic, but believable grandfather/pioneer: a man as capable of venting his anger on a phone booth as of listening tirelessly to the problems and dreams of just about everybody in sight.

While Harry is credible in the emotional sense, he is by no means realistic. We don't listen to his aging bones creak and spend minimal time worrying about his health. Even his journey toward Death — the Unknown, is seen as a variation on youth's journey toward life — the Unknown. If Harry finds it easier to comprehend his grandson's interest in Zen than his daughter's disinclination to bear children, it is not just because of the proverbial bond of the very young and the very old, however. The subtle tragedy in this carefully up-beat, irreverent view of old age is the failure of humans of all ages to communicate with those they are closest to and whom they love best. Harry faces old age alone not just because of a tenaciously eager and independent spirit, but because he can't live with any of his children.

Harry and Tonto is surely the film in which Mazursky skids closest to sentimentality, and there are certain scenes — particularly with the fifteen-year-old girl — in which he crashes. Many of the episodes — such as Harry's encounter with an old Indian — are also as unlikely as Alex's fantasies; but they are all tenable on an emotional level.

Harry and Tonto begins as Harry, a seventy-two-year-old widower and ex-professor, is evicted from his Upper West Side apartment in New York City. Not that he takes this change of life with equanimity: the police are forced to carry the unwilling Harry out in a chair. Harry consoles himself and his cat Tonto with the thought that Lear too gave up his real estate, and moves with this speechless fool to live in the suburbs with son no. 1. His daughter-in-law greets his arrival as an occasion about as felicitous as Doomsday, and the feeling is more or less mutual. Despite a *rapport* with his grandson Norman, presently into a Zen diet and Zen silence, Harry feels it is time to leave and make the cross-country trip he never took in his youth. He sets off to visit his daughter, a four-time divorcee, in Chicago.

On the way, Harry encounters a fifteen-year-old hitch-hiker, whom he adopts, and visits an old girlfriend who once danced with Isadora Duncan. Norman soon joins them and spirits the young girl off to a commune, while Harry, finding his daughter little better on a permanent basis than son no. 1, heads on to California and son no. 2. Predictably, this second son turns out another failure, presently burying his pain in liquor, and after some fatherly advice and financial assistance, Harry once again opts for independence and the ancillary loneliness that, like capitalism, is the worst system except for all the rest. Tonto dies in the West, and in the final scene we see Harry alone, chasing a cat that resembles Tonto and coming upon

the ocean and a child building a sand castle. Despite the disappointment of all his children, children obviously still hold an allure for
Harry, a mystery and perhaps even a compensation for death.

Molly Haskell has said of *Harry:* "He [Mazursky] regards
families as he regards cities with the same quizzical ironic glance.
What the rest of us call hopeless, he loves, and he leads us to suspect
that perhaps the future is not in the institution itself but in the
expectations we bring to it . . ."[16] This clash between the rigid role
or institution (marriage, parent, professor, etc.) and the malleable
expectations of the humans who squeeze in, out, and around them is
best portrayed in *Harry*. Harry is not the mythic Lear, for instance:
his lack of property does not relegate him to subjugation in either
fact or feeling. He is no more the conventional father than Shirley is
the conventional woman; but neither are they revolutionaries.
Shirley has watched marriage fail at first-hand, but she has continued
to marry nonetheless. Harry saw what it was like living with his first
child, but he persisted in trying out life with all the others.

My favourite scene in *Harry* takes place in the old age home
where he waltzes with an old girlfriend who mistakes him for a
subsequent admirer. In this scene, beautifully portrayed by Art
Carney as Harry and Geraldine Fitzgerald as the lovely, dignified,
senile woman who once danced with Isadora Duncan, Mazursky
evokes the ineffability of memory without underestimating
inevitable decay. These two can never call back the past, but the
present need not efface it. As it turns out, this vignette was actually
based on real-life experience. Twenty-one years before *Harry,*
Mazursky went with his wife to visit her grandmother in a nursing
home in Pleasantville, New York. A beautiful woman, she was "senile
in the sense that her mind was clear one minute and blurred the next.
And she thought I was her husband who'd been dead for twenty-five
years."

There are, however, many lovely sequences in *Harry:* in one
Harry discusses his sex life with his old friend Jacob: in another he
irascibly insists that a Greyhound bus stop in order that Tonto may
pee. The scene between Shirley and Harry, discussed earlier,
encapsulates the reverse magnetism of two bright, independent
minds, while the breakdown scene of Harry's younger son beautifully
portrays the chasm that can exist between those of the same blood.

Like *Blume* and *Alex, Harry* moves disjointedly and unpredict-
ably from one episode to the next, eschewing the smooth narrative
techniques of *Bob and Carol* for a more life-like rhythm. The
characters, particularly Harry, creep up on us and render *Harry and
Tonto* Mazursky's most moving film to date.

Art Carney with Chief Dan George in HARRY AND TONTO

NEXT STOP, GREENWICH VILLAGE

Like *American Graffiti, Next Stop, Greenwich Village* is a rites of passage film, based on the "to go or not to go" dilemma – or in this case two such dilemmas. In the opening scene we watch Larry Lapinsky, nice Jewish boy from Brooklyn, assiduously coming to terms with his past and the necessity of leaving the nest to "find himself" in New York's Greenwich Village. In the final scene Mazursky presents us with a second parting – this time Larry leaving for Hollywood – and Larry recognising his failure to come to terms with the past: his hope being instead to grow with it. In between is the body of Mazursky's most comprehensive, most searing film thus far. Unlike George Lucas, he does not portray the past as innocence precipitately colliding with a watershed of Vietnam, Presidential assassination, etc. Rather, Mazursky sees the seed of the Sixties within the apparent ingenuousness of the previous decade. "It's the feeling that Salinger captured a long time before the media picked it up: the strange kind of confusion that I think led to the drug cult. It's the kind of self-pitying emotion that the lower middle class – the working community — doesn't have time for. It's a luxury — finding yourself — and their response to it is, 'So who cares? Get a job.' They're right in many ways."

Mazursky's first totally "New York" film, *Greenwich Village* is set in the early Fifties (1953) when cabs were yellow and red, rents were $25, abortions were illegal, and emotions were pretty much the way they are now. Would-be star Larry, graduated from Brooklyn College, takes leave of his hysterical mother and stolid, unimaginative father to find fame and adulthood in the nearby Village. Larry bluffs his way into a job squeezing vegetable juice at a counter and spends his free moments at acting lessons, with his beautiful Jewish girlfriend Sarah, discussing the Rosenbergs or Ezra Pound with a coterie of friends: Bernstein — a gay black with pretensions to aristocracy; Robert, a womanising poet; Connie — a grown-up Tomboy; Anita — a suicidal Village Holly-Go-Lightly. A series of small events re-shape many of Larry's attitudes. Sarah gets pregnant, but prefers abortion to marriage; Anita finally does kill herself; Larry's acting class decries his continual joking as an inability to get in touch with his feelings. Later Sarah sleeps with Robert and chooses a fleeting affair rather than a permanent relationship with

An impossible mating: Sarah, the liberated intellectual, will never come around to Larry's way of thinking

Larry takes leave of Brooklyn and his hysterical mother (Shelley Winters) in the opening scene of NEXT STOP, GREENWICH VILLAGE

Larry. The gang sets off for vacation in Mexico, while Larry leaves for a bit part in Hollywood.

As a skeletal plot, *Greenwich Village* sounds routine: it is Mazursky's flair for atmosphere and character that renders it exceptional. The stars, with the exception of Shelley Winters as Mrs. Lapinsky, are young, relatively unknown faces (Lois Smith who plays Anita, had already given a lovely performance as the sister in

Five Easy Pieces) who share the ambivalence of their more worldly counterparts in the earlier California films. In the opening scene, Larry (Lenny Baker), the embodiment of Great Expectations with a slide for a nose assures his tearful mother that she will not succeed in making him feel guilty. When he arrives on his deserted new block moments later, he announces to the city at large, "Oy, boy am I guilty!"

The sexual relationships are particularly well evoked in *Greenwich Village*. As Larry points out in a comic routine designed to cheer up Bernstein, "Sex is not funny; sex is serious." Bodily functions as a rule are funny, as Mazursky/Larry points out, but where is the man who treats impotence like constipation? This discrepancy has played a major role in the humour of all Mazursky's films. In *Bob and Carol* for instance, we laugh as Ted finds it not the least bit amusing that Alice is disinclined to make love. We laugh, not because he is peculiar, but because we would doubtless react in the same manner. In *Greenwich Village,* Larry probes Sarah for an analysis of his sexual prowess. "Fine," she says, without interest. Larry replies, only half-kiddingly, "Larry Lapinsky is either a sexual brute or a tender poet; Larry Lapinsky is *not* fine."

Ironically, it is in Mazursky's youth film that he portrays the intransigeance of life which has eluded his earlier, older heroes. Romantically, Blume and Nina, Bob and Carol, Alex and Betsy, are well-matched: they love each other and share variations on the same confused values. It never really enters our minds that Bill will fail to get Nina back, any more than we consider Cary Grant and Irene Dunne permanently split in *The Awful Truth.* Reunion is merely a matter of time and tribulations.

But *Greenwich Village* is full of impossible matings. Anita will never get on with life — she has to die. Robert is not just a pompous poet with a deep-down heart of gold. As Larry aptly observes: "I'll tell you something, Robert — underneath that pose, there's just more pose." Most important, Sarah will never come around to Larry's way of thinking. She is a "semitic beauty" as a friend observes, and a smart one, marvellously portrayed by Ellen Greene. Whether or not she ever really loves Larry is questionable. She will never say as much (instead, when he repeatedly asks, she holds up her diaphragm as proof of devotion), while she freely confesses her love for the shallow Robert.

She, unlike Blume or Bob or Ted or even Harry, is the liberated intellect; and as such her body is at one with her mind. It is the idea of freedom — naively epitomised in her mind by Mexico — that is incompatible with marriage or permanent relationships, and not the perennial sexual itches that crop up like common colds in the promiscuous bodies and monogamous minds of the earlier characters. Anality – or the discrepancy between mind and body – is not her problem: her spirit is in there with her body, and this is the revelation that seems to disturb Mazursky as much as it does Larry. In *Harry,* the father tells Shirley that he can't understand women who don't want children; Larry can't understand *people* who don't want monogamous love. For Larry, and for Mazursky, this is the most intractable and unpalatable fact of life yet encountered.

The other major dilemma in *Greenwich Village* [handled with equal deftness] is the more conventional tension between past and future. Like Harry, Larry is confronted with mortality. His parents – and particularly his soul-mate mother – are being taken away from him by a natural process. Not only will his mother die, but, much as they love each other, they could no more subsist under the same roof than Harry and Shirley. During the course of the film, Larry comes to accept her more fully on her own terms, as he comes to recognise himself without the umbilical chord. In a superb dream sequence, he acknowledges an innate jealousy of his mother as he imagines Mrs. Lapinsky performing in a hypothetical acting class, while he has been doing rather mediocre work in the class. Perhaps, he will never live up either to her potential or her expectations, now transferred to him.

Significantly, Larry's second parting is less abrasive than the first: he has less to prove. He can accept the apple strudel and the demand for phone calls without feeling his independence threatened. He does not need to divest himself of the past in order to embrace the future; and a glint in his eye as he looks back suggests that he, like Frédérick of *Les enfants de paradis* and, doubtless, Mazursky, will use his experiences in his art as well as his heart.

This factor is interesting in all Mazursky's works, and distinguishes him from almost all the other directors I've discussed. For Cassavetes, relationships are necessary evils, but they are generally unsatisfying. Scorsese, Coppola, and especially Altman, view relationships as diversion from ambition or business or the "right" course of action. Women as a rule are betrayers or predators. Love deters men from safety or success. (In rare instances like *Alice Doesn't Live Here Anymore* or *The Rain People,* it is women who are thus afflicted by relationships, although, significantly, their men look more appealing than the freedom these women *think* they're after.)

The inability to be happy both in love and in life is a theme happily absent from all Mazursky's films, and while he has never geared the main plot of a film toward the woman's viewpoint, neither has he shown woman as anything other than necessary. His characters don't yearn for greatness so much as they aspire to total fulfilment. One is tempted to look autobiographically toward the twenty-three years of Mazursky's own happy marriage when analysing his films through *Greenwich Village.* Sarah and Hollywood, for instance, are never regarded as mutually exclusive to Larry, any more than Nina and law were mutually exclusive to Blume. Indeed, it seems as though Blume will not be able to function in the world at *all* if he doesn't have Nina by his side. Like Curt of *American Graffiti,* Larry must leave the womb of family in order to develop an individuality; but the subtle difference between the two is that Larry could easily have brought his romantic interest along with him. We would never see a Mazursky hero gazing longingly back at an elusive blonde: if he loved her, he'd run (probably trip), and get her.

Sarah's rejection of Larry is the most pessimistic note in the Mazursky *oeuvre;* and yet we are encouraged to see it not as a termination of romance in favour of career, but rather as experience on the road to wisdom. "I'll always love you, Sarah," Larry says. "No, you won't," she retorts, and she's right. But one senses that he will always love someone and not just the star of his ambition. He will not, like Scorsese's Alice, see the necessity of chosing between love and career, and the difference is not exclusively one of sex. Scorsese is a hopeful pessimist; Mazursky a tempered optimist. Forever spoofing the anality and the contradictions of mind and body, instinct and intellect, yearning and inevitability, he is the new director most capable of envisioning a viable truce between both camps.

Bibliography

1. Adler, John. Interview with John Cassavetes in *Viva Magazine,* December 1974.

2. Agee, James. *Agee on Film,* Volume One (Grosset's Universal Library, New York, 1969).

3. Atlas, Jacoba; Guerin, Ann. "Robert Altman, Julie Christie and Warren Beatty Make the Western Real," in *Show,* August 1971.

4. Bazin, André. *What Is Cinema?* Volume II (University of California Press, Berkeley, Los Angeles/London, 1971).

5. De Beauvoir, Simone. *Force of Circumstance* (English translation: Andre Deutsch and Weidenfeld & Nicholson, London, 1965).

6. Blume, Mary. "Robert Altman's 'Pipedream'," in The International *Herald Tribune,,* January 8, 1972.

7. Corliss, Richard. "The Horace with the Heart of Gold," in *Film Comment,* March-April 1975, Volume II, number 2.

8. Cowie, Peter. "Francis Ford Coppola," in *International Film Guide, 1976,* (The Tantivy Press, London; A.S. Barnes & Co., South Brunswick and New York, 1975).

9. De Palma, Brian. "The Making of *The Conversation,"* in *Filmmakers Newsletter,* May 1974, Volume 7, number 7.

[10] Farber, Stephen. Interview with Francis Ford Coppola, in *Sight and Sound*, Autumn, 1972.

[11] Gardner, Paul. "'Graffiti' Reflects Its Director's Youth," in *The New York Times*, September 19, 1973.

[12] Gelmis, Joseph. *The Film Director as Superstar* (Doubleday & Company, New York, 1970).

[13] Gill, Brendan. Review of *A Child Is Waiting*, in *The New Yorker*, 1962.

[14] Greenspun, Roger. Review of *M*A*S*H*, in *The New York Times*, January 26, 1970.

[15] Haskell, Molly. *From Reverence to Rape* (Holt, Rinehart and Winston, New York, Chicago, San Francisco, 1973).

[16] ———. "The Extended Family, American Style," in *The Village Magazine*, March, 1976.

[17] Jacobs, Diane. "Martin Scorsese Doesn't Live Here Anymore," in *Viva Magazine*, March, 1976.

[18] Kerwin, Robert. Interview with Robert Altman, in *The Chicago Tribune*, October 13, 1974.

[19] Labarthe, André S. Interview with John Cassavetes, in *Cahiers du Cinéma*, October 1968, Volume 205.

[20] Martin, James. Interview with Robert Altman, in *Touch Magazine*, July, 1974.

[21] Rosen, Marjorie. Interview with Francis Ford Coppola, in *Film Comment*, July-August, 1974.

[22] Rosenbaum, Jonathan. "Improvisations and Interactions in Altmanville," in *Sight and Sound*, Spring 1975.

[23] Sarris, Andrew. "Films in Focus," in *The Village Voice*, January 24, 1974.

24 "Films in Focus," in *The Village Voice,* September 10, 1970.

25 "Films in Focus," in *The Village Voice,* December 10, 1970.

26 "Films in Focus," in *The Village Voice,* December 24, 1970.

27 "Films in Focus," in *The Village Voice,* March 15, 1973.

28 Scorsese, Martin. Conversation transcribed in *Dialog: The American Film Institute,* Beverly Hills, California, April, 1975, Volume 4, number 7.

29 Sterrit, David. Interview with John Cassavetes, in *The Christian Science Monitor,* March 25, 1975.

30 Toeplitz, Jerzy. *Hollywood and After* (Henry Regenery Company, Chicago, 1974).

31 Updike, John. *Rabbit Run* (Alfred A. Knopf, Inc., New York, 1960).

32 Warshow, Robert. *The Immediate Experience* (Atheneum, New York, 1970).

33 Waugh, John C. Interview with John Cassavetes, in *The Christian Science Monitor,* February 14, 1961.

34 Welles, Orson. "But Where Are We Going?," in *Look,* November 3, 1970.

Gena Rowlands in A WOMAN UNDER THE INFLUENCE

Filmographies

JOHN CASSAVETES FILMOGRAPHY

Cassavetes's acting appearances in films other than his own are as follows: *Taxi* (1953), *The Night Holds Terror* (1955), *Crime in the Streets* (1956), *Edge of the City/A Man Is Ten Feet Tall* (1957), *Affair in Havana* (1957), *Saddle the Wind* (1958), *Virgin Island* (1958), *The Webster Boy* (1962), *The Killers* (1964; made for TV), *The Devil's Angels* (1967), *The Dirty Dozen* (1967), *Rosemary's Baby* (1968), *Gli intoccabili/Machine Gun McCain* (1968) *Roma come Chicago/Bandits in Rome* (1968), *If It's Tuesday, This Must be Belgium* (1969), *Capone* (1975), *Two-Minute Warning* (1976).

1960

SHADOWS. Script and direction: JC. Photography (16mm): Erich Kollmar. Editing: Len Appelson, Maurice McEndree. Music: Charles Mingus (saxophone: Shafi Hadi). Players: Lelia Goldoni *(Lelia)*, Ben Carruthers *(Ben)*, Hugh Hurd *(Hugh)*, Anthony Ray *(Tony)*, Rupert Crosse *(Rupe)*, Tom Allen *(Tom)*, Dennis Sallas *(Dennis)*, David Pokitellow *(David)*. Produced by Maurice McEndree-Cassel. 81 mins.

1961

TOO LATE BLUES. Script: JC, Richard Carr. Direction: JC. Photography: Lionel Lindon. Editing: Frank Bracht. Music:

David Raksin. Art Direction: Tambi Larsen. Players: Bobby Darin *(John "Ghost" Wakefield)*, Stella Stevens *(Jess Polanski)*, Everett Chambers *(Benny Flowers)*, Nick Dennis *(Nick)*, Rupert Crosse *(Baby Jackson)*, Vince Edwards *(Tommy)*, Val Avery *(Frielobe)*, J. Allen Hopkins *(Skipper)*, James Joyce *(Reno, the Barman)*, Marilyn Clark *(Countess)*, Allyson Ames *(Billie Gray)*, June Wilkinson *(Girl at Bar)*, Cliff Carnell *(Charlie, the Saxophonist)*, Seymour Cassel *(Red, the Bassist)*, Dan Stafford *(Shelley, the Drummer)*, Richard Chambers *(Pete, the Trumpet-Player)*. Produced by JC for Paramount. 103 mins.

1962

A CHILD IS WAITING. Script: Abby Mann, from his own story. Direction: JC. Photography: Joseph LaShelle. Editing: Gene Fowler Jr. Music: Ernest Gold. Production Design: Rudolph Sternad. Players: Burt Lancaster *(Dr. Matthew Clark)*, Judy Garland *(Jean Hansen)*, Gena Rowlands *(Sophie Widdicombe)*, Steven Hill *(Ted Widdicombe)*, Bruce Ritchey *(Reuben Widdiacombe)*, Gloria McGehee *(Mattie)*, Paul Stewart *(Goodman)*, Lawrence Tierney *(Douglas Benham)*, Elizabeth Wilson *(Miss Fogarty)*, Barbara Pepper *(Miss Brown)*, John Marley *(Holland)*, June Walker *(Mrs. McDonald)*, Mario Gallo *(Dr. Lombardi)*, Frederick Draper *(Dr. Sack)*. Produced by Stanley Kramer *(Larcas Productions)* for United Artists. 104 mins.

1968

FACES. Script and direction: JC. Photography: Al Ruban. Editing: Al Ruban, Maurice

McEndree. Music: Jack Ackerman. Song: Charles Smalls ("Never Felt Like This Before"). Art Direction: Phedon Papamichael. Players: John Marley *(Richard Forst)*, Gena Rowlands *(Jeannie Rapp)*, Lynn Carlin *(Maria Forst)*, Fred Draper *(Freddie)*, Seymour Cassel *(Chet)*, Val Avery *(McCarthy)*, Dorothy Gulliver *(Florence)*, Joanne Moore Jordan *(Louise)*, Darlene Conley *(Billy Mae)*, Gene Darfler *(Jackson)*, Elizabeth Deering *(Stella)*, Dave Mazzie, Julie Gambol. Produced by Maurice McEndree. 130 mins.

1970

HUSBANDS. Script and direction: JC. Photography (DeLuxe Color): Victor Kemper. Sup. Editing: Peter Tanner. Art Direction: René D'Auriac. Players: Ben Gazzara *(Harry)*, Peter Falk *(Archie)*, JC *(Gus)*, Jenny Runacre *(Mary Tynan)*, Jenny Lee Wright *(Pearl Billingham)*, Noelle Kao *(Julie)*, Leola Harlow *(Leola)*, Meta Shaw *(Annie)*, John Kullers *(Red)*, Delores Delmar *(Countess)*, Peggy Lashbrook *(Diana Mallabee)*, Eleanor Zee *(Mrs. Hines)*, Claire Malis *(Stuart's Wife)*, Lorraine McMartin *(Annie's Mother)*, Edgar Franken *(Ed Weintraub)*, Sarah Felcher *(Sarah)*, Antoinette Kray *("Jesus Loves Me")*, Gwen Van Dam *("Jeannie")*, John Armstrong *("Happy Birthday")*, Eleanor Gould *("Normandy")*, Carinthia West *(Susanna)*, Rhonda Parker *(Margaret)*, Joseph Boley *(Minister)*, Judith Lowrey *(Stuart's Grandmother)*, Joseph Hardy *("Shaghai Lil")*, K. C. Townsend *(Barmaid)*, Anne O'Donnell *(Nurse)*, Gena Wheeler *(Nurse)*. David Rowlands *(Stuart Jackson)*. Produced by Al Ruban for Columbia. 154 mins. (G.B.: 142 mins).

1971

MINNIE AND MOSKOWITZ. Script and direction: JC. Photography (Technicolor): Arthur J. Ornitz, Alric Edens, Michael Margulies. Editing: Fred Knudtson. Music: Bob Harwood. Players: Gena Rowlands *(Minnie Moore)*, Seymour Cassel *(Seymour*

Moskowitz), Val Avery *(Zelmo Swift)*, Tim Carey *(Morgan Morgan)*, Katherine Cassavetes *(Sheba Moskowitz)*, Elizabeth Deering *(Girl)*, Elsie Ames *(Florence)*, Lady Rowlands *(Georgia Moore)*, Holly Near *(Irish)*, Judith Roberts *(Wife)*, JC *(Husband)*, Jack Danskin *(Dick Henderson)*, Eleanor Zee *(Mrs. Grass)*, Sean Joyce *(Ned)*, David Rowlands *(Minister)*. Produced by Al Ruban for Universal 115 mins.

1974

A WOMAN UNDER THE INFLUENCE. Script and direction: JC. Photography (M-G-M Color): Mitch Breit, Chris Taylor, Bo Taylor, Merv Dayan, Caleb Deschanel. Editing: Tom Cornwell, Elizabeth Bergeron, David Armstrong, Sheila Viseltear. Music: Bo Harwood. Art Direction: Phedon Papamichael. Players: Peter Falk *(Nick Longhetti)*, Gena Rowlands *(Mabel Longhetti)*, Matthew Cassel *(Tony Longhetti)*, Matthew Laborteaux *(Angelo Longhetti)*, Christina Grisanti *(Maria Longhetti)*, Katherine Cassavetes *(Mama Longhetti)*, Lady Rowlands *(Martha Mortensen)*, Fred Draper *(George Mortensen)*, O. G. Dunn *(Garson Cross)*, Mario Gallo *(Harold Jensen)*, Eddie Shaw *(Doctor Zepp)*, Angelo Grisanti *(Vito Grimaldi)*, James Joyce *(Bowman)*, John Finnegan *(Clancy)*, Hugh Hurd *(Willie Johnson)*, Leon Wagner *(Billy Tidrow)*, John Hawker *(Joseph Morton)*, Sil Words *(James Turner)*, Elizabeth Deering *(Angela)*, Jacki Peters *(Tina)*, Elsie Ames *(Principle)*. Produced by Faces International Films (Sam Shaw). 155 mins.

1976

THE KILLING OF A CHINESE BOOKIE. Script and direction: JC. Photography (colour): Fred Elmes and Mike Ferris. Editing: Tom Cornwell. Music: Bo Harwood. Production Design: Sam Shaw. Players: Ben Gazzara *(Cosmo Vitelli)*, Timothy Agoglia Carey *(Flo)*, Azizi Johari *(Rachel)*, Meade Roberts *(Mr. Sophistication)*, Seymour Cassel *(Mort*

Weil), Alice Friedland *(Sherry)*, Donna Gordon *(Margo)*, Robert Phillips *(Phil)*, Morgan Woodward *(John the Boss)*, Virginia Carrington *(Betty)*, John Red Kullers *(Eddie–Red)*, Al Ruban *(Marty Reitz)*, Soto Joe Hugh *(Chinese Bookie)*, Haji *(Haji)*, Carol Warren *(Carol)*, Derna Wong Davis *(Derna)*, Kathalina Veniero *(Annie)*, Yvette Morris *(Yvette)*, Jack Ackerman *(Musical director)*. Produced by Al Ruban for Faces Distribution Corp. 135 mins.

ROBERT ALTMAN FILMOGRAPHY

With George W. George, Altman apparently wrote part of the story for *Christmas Eve* (1947) (uncredited) as well as the story of *Bodyguard* (1948). Altman's work for American TV includes *The Young One* and *Together* (both 1961 for "Alfred Hitchcock Presents"); *County General, The Covering Darkness, The Door Without a Key, Summer Lightning,* and *The Pursuit of Evil* (all 1961 for "Bus Stop"); *The Long Lost Life of Edward Smalley* (for "Kraft Suspense Theatre," 12 December 1963); and *Once Upon a Savage Night* (detailed below in feature version, *Nightmare in Chicago).* Altman produced Alan Rudolph's *Welcome to L.A.* (1976).

1957

THE DELINQUENTS. Script and direction: RA. Photography: Charles Paddock (or Harry Birch). Editing: Helene Turner. Music: Bill Nolan Quintet Minus Two. Song: Bill Nolan, Ronnie Norman ("The Dirty Rock Boogie"), sung by Julia Lee. Art direction: Chet Allen. Players: Tom Laughlin *(Scotty)*, Peter Miller *(Cholly)*, Richard Bakalyn *(Eddy)*, Rosemary Howard *(Janice)*, Helene Hawley *(Mrs. White)*, Leonard Belove *(Mr. White)*, Lotus Corelli *(Mrs. Wilson)*, James Lantz *(Mr. Wilson)*, Christine Altman *(Sissy)*, George Kuhn *(Jay)*, Pat Stedman *(Meg)*, Norman Zands *(Chizzy)*, James Leria *(Steve)*, Jet Pinkston *(Molly)*, Kermit Echols *(Barman)*, Joe Adleman *(Station Attendant).*

Produced by RA (Imperial Productions) for United Artists. 72 mins.

THE JAMES DEAN STORY. Script: Stewart Stern. Direction: RA and George W. George. Photography: twenty-nine various cameramen (still ph.: Camera Eye Pictures). Music: Leith Stevens. Song: Jay Livingston, Ray Evans. Production design: Louis Clyde Stoumen. Narrator: Martin Gabel. Players: Marcus, Ortense and Markie Winslow *(Dean's Aunt, Uncle and Cousin)*, Mr. and Mrs. Dean *(His Grandparents)*, Adeline Hall *(His Drama Teacher)*, Bing Traster, Mr. Carter, Jerry Luce, Louis de Liso, Arnie Langer, Arline Sax, Chris White, George Ross, Robert Jewett, John Kalin, Lew Bracker, Glenn Kramer, Patsy d'Amore, Billy Karen, Lille Kardell *(His Friends)*, Officer Nelson *(Highway Patrolman).* Produced by RA and George W. George for Warner Bros. 83 mins.

1968

COUNTDOWN. Script: Loring Mandel, from the novel by Hank Searls. Direction: RA. Photography (Technicolor, Panavision): William W. Spencer. Editing: Gene Milford. Music: Leonard Rosenman. Art direction: Jack Poplin. Set decoration: Ralph S. Hurst. Players: James Caan *(Lee)*, Robert Duvall *(Chiz)*, Joanna Moore *(Mickey)*, Barbara Baxley *(Jean)*, Charles Aidman *(Gus)*, Steve Ihnat *(Ross)*, Michael Murphy *(Rick)*, Ted Knight *(Larson)*, Stephen Coit *(Ehrman)*, John Rayner *(Dunc)*, Charles Irving *(Seidel)*, Bobby Riha Jr. *(Stevie).* Produced by William Conrad (Productions) for Warner Bros. 101 mins. (G.B.: 73 mins.).

1969

NIGHTMARE IN CHICAGO. Script: Donald Moessinger, from the novel "Killer on the Turnpike" by William P. McGivern. Direction: RA. Photography (colour): Bud Thackery. Music: Johnny Williams. Players: Charles McGraw, Robert Ridgely, Ted Knight, Philip Abbott, Barbara Turner, Charlene Lee, Arlene Kieta. Produced by RA for Roncom/Universal. 81 mins. This was a version for release to American cinemas of the TV movie, *Once Upon a Savage Night*, expanded with out-takes from an original 54 mins. to 81 mins. The shorter version was first televised on April 2, 1964.

THAT COLD DAY IN THE PARK. Script: Gillian Freeman, from the novel by Richard Miles. Direction: RA. Photography (Eastmancolor): László Kovács. Editing: Danford Greene. Music: Johnny Mandel. Art direction: Leon Erickson. Players: Sandy Dennis *(Frances Austen)*, Michael Burns *(The Boy)*. Susanne Benton *(Nina)*, Luana Anders *(Sylvie)*, John Garfield Jr. *(Nick)*. Produced by Donald Factor and Leon Mirell for (Factor—Altman—Mirell Films). 115 mins. (G.B.: 105 mins.). 1970

1970

M*A*S*H. Script: Ring Lardner Jr., from the novel by Richard Hooker. Direction: RA. Photography (DeLuxe Color, Panavision): Harold E. Stine. Editing: Danford B. Greene. Music: Johnny Mandel. Song: Johnny Mandel and Mike Altman ("Suicide Is Painless"). Art direction: Jack Martin Smith, Arthur Lonergan. Set decoration: Walter M. Scott, Stuart A. Reiss. Players: Donald Sutherland *(Hawkeye Pierce)*, Elliott Gould *(Trapper John McIntyre)*, Tom Skerritt *(Duke Forrest)*, Sally Kellerman *(Major Hot Lips)*, Robert Duvall *(Major Frank Burns)*, Jo Ann Pflug *(Lt. Dish)*, Rene Auberjonois *(Dago Red)*, Roger Bowen *(Col. Henry Blake)*, Gary Burghoff *(Radar O'Reilly)*, David Arkin *(Sgt. Major Vollmer)*, Fred Williamson *(Spearchucker)*, Michael Murphy *(Me Lay)*, Kim Atwood *(Ho-Jon)*, Tim Brown *(Corporal Judson)*, Indus Arthur *(Lt. Leslie)*, John Schuck *(Painless Pole)*, Ken Prymus *(Pfc. Seidman)*, Dawne Damon *(Capt. Scorch)*, Carl Gottlieb *(Ugly John)*, Tamara Horrocks *(Capt. Knocko)*, G. Wood *(General Hammond)*, Bobby Troup *(Sgt. Gorman)*, Bud Cort *(Private Boone)*, Danny Goldman. *(Capt. Murrhardt)*, Corey Fischer

(Capt. Bandini), J. B. Douglas, Yoko Young. Produced by Ingo Preminger for Aspen/20th Century-Fox. 116 mins.

BREWSTER McCLOUD. Script: Brian McKay (uncredited), Doran William Cannon. Direction: RA. Photography (Metrocolor, Panavision): Lamar Boren, Jordan Cronenweth. Editing: Lou Lombardo. Music: Gene Page. Songs: Francis Scott Key, Rosamund Johnson and James Weldon Johnson, John Phillips, sung by Merry Clayton, John Phillips. Art direction: Preston Ames, George W. Davis. Players: Bud Cort *(Brewster McCloud)*, Sally Kellerman *(Louise)*, Michael Murphy *(Frank Shaft)*, William Windom *(Haskel Weeks)*, Shelley Duvall *(Suzanne Davis)*, Rene Auberjonois *(Lecturer)*, Stacy Keach *(Abraham Wright)*, John Schuck *(Lt. Alvin Johnson)*, Margaret Hamilton *(Daphne Heap)*, Jennifer Salt *(Hope)*, Corey Fischer *(Lt. Hines)*, G. Wood *(Capt. Crandall)*, Bert Remsen *(Douglas Breen)*, Angelin Johnson *(Mrs. Breen)*, William Baldwin *(Bernard)*, William Henry Bennet *(Band Conductor)*, Gary Wayne Chason *(Camera Shop Clerk)*, Ellis Gilbert *(Butler)*, Verdie Henshaw *(Feathered Nest Sanatorium Manager)*, Robert Warner *(Camera Shop Assistant Manager)*, Dean Goss *(Eugene Ledbetter)*, Keith V. Erickson *(Prof. Aggnout)*, Thomas Danko *(Colour Lab Man)*, W. E. Terry Jnr. *(Police Chaplain)*, Ronnie Cammack *(Wendell)*, Dixie M. Taylor *(Nursing Home Manager)*, Pearl Coffey Chason *(Nursing Home Attendant)*, Amelia Parker *(Nursing Home Manageress)*, David Welch *(Breen's Son)*. Produced by Lou Adler (Adler—Phillips/Lion's Gate) for M-G-M. 105 mins.

1971

McCABE AND MRS. MILLER. Script: RA and Brian McKay, from the novel "McCabe" by Edmund Naughton. Direction: R.A. Photography (Technicolor, Panavision): Vilmos Zsigmond. Editing: Lou Lombardo. Music: songs by Leonard Cohen. Production design: Leon Ericksen. Art direction: Phillip

Elliott Gould and Nina van Pallandt in THE LONG GOODBYE

Thomas. Players: Warren Beatty *(John McCabe)*, Julie Christie *(Constance Miller)*, Rene Auberjonois *(Sheehan)*, Hugh Millais *(Dog Butler)*, Shelley Duvall *(Ida Coyle)*, Michael Murphy *(Sears)*, John Schuck *(Smalley)*, Corey Fischer *(Mr. Elliott)*. Produced by David Foster, Mitchell Brower for Warner Bros. 121 mins. On 16mm: Warner (U.S.).

1972

IMAGES. Script and direction: RA (with passages from "In Search of Unicorns" by Susannah York). Photography (Technicolor, Panavision): Vilmos Zsigmond. Editing: Graeme Clifford. Music: John Williams (with sounds by Stomu Yamash'ta). Art direction: Leon Ericksen. Players: Susannah York *(Cathryn)*, Rene Auberjonois *(Hugh)*, Marcel Bozzuffi *(René)*, Hugh Millais *(Marcel)*, Cathryn Harrison *(Susannah)*, John Morley *(Old Man)*. Produced by Tommy Thompson for Lion's Gate Film/The Hemdale Group. 101 mins.

1973

THE LONG GOODBYE. Script. Leigh Brackett, from the novel by Raymond Chandler. Direction: RA. Photography (Technicolor, Panavision): Vilmos Zsigmond. Editing: Lou Lombardo. Music: John Williams. Art Direction: none. Players: Elliott Gould *(Philip Marlowe)*, Nina van Pallandt *(Eileen Wade)*, Sterling Hayden *(Roger Wade)*, Mark Rydell *(Marty Augustine)*, Henry Gibson *(Dr. Verringer)*, David Arkin *(Harry)*, Jim Bouton *(Terry Lennox)*, Warren Berlinger *(Morgan)*, Jo Ann Brody *(Jo Ann Eggenweiler)*, Steve Coit *(Detective Farmer)*, Jack Knight *(Mabel)*, Pepe Callahan *(Pepe)*, Vince Palmieri *(Vince)*, Pancho Cordoba *(Doctor)*, Enrique Lucero *(Jefe)*, Rutanya Alda *(Rutanya Sweet)*, Tammy Shaw *(Dancer)*, Jack Riley *(Piano Player)*, Ken Sansom *(Colony Guard)*, Jerry Jones *(Detective Green)*, John Davies *(Detective Dayton)*, Rodney Moss *(Supermarket Clerk)*, Sybil Scotford *(Real Estate Lady)*, Herb Kerns *(Herbie)*. Produced by Jerry Bick (Lion's Gate Films) for United Artists. 111 mins.

1974

THIEVES LIKE US. Script: Calder Willingham, Joan Tewkesbury and RA, from the novel by Edward Anderson. Direction: RA. Photography (colour): Jean Boffety. Editing: Lou Lombardo. Visual consultant: Jack DeGovia. Radio research: John Dunning. Players: Keith Carradine *(Bowie)*, Shelley Duvall *(Keechie)*, John Schuck *(Chicamaw)*, Bert Remsen *(T-Dub)*, Louise Fletcher *(Mattie)*, Ann Latham *(Lula)*, Tom Skerritt *(Doc Mobley)*, Al Scott *(Capt. Stammers)*, John Roper *(Jasbo)*, Mary Waits *(Noel)*, Rodney Lee Jr. *(James Mattingly)*, William Watters *(Alvin)*, Joan Tewkesbury *(Lady in Train Station)*, Eleanor Matthews *(Mrs. Stammers)*, Pam Warner *(Woman in Accident)*, Suzanne Majure *(Coca-Cola Girl)*, Walter Cooper and Lloyd Jones *(Sheriffs)*. Produced by Jerry Bick and George Litto for United Artists. 123 mins.

CALIFORNIA SPLIT. Script: Joseph Walsh. Direction: RA. Photography (Metrocolor, Panavision): Paul Lohmann. Editing: Lou Lombardo. Production Design: Leon Ericksen. Players: Elliott Gould *(Charlie Waters)*, George Segal *(Bill Denny)*, Ann Prentiss *(Barbara Miller)*, Gwen Welles *(Susan Peters)*, Edward Walsh *(Lew)*, Joseph Walsh *(Sparkie)*, Bert Remsen *("Helen Brown")*, Barbara London *(Lady on the bus)*, Barbara Ruick *(Reno barmaid)*, Jay Fletcher *(Robber)*, Jeff Goldblum *(Lloyd Harris)*, Barbara Colby *(Receptionist)*, Vince Palmieri *(First bartender)*, Alyce Passman *(Go-go girl)*, Joanne Strauss *(Mother)*, Jack Riley *(Second bartender)*, Sierra Bandit *(Woman at bar)*, John Considine *(Man at bar)*, Eugene Troobnick *(Harvey)*, Richard Kennedy *(Used car salesman)*, John Winston *(Tenor)*, Bill Duffy *(Kenny)*, Mike Greene *(Reno dealer)*, Tom Signorelli *(Nugie)*, Sharon Compton *(Nugie's wife)*, Arnold Herzstein, Marc Cavell, Alvin Weissman, Mickey Fox and Carolyn Lohmann *(California Club poker players)*, "Amarillo Slim" Preston, Winston Lee, Harry Drackett, Thomas Hal Phillips, Ted Say, A. J. Hood *(Reno poker players)*. Produced by RA and

Joseph Walsh (Won World/Persky Bright/ Reno - executive producers: Aaron Spelling, Leonard Goldberg) for Columbia. 109 mins.

1975

NASHVILLE. Script: Joan Tewkesbury. Direction: RA. Photography (Colour, Panavision): Paul Lohmann. Editing: Sidney Levin, Dennis Hill. Political Campaign: Thomas Hal Phillips. Songs: "200 Years" (lyrics by Henry Gibson, music by Richard Baskin), "Yes, I Do" (lyrics and music by Richard Baskin and Lily Tomlin), "Down to the River" (lyrics and music by Ronee Blakley), "Let Me Be the One" (lyrics and music by Richard Baskin), "Sing a Song" (lyrics and music by Joe Raposo), "The Heart of a Gentle Woman" (lyrics and music by Dave Peel), "Bluebird" (lyrics and music by Ronee Blakley), "The Day I Looked Jesus in the Eye" (lyrics and music by Richard Baskin and Robert Altman), "Memphis" (lyrics and music by Daren Black), "I Don't Know If I Found It in You" (lyrics and music by Karen Black), "For the Sake of the Children" (lyrics and music by Richard Baskin and Richard Reicheg), "Keep a Goin' " (lyrics by Henry Gibson, music by Richard Baskin and Henry Gibson), "Swing Low Sweet Chariot" (arrangements by Millie Clements), "Rolling Stone" (lyrics and music by Karen Black), "Honey" (lyrics and music by Keith Carradine), "Tapedeck in his Tractor (The Cowboy Song)" (lyrics and music by Ronee Blakley), "Dues" (lyrics and music by Ronne Blakley), "I Never Get Enough" (lyrics and music by Richard Baskin and Ben Raleigh), "Rose's Cafe" (lyrics and music by Allan Nicholls), "Old Man Mississippi" (lyrics and music by Juan Grizzle), "Mr Baby's Cookin' in Another Man's Pan" (lyrics and music by Jonnie Barnett), "One, I Love You" (lyrics and music by Richard Baskin), "I'm Easy" (lyrics and music by Keith Carradine), "It Don't Worry Me" (lyrics and music by Keith Carradine), "Since You've Gone" (lyrics and music by Gary Busey), "Trouble in the U.S.A." (lyrics and music by Arlene Barnett), "My Idaho Home" (lyrics and music by Ronee Blakley).

Players: David Arkin *(Norman)*, Barbara Baxley *(Lady Pearl)*, Ned Beatty *(Delbert Reese)*, Karen Black *(Connie White)*, Ronee Blakley *(Barbara Jean)*, Timothy Brown *(Tommy Brown)*, Keith Carradine *(Tom Frank)*, Geraldine Chaplin *(Opal)*, Robert Doqui *(Wade)*, Shelley Duvall *(L. A. Joan)*, Allen Garfield *(Barnett)*, Henry Gibson *(Haven Hamilton)*, Scott Glenn *(Pfc. Glenn Kelly)*, Jeff Goldblum *(Tricycle Man)*, Barbara Harris *(Albuquerque)*, David Hayward *(Kenny Fraiser)*, Michael Murphy *(John Triplette)*, Allan Nicholls *(Bill)*, Dave Peel *(Bud Hamilton)*, Cristina Raines *(Mary)*, Bert Remsen *(Star)*, Lily Tomlin *(Linnea Reese)*, Gwen Welles *(Sueleen Gay)*, Keenan Wynn *(Mr. Green)*, James Dan Calvert *(Jimmy Reese)*, Donna Denton *(Donna Reese)*, Merle Kilgore *(Trout)*, Carol McGinnis *(Jewel)*, Sheila Bailey and Patti Bryant *(Smokey Mountain Laurel)*, Richard Baskin *(Frog)*, Jonnie Barnett, Vassar Clements, Misty Mountain Boys, Sue Barton, Elliott Gould and Julie Christie *(Themselves)*. Produced by RA (associate producers: Robert Eggenweiler, Scott Bushnell) (executive producers: Martin Starger, Jerry Weintraub) (ABC Entertainment) for Paramount. 161 mins.

FRANCIS FORD COPPOLA FILMOGRAPHY

Coppola is reported to have directed three "nudie pix" in the late Fifties (titles unknown). In 1961, he wrote and directed *Come On Out*, a compilation of three unidentified films. He wrote a screenplay — *Pilma, Pilma* — which won a Samuel Goldwyn award in 1962 but was never filmed. While working for Roger Corman in sundry capacities, he apparently wrote the English dubbed version of the Russian *Nebo Zowet* (1959), released in 1963 as *Battle Beyond the Sun* but was not credited (or only under a pseudonym). He similarly wrote the English version of the Russian *Sadko* (1953), released in 1963 as *The Magic Voyage of Sinbad.* For Corman he also

Marlon Brando and Al Pacino in THE GODFATHER

worked as assistant director on *The Premature Burial* (1962), dialogue director on *The Tower of London* (1962), was in charge of sound and second unit director for *The Young Racers* (1963), associate producer and uncredited second unit director on *The Terror* (1963). Coppola also wrote unfilmed scripts, *The Disenchanted* and *The Fifth Coin*, worked on *My Last Duchess* (filmed as *Drop Dead, Darling*, but apparently discarding all his work), and collaborated on *Reflections in a Golden Eye* (1967) during the early stages. He is credited for his work on the filmed screenplays of *This Property Is Condemned* (1966), *Paris brûle−t−il?/Is Paris Burning?* (1966), *Patton: Salute to a Rebel/Patton:Lust for Glory* (1970) and *The Great Gatsby* (1974). He set up his own studios, American Zoetrope, in San Francisco and arranged production there of George Lucas's *THX 1138* (1971), on which he was billed as executive producer. He was also involved in the production of Lucas's second film, *American Graffiti* (1973).

1963

DEMENTIA 13/THE HAUNTED AND THE HUNTED. Script and direction: FFC. Photography: Charles Hannawalt. Editing: Stewart O'Brien. Music: Ronald Stein. Art Direction: Albert Locatelli. Players: William Campbell *(Richard Haloran)*, Luana Anders *(Louise Harloran)*, Bart Patton *(Billy Haloran)*, Mary Mitchell *(Kane)*, Patrick Magee *(Justin Caleb)*, Eithne Dunn *(Lady Haloran)*, Peter Reed *(John Haloran)*, Karl Schanzer *(Simon)*, Ron Perry *(Arthur)*, Derry O'Donovan *(Lillian)*, Barbara Dowling *(Kathleen)*. Produced by Roger Corman for Filmgroup/AIP. 81 mins. (G.B: 73 mins.).

1967

YOU'RE A BIG BOY NOW. Script: FFC, from the novel by David Benedictus. Direction: FFC. Photography (Eastmancolor): Andy Laszlo. Editing: Aram Avakian. Music: Bob Prince. Songs: John Sebastian (sung by The Lovin' Spoonful). Art Direction:

Vassele Fotopoulos. Choreography: Robert Tucker. Players: Peter Kastner *(Bernard Chanticleer)*, Elizabeth Hartman *(Barbara Darling)*, Geraldine Page *(Margery Chanticleer)*, Julie Harris *(Miss Thing)*, Rip Torn *(I.H. Chanticleer)*, Tony Bill *(Raef)*, Karen Black *(Amy)*, Michael Dunn *(Richard Mudd)*, Dolph Sweet *(Policeman Francis Graf)*, Michael O'Sullivan *(Kurt Doughty)*. Produced by Phil Feldman (Seven Arts) for Warner-Pathé. 97 mins.

1968

FINIAN'S RAINBOW. Script: E. Y. Harburg, Fred Saidy, based on their musical play (music: Burton Lane; lyrics: E. Y. Harburg). Direction: FFC. Photography (Technicolor, Panavision, presented in 70 mm): Philip Lathrop. Editing: Melvin Shapiro. Music Direction: Ray Heindorf. Production Design: Hilyard M. Brown. Choreography: Hermes Pan. Players: Fred Astaire *(Finian McLonergan)*, Petula Clark *(Sharon McLonergan)*, Tommy Steele *(Og)*, Don Francks *(Woody)*, Barbara Hancock *(Susan the Silent)*, Keenan Wynn *(Judge Billboard Rawkins)*, Al Freeman Jr. *(Howard)*, Brenda Arnau *(Sharecropper)*, Avon Long, Roy Glenn, Jerster Hairston *(Passion Pilgrim Gospellers)*, Louis Silas *(Henry)*, Dolph Sweet *(Sheriff)*, Wright King *(District Attorney)*. Produced by Joseph Landon (Warner Bros./Seven Arts) for Warner-Pathé. 144 mins.

1969

THE RAIN PEOPLE. Script and direction. FFC. Photography (Technicolor): Wilmer Butler. Editing: Blackie Malkin. Music: Ronald Stein. Art Direction: Leon Ericksen. Players: James Caan *(Kilgannon)*, Shirley Knight *(Natalie)*, Robert Duvall *(Gordon)*, Marya Zimmet *(Rosalie)*, Tom Aldredge *(Mr. Alfred)*, Laurie Crews *(Ellen)*, Andrew Duncan *(Artie)*, Margaret Fairchild *(Marion)*, Sally Gracie *(Beth)*, Alan Manson *(Lou)*, Robert Modica *(Vinny)*, Produced by Bart

Patton and Ronald Colby (Coppola Company Presentation) for Warner Bros./Seven Arts. 101 mins.

1972

THE GODFATHER. Script: Mario Puzo, FFC, based on the novel by Puzo. Direction: FFC. Photography (Technicolor): Gordon Willis. Editing: William Reynolds, Peter Zinner, Marc Laub, Murray Solomon. Music: Nino Rota (conducted by Carlo Savina). Production Design: Dean Tavoularis. Art Direction: Warren Clymer. Players: Marlon Brando *(Don Vito Corleone)*, Al Pacino *(Michael Corleone)*, James Caan *(Sonny Corleone)*, Richard Castellano *(Clemenza)*, Robert Duvall *(Tom Hagan)*, Sterling Hayden *(McClusky)*, John Marley *(Jack Woltz)*, Richard Conte *(Barzini)*, Diane Keaton *(Kay Adams)*, Al Lettieri *(Sollozzo)*, Abe Vigoda *(Tessio)*, Talia Shire *(Connie Rizzi)*, Gianni Russo *(Carlo Rizzi)*, John Cazale *(Fredo Corleone)*, Rudy Bond *(Cuneo)*, Al Martino *(Johnny Fontane)*, Morgana King *(Mama Corleone)*, Lenny Montana *(Luca Brasi)*, John Martino *(Paulie Gatto)*, Salvatore Corsitto *(Bonasera)*, Richard Bright *(Neri)*, Alex Rocco *(Moe Greene)*, Tony Giorgio *(Bruno Tattaglia)*, Vito Scottia *(Nazorine)*, Tere Livrano *(Theresa Hagen,)* Victor Rendina *(Philip Tattaglia)*, Jeannie Linero *(Lucy Mancini)*, Julie Gregg *(Sandra Corleone)*, Ardell Sheridan *(Mrs. Clemenza)*, Simonetta Stefanelli *(Apollonia)*, Angelo Infanti *(Fabrizio)*, Corrado Gaipa *(Don Tommasino)* Franco Citti *(Calo)*, Saro Urzi *(Vitelli)*. Produced by Albert S. Ruddy (Alfran Productions) for Paramount. 175 mins.

1974

THE CONVERSATION. Script and direction: FFC. Photography (Technicolor): Bill Butler. Editing: Walter Murch, Richard Chew. Music: David Shire. Production Design: Dean Tavoularis. Technical Advisors: Hal Lipset, Leo Jones. Players: Gene Hackman *(Harry Caul)*, John Cazale *(Stan)*, Allen Garfield *(Bernie Moran)*, Frederic Forrest *(Mark)*, Cindy Williams *(Ann)*, Michael Higgins *(Paul)*, Elizabeth MacRae *(Meredith)*, Harrison Ford *(Martin Stett)*, Mark Wheeler *(Receptionist)*, Teri Garr *(Amy)*, Robert Shields *(Mime)*, Phoebe Alexander *(Lurleen)*, Robert Duvall *(The Director)*. Produced by FFC and Fred Roos (Coppola Company/Paramount) for CIC. 113 mins.

1974

THE GODFATHER Part II. Script: FFC, Mario Puzo, from the novel by Puzo. Direction: FFC. Photography (Technicolor): Gordon Willis. Editing: Peter Zinner, Barry Malkin, Richard Marks. Music: Nino Rota (conducted by Carmine Coppola). Production Design: Dean Tavoularis. Art Direction: Angelo Graham. Players: Al Pacino *(Michael Corleone)*, Robert Duvall *(Tom Hagen)*, Diane Keaton *(Kay Adams)*, Robert De Niro *(Vito Corleone)*, John Cazale *(Fredo Corleone)*, Talia Shire *(Connie Corleone)*, Lee Strasberg *(Hyman Roth)*, Michael V. Gazzo *(Frankie Pentangeli)*, G. D. Spradlin *(Seantor Pat Geary)*, Richard Bright *(Al Neri)*, Gaston Moschin *(Fanucci)*, Tom Rosqui *(Rocco Lampone)*, B. Kirby Jr. *(Young Clemenza)*, Frank Sivero *(Genco)*, Francesca De Sapio *(Young Mama Corleone)*, Morgana King *(Mama Corleone)*, Mariana Hill *(Deanna Corleone)*, Leopoldo Trieste *(Signor Roberto)*, Dominic Chianese *(Johnny Ola)*, Amerigo Tot *(Michael's Bodyguard)*, Troy Donahue *(Merle Johnson)*, John Aprea *(Young Tessio)*, Joe Spinell *(Willi Cicci)*, Abe Vigoda *(Tessio)*, Tere Livrano *(Theresa Hagen)*, Gianni Russo *(Carlo Rizzi)*, Maria Carta *(Vito's Mother)*, Oreste Baldini *(Vito Andolini, as a Boy)*, Giuseppe Sillato *(Don Francesco)*, Mario Cotone *(Don Tommasino)*, James Gounaris *(Anthony Corleone)*, Fay Spain *(Mrs. Marcia Roth)*, Harry Dean Stanton *(First FBI Man)*, David Baker *(Second FBI Man)*, Carmine Caridi *(Carmine Rosato)*, Danny Aiello *(Tony Rosato)*, Carmine Foresta

(Policeman), Nick Discenza *(Barman)*, Father Joseph Medeglia *(Father Carmelo)*, William Bowers *(Senate Committee Chairman)*, Joe Della Sorte, Carmen Argenziano, Joe Lo Grippo *(Michael's Buttonmen)*, Ezio Flagello *(Impresario)*, Livio Giorgi *(Tenor in "Senza Mamma")*, Kathy Beller *(Girl in "Senza Mamma")*, Saveria Mazzola *(Signora Colombo)*, Tito Alba *(Cuban President)*, Johnny Naranjo *(Cuban Translator)*, Elda Maida *(Pentangeli's Wife)*, Salvatore Po *(Pentangeli's Brother)*, Ignazio Pappalardo *(Mosca)*, Andrea Maugeri *(Strollo)*, Peter La Corte *(Signor Abbandando)*, Vincent Coppola *(Street Salesman)*, Peter Donat *(Questadt)*, Tom Dahlgren *(Fred Corngold)*, Paul B. Brown *(Senator Ream)*, Phil Feldman *(First Senator)*, Roger Corman *(Second Senator)*, Yvonne Coll *(Yolanda)*, J. D. Nichols *(Attendant at Brothel)*, Edward Van Sickle *(Ellis Island Doctor)*, Gabria Belloni *(Ellis Island Nurse)*, Richard Watson *(Custom Official)*, Venancia Grangerard *(Cuban Nurse)*, Erica Yohn *(Governess)*, Theresa Tirelli *(Midwife)*, and James Caan *(Sonny Corleone)*. Produced by FFC (A Coppola Company Production) for Paramount. 200 mins.

MARTIN SCORSESE FILMOGRAPHY

Besides making commercials in Britain in 1968, Scorsese worked on the screenplay of *Obsessions* (1968, Pim de la Parra), began directing *The Honeymoon Killers* (1968) but was replaced by Leonard Kastle, worked on *Woodstock* (1969) as assistant director and supervising editor, on *Medicine Ball Caravan/We Have Come for Your Daughters* (1971) as associate producer and supervising editor, as supervisor of montages for *Elvis on Tour* (1972), and as supervising editor of *Unholy Rollers* (1973, Vernon Zimmerman).

1963

WHAT'S A NICE GIRL LIKE YOU DOING

IN A PLACE LIKE THIS? Script and direction: MS. Music: Richard Coll (lyrics by Sandor Reich). Players: Zeph Michaelis *(Harry)*, Mimi Stark *(His wife)*, Sarah Braverman *(Psychoanalyst)*, Fred Sica *(Friend)*, Robert Uricola *(The singer)*. Produced for the Cinema Dept. of the University of New York. 9 mins. (16mm.)

1964

IT'S NOT JUST YOU, MURRAY. Script: MS and Mardik Martin. Direction: MS. Photography (16mm): Richard Coll. Editing: Eli Bleich. Art Direction: Lancelot Braithwaite, Victor Magnotta. Players: Ira Rubin *(Murray)*, Sam DeFazio *(Joe)*, Andrea Martin *(The wife)*, Catherine Scorsese *(The mother)*, Robert Uricola *(The singer)*, Bernard Weisberger, Victor Magnotta, Richard Sweeton, John Bivona, Mardik Martin, Richard Coll, Martin Scorsese. Produced by the Cinema Dept. of the University of New York. 15 mins.

1967

THE BIG SHAVE. Script and direction: MS. Photography (colour, 16mm): Ares Demertzis. Music: Bunny Berigan. Player: Peter Bernuth. Sponsored by the Cinémathèque Royale de Belgique. 6 mins.

1969

WHO'S THAT KNOCKING AT MY DOOR? Script and direction: MS. (additional dialogue by Betzi Manoogian) Photography: Michael Wadleigh, Richard Coll, Max Fisher. Editing: Thelma Schoonmaker. Art Direction: Victor Magnotta. Players: Zina Bethune *(The young girl)*, Harvey Keitel *(J.R.)*, Anne Collette *(Young girl in dream)*, Lennard Kuras *(Joey)*, Michael Scala *(Sally Gaga)*, Harry Northup *(Harry)*, Bill Minkin *(Iggy)*, Phil Carlson *(The guide)*, Wendy Russell *(Gaga's small friend)*, Robert Uricola *(The armed young man)*, Susan Wood

(Susan), Marissa Joffrey *(Rosie)*, Catherine Scorsese *(J. R.'s mother)*, Victor Magnotta and Paul De Bionde *(Waiters)*, Saskia Holleman, Tsuai Yu–Lan and Marieka *(Dream girls)*, Martin Scorsese *(Gangster)*, Thomas Aiello. Produced by Joseph Weill, Betzi Manoogian and Haig Manoogian (Trimrod) for release by Joseph Brenner Associates. 90 mins. Earlier versions known as *Bring on the Dancing Girls* (1965) and *I Call First* (1967). Also released as *J. R.*

1972

BOXCAR BERTHA. Script: Joyce H. Corrington and John William Corrington from the book "Sister of the Road" by Boxcar Bertha Thompson as told to Ben L. Reitman. Direction: MS. Photography (DeLuxe colour): John Stephens. Editing: Buzz Feitshans. Music: Gib Guilbeau, Thad Maxwell. Players: Barbara Hershey *(Bertha)*, David Carradine *(Bill Shelley)*, Barry Primus *(Rake Brown)*, Bernie Casey *(Von Morton)*, John Carradine *(H. Buckram Sartoris)*, Victor Argo and David R. Osterhout *(The McIvers)*, "Chicken" Holleman *(Michael Powell)*, Grahame Pratt *(Emeric Pressburger)*, Harry Northup *(Harvey Hall)*, Ann Morell *(Tillie)*, Marianne Dole *(Mrs. Mailer)*, Joe Reynolds *(Joe)*, Gayne Rescher and Martin Scorsese *(Brothel clients)*. Produced by Roger Corman for American International. 88 mins.

1973

MEAN STREETS. Script: MS and Mardik Martin. Direction: MS. Photography (Technicolor): Kent Wakeford. Editing: Sid Levin. Players: Harvey Keitel *(Charlie)*, Robert De Niro *(Johnny Boy)*, Amy Robinson *(Teresa)*, David Proval *(Tony)*, Richard Romanus *(Michael)*, Cesare Danova *(Giovanni)*, Victor Argo *(Mario)*, George Memmoli *(Joey Catucci)*, Lenny Scaletta *(Jimmy)*, Jeannie Bell *(Diane)*, Murray Mosten *(Oscar)*, David Carradine *(Drunk)*, Robert Carradine *(The*

young assassin), Lois Walden *(Jewish girl)*, Harry Northup *(Vietnam veteran)*, Dino Seragusa *(Old Man)*, D'Mitch Davis *(Black cop)*, Peter Fain *(George)*, Julie Andelman *(Girl at Party)*, Robert Wilder *(Benton)*, Ken Sinclair *(Sammy)*, Catherine Scorsese *(Woman on the landing)*, Martin Scorsese *(Shorty, the killer in the car)*. Produced by Jonathan T. Taplin (Taplin–Perry–Scrosese) for Warner Bros. 110 mins.

1974

ITALIANAMERICAN. Script: Mardik Martin, Larry Cohen. Direction: MS. Photography (16mm, colour): Alex Hirschfeld. Editing: B. Lovitt. Players: Catherine, Charles and Martin Scorsese. Produced by Saul Rubin and Elaine Attias. 48 mins. Although shown at the New York Film Festival, this was part of a TV series "Storm of Strangers" scheduled for transmission in 1976.

ALICE DOESN'T LIVE HERE ANYMORE. Script: Robert Getchell. Direction: MS. Photography (Technicolor): Kent Wakeford. Editing: Marcia Lucas. Original music: Richard LaSalle. Production Design: Toby Carr Rafelson. Players: Ellen Burstyn *(Alice Hyatt)*, Kris Kristofferson *(David)*, Alfred Lutter *(Tommy)*, Billy Green Bush *(Donald)*, Diane Ladd *(Flo)*, Lelia Goldoni *(Bea)*, Lane Bradbury *(Rita)*, Vic Tayback *(Mel)*, Jodie Foster *(Audrey)*, Harvey Keitel *(Ben)*, Valerie Curtin *(Vera)*, Murray Moston *(Jacobs)*, Harry Northup *(Joe and Jim's bartender)*, Mia Bendixsen *(Alice aged 8)*, Ola Moore *(Old woman)*, Martin Brinton *(Lenny)*, Dean Casper *(Chicken)*, Henry M. Kendrick *(Shop assistant)*, Martin Scorsese and Larry Cohen *(Diners at Mel and Ruby's)*, Mardik Martin *(Customer in club during audition)*. Produced by David Susskind and Audrey Maas for Warner Bros. 112 mins.

1976

TAXI DRIVER. Script: Paul Schrader.

Direction: MS. Photography (colour): Michael Chapman. Editing: Marcia Lucas, Tom Rolf, Melvin Shapiro. Music: Bernard Herrmann. Art direction: Charles Rosen. Players: Robert De Niro *(Travis Bickle)*, Cybill Shepherd *(Betsy)*, Jodie Foster *(Iris)*, Harvey Keitel *(Sport)*, Peter Boyle *(Wizard)*, Albert Brooks *(Tom)*, Leonard Harris *(Charles Palantine)*, Diahnne Abbott *(Concession girl)*, Frank Adu *(Angry black man)*, Vic Argo *(Melio)*, Gino Ardito *(Policeman at rally)*, Garth Avery *(Iris's friend)*, Harry Cohn *(Cabbie in Bellmore)*, Copper Cunningham *(Hooker in cab)*, Brenda Dickson *(Soap opera woman)*, Harry Fischler *(Dispatcher)*, Nat Grant *(Stick-up man)*, Richard Higgs *(Tall Secret Service man)*, Beau Kayser *(Soap opera man)*, Vic Magnotta *(Secret Service photographer)*, Robert Maroff *(Mafioso)*, Norman Matlock *(Charlie T)*, Bill Minkin *(Tom's assistant)*, Murray Moston *(Iris's timekeeper)*, Harry Northup *(Doughboy)*, Gene Palma *(Street drummer)*, Carey Poe *(Campaign worker)*, Steven Prince *(Andy, gun salesman)*, Peter Savage *(The John)*, Martin Scorsese *(Passenger watching silhouette)*, Robert Shields *(Palantine aide)*, Ralph Singleton *(TV interviewer)*, Joe Spinell *(Personnel officer)*, Maria Turner *(Angry hooker on street)*, Robin Utt *(Campaign worker)*. Produced by Michael and Julia Phillips *(Bill/Phillips* production) for Columbia. 112 mins.

PAUL MAZURSKY FILMOGRAPHY

Mazursky wrote with Larry Tucker the screenplay of *I Love You, Alice B. Toklas!* (1969, Hy Averback).

1969

BOB AND CAROL AND TED AND ALICE. Script: PM and Larry Tucker. Direction: PM. Photography (Technicolor): Charles Lang. Editing: Stuart H. Pappe. Music: Quincy Jones. Art Direction: Pato Guzman. Players: Natalie Wood *(Carol)*, Robert Culp *(Bob)*, Elliott Gould *(Ted)*, Dyan Cannon *(Alice)*,

Horst Ebersberg *(Horst)*, Lee Bergere *(Emelio)*, Donald F. Muhich *(Psychiatrist)*, Noble Lee Holderreal Jr. *(Sean)*, K. T. Stevens *(Phyllis)*, Celeste Yarnall *(Susan)*, Grey Mullavey *(Group leader)*. Produced by Larry Tucker (A Frankovich production) for Columbia. 105 mins.

1970

ALEX IN WONDERLAND. Script: PM and Larry Tucker. Direction: PM. Photography (Metrocolor): Laszlo Kovacs. Editing: Stuart H. Pappe. Music: Tom O'Horgan. Production Design: Pato Guzman. Players: Donald Sutherland *(Alex)*, Ellen Burstyn *(Beth)*, Meg Mazursky *(Amy)*, Glenna Sergent *(Nancy)*, Viola Spolin *(Mother)*, Federico Fellini and Jeanne Moreau *(Themselves)*, André Philippe *(André)*, Michael Lerner *(Leo)*, Joan Delaney *(Jane)*, Neil Burstyn *(Norman)*, Leon Frederick *(Lewis)*, Carol O'Leary *(Marlene)*, Paul Mazursky *(Hal Stern)*, Moss Mabry *(Mr. Wayne)*. Produced by Larry Tucker for MGM. 109 mins.

1973

BLUME IN LOVE. Script: PM. Direction: PM. Photography (Technicolor): Bruce Surtees. Editing: Donn Cambern. Music and songs: Kris Kristofferson, Bob Dylan, Richard Wagner, Van Morrison, Zelma and Otis Redding, Carole King, Carosone, Amilcare Ponchielli, Giocchino Rossini, Rudolf Sieczynski, Wolfgang Amadeus Mozart, etc. Production Design: Pato Guzman. Players: George Segal *(Stephen Blume)*, Susan Anspach *(Nina Blume)*, Kris Kristofferson *(Elmo)*, Marsha Mason *(Arlene)*, Shelley Winters *(Mrs. Cramer)*, Donald F. Muhlich *(Analyst)*, Paul Mazursky *(Hellman)*, Erin O'Reilly *(Cindy)*, Annazette Chase *(Gloria)*, Shelley Morrison *(Mrs. Greco)*, Mary Jackson *(Louise)*, Ed Peck *(Ed Goober)*, Jo Morrow *(Bar hostess)*, Gigi Ballista *(Old Man)*, Ian Linhart *(Young boy)*, Mario Demo *(Venice waiter)*, Erika Von Kessler *(Girl at party)*, Dennis Kort *(Boy at party)*, Judy Ann Elder *(Lulu)*, Carol Worthington *(Annie Goober)*, Lou Gottlieb *(Party* *guru)*, Ray Schmidt *(Party guest)*, Virginia Dension *(Yoga leader)*. Produced by PM (associate producer: Tony Ray) for Warner Bros. 116 mins.

1974

HARRY AND TONTO. Script: PM and Josh Greenfeld. Direction: PM. Photography (De-Luxe colour): Michael Butler. Editing: Richard Halsey. Music: Bill Conti. Art Direction: Ted Haworth. Players: Art Carney *(Harry Coombs)*, Ellen Burstyn *(Shirley)*, Chief Dan George *(Sam Two Feathers)*, Geraldine Fitzgerald *(Jessie)*, Larry Hagman *(Eddie)*, Arthur Hunnicutt *(Wade)*, Phil Burns *(Burt)*, Joshua Mostel *(Norman)*, Melanie Mayron *(Ginger)*, Dolly Jonah *(Elaine)*, Herbert Berghof *(Rivetowski)*, Avon Long *(Leroy)*, Barbara Rhoades *(Happy Hooker)*, Cliff DeYoung *(Burt Jr.)*, Lou Guss *(Dominic)*, Mike Nussbaum *(Old Age Home Clerk)*, Rene Enriquez *(Grocery clerk)*, Michael McCleery *(Mugger)*, Rashel Novikoff *(Mrs. Rothman)*, Sybil Bowan *(Old landlady)*, Michael Butler *(Hitchhiker)*. Pro-duced by PM (associate producer: Tony Ray) for 20th Century—Fox. 115 mins.

1976

NEXT STOP, GREENWICH VILLAGE. Script: PM. Direction: PM. Photography (Colour, Panavision): Arthur Ornitz. Editing: Richard Halsey. Production Design: Philip Rosenberg. Players: Lenny Baker *(Larry Lapinsky)*, Ellen Greene *(Sarah)*, Shelley Winters *(Mom)*, Mike Kellin *(Pop)*, Christopher Walken *(Robert)*, Dori Brenner *(Connie)*, Antonio Fargas *(Bernstein)*, Lois Smith *(Anita)*, Lou Jacobi *(Herb)*, Helen Hanft *(Herb's wife)*, John Ford Noonan *(Barney)*, Rashel Novikoff *(Mrs. Tupper-man)*, Joe Madden *(Jake the Poet)*, Joe Spinnell *(Cop)*, Rochelle Oliver *(Doctor)*, Michael Egan *(Herbert)*, Gui Andrisano *(Marco)*, Denise Galik *(Ellen)*, Carole Man-ferdini *(Southern girl)*, Jeff Goldblum *(Clyde)*, John C. Becher *(Sid Weinberg)*, Rutanya Alda *(Party person)*. Produced by PM and Tony Ray for 20th Century—Fox. 110 mins.